PRAISE FOR WIRED AND CONNECTED

"*Wired and Connected* is packed with cutting-edge brain research and great wisdom about how to help children develop empathy and self-control. It is Craig Knippenberg's special gift to weave together his vast experience as a therapist, along with brain-based research and anecdotes into a helpful and readable guide for parents. A must read for parents wanting to understand their child."

Michael Thompson, PhD
New York Times **Bestselling Author and International speaker**
Coauthor of Raising Cain and Best Friends, Worst Enemies

"Craig's work captures the uniqueness of every child's social brain, including the neurologically based abilities of boys and girls. The Child Support System makes it easy to determine the parenting and educational strategies that will fit best for each child. Craig writes accessibly and powerfully for parents, educators, and clinicians, and his inclusion of sports in the book provides wonderful stories and anecdotes for dads and anyone who loves athletics. I highly recommend this book!"

Michael Gurian,
New York Times **bestselling author of**
The Wonder of Boys and the Minds of Girls

"The past 30 years has witnessed enormous strides in our understanding of the human brain, how it develops in childhood, and the importance of functional brain networks for understanding human behavior, child development, and the neurodevelopment disorders likely to adverse impact such development, such as autism spectrum, learning, language, and attention deficit hyperactivity disorders, among others. But how can parents or teachers benefit from this highly technical, and massive amount of research findings when it comes to parenting and teaching children today? By reading books like this one where authors like Craig Knippenberg have taken the time to translate these findings into viable strategies and metaphors to use in the important areas of educating and raising adaptive, effective, successful, and healthy children. This book is chock full of useful ideas parents and teachers can put into practice right away to help children adjust and succeed."

Russell A. Barkley, Ph.D.
Clinical Professor of Psychiatry
Virginia Treatment Center for Children and
Virginia Commonwealth University School of Medicine
Richmond, VA

"Craig's brain-based approach will make it easy for parents to understand their individual child. His many faceted solutions for self-control, emotional regulation and social development will help your child gain the 'empathy advantage.' It will also bring easy to understand brain concepts into the classroom and the clinical office setting. Simply extraordinary!"

Michele Borba, Ed.D.
UnSelfie: Why Empathetic Kids Succeed in Our All-About-Me World

"*Wired and Connected* is a ground-breaking, practical but penetrating owner's manual for the only assignment with eternal consequences—raising a soul! Craig Knippenberg continues to guide parents through the class five water rapids adventure of parenting. He packed in everything on developing a deeper understanding of each kiddo while empowering parents to guide our children into their own, individual social success in a book! #prayersanswered"

Stephanie Riggs,
Emmy award–winning television journalist,
producer, author, and mom

"With lively and engaging storytelling, Craig Knippenberg provides a useful framework for understanding how and why the developing brain produces thoughts, feelings, and behaviors. Grounded in empirical research and his many years of professional practice, his approach is a wonderful heuristic for working with children as unique, intentional persons. Parents and professionals alike will find the many growth activities in this book to be a great resource."

Jeff Howard, Ph. D.
Developmental Psychology Eckerd College

"In *Wired and Connected*, Mr. Knippenberg integrates the science of brain development with his diverse and compassionate experiences in counseling and education to produce a guide that empowers parents to help their children develop emotional regulation, improve social skills, and build self-awareness. Complex concepts related to brain functioning and neuroscience research are carefully explained with language and analogies that are easy to understand and help parents to conceptualize their child's development and behavior. With an understanding that children come with all different temperaments and unique strengths and weaknesses, this book provides tools for parents to provide a behavioral and emotional environment supportive of their individual child, including specific ideas and exercises for parents to use with children. The chapters are littered with interesting examples, thoughtful anecdotes, relevant research, as well as humor and compassion. As a physician specializing in child development and behavior, I recommend this book for parents who wish to broaden their understanding of their child's behavior and learn tools to support their social and emotional development."

Nicole Tartaglia, MD, MS,
Developmental-Behavioral Pediatrician
Associate Professor of Pediatrics,
Section of Developmental Pediatrics,
University of Colorado School of Medicine

"If you're wondering what's going on in your child's brain, at last you hold the X-ray machine in your hands. Craig Knippenberg's nearly four decades of watching, studying and helping kids afford him uncommon insight into happy kids, as well as into kids feeling lonely, frustrated, or angry—and how they can work their way through to feeling connected."

Lenore Skenazy,
President of Let Grow,
Founder of Free-Range Kids

"Listening to Craig speak is to listen to a wise man. That same voice is apparent on these pages. Craig knows kids and what makes them tick. As a college counselor, I know the importance of self-control, empathy, handling failure, and community service to college admission and life success. I trust him as a guide through the rewards and challenges of raising a healthy, value-centered child."

Dr. Steven R. Antonoff, Independent Educational Consultant
Distinguished Instructor, University of California,
Irvine Educational Consultant Certificate Program
Author, College Match, College Finder,
and A Student of Colleges

"*Wired and Connected* is a manual that provides insider knowledge and strategies, a bona fide decoder ring that allows parents and teachers to guide and foster children to be their best. Unfortunately, our children do not come with manuals. This book is the closest thing. Balancing story, spirit, and strategies, not to mention a comprehensive synthesis of the best educational and parenting research of the last hundred years, this manual should be required reading for parents and teachers."

"My life's work has been to increase economic development around the world. Having traveled to the most remote regions of the earth, I know the consequences on an inadequate environment on child growth and wellbeing. Economic development and equality mean that all children can live in an adequate environment where their brains can develop to their fullest potential. Craig's emphasis on empathy, community service and volunteerism help you and your children to live a life of service that makes this dream a possibility. My personal motivation comes from the book of Matthew: 'Whatever you did for the least of these brothers and sisters of mine, you did for me' (Matthew 25:40)."

"In this book, Craig Knippenberg combines his many years as a skilled child therapist with the latest in neurobehavioral science. This is presented in a manner that is helpful to physicians, educators, and most importantly parents of elementary school aged children. The insight to understand each child as a unique individual will give parents the tools to help their children succeed academically and socially. This book has helped me gain a new approach to address my patient's needs."

Greg Arfsten, MD
Academy Park Pediatrics,
Clinical Professor of Pediatrics,
University of Colorado School of Medicine
President, Uplift Internationale

"Being a bookseller causes me to be involved with many attempts to describe a psychological position, theory and helpful practices. Craig's work is among the best I have read allowing me to promote/sell his work to any person with confidence in content and style. I think the book will be helpful to parents and children as they determine who they wish to be as a person. Simply stated, this is a good, helpful and readable book well worth its cost."

Larry Yoder,
Buyer/Bookseller,
the Bookies, Denver

WIRED AND CONNECTED

8/8/19

Brenda,
Thank you so much
for your advanced support
of my book! Happy Reading,

[signature]

Make your empathy a verb!

Make your empathy a verb!

WIRED AND CONNECTED
Brain-Based Solutions
To Ensure Your Child's Social and Emotional Success

Why They Work and How to Teach Them to Children

CRAIG A. KNIPPENBERG
LCSW, M.Div.

ILLUMIFY MEDIA GLOBAL
Littleton, Colorado

WIRED AND CONNECTED

Copyright © 2019 Craig A. Knippenberg

The views and opinions expressed in this book are those of the author and do not necessarily reflect the official policy or position of Illumify Media Global.

Published by
Illumify Media Global
www.IllumifyMedia.com
"Write. Publish. Market. *SELL!*"

Library of Congress Control Number: 2019938566

Paperback ISBN: 978-1-949021-50-9
eBook ISBN: 978-1-949021-52-3

Printed in the United States of America

CONTENTS

Section III: How Does Your Child Respond Emotionally?

PREFACE

Wired and Connected emerged from the brain-based curriculum that I've developed over the past twenty-three years while working in the K-8 classrooms at St. Anne's Episcopal School in Denver. Each child is unique, so applying the same strategies for the "average" child isn't effective. Children need strategies based on their unique nature.

Written as a how-to manual for parents, teachers, and clinicians, this book simplifies the social brain's complexities and combines time-honored parenting tips with the latest brain research into today's problems that our children are faced with. You can read the whole book cover to cover or use it as a handbook to look up specific issues.

Interspersed throughout the five sections of the book are strategies for proper brain nutrition, electronics impact on sleep, utilizing visualization and breath work, managing stress, learning to handle failure, media awareness, gaming's impact on the brain, creating family adventures, and the importance of community service for your entire family.

This book instructs by using a combination of metaphors, entertaining anecdotes, and exercises to share with children, students, and clients for a host of emotional and social situations. You will learn the root causes for a child's distinctive personality on a neurological level, which results in more parents and mentors who can navigate the ups and downs of different developmental stages with patience and understanding. The Child Support System (section V) is based on each child's Presidential, Factory, and Mirror functioning (my names for the frontal lobe, limbic system, and mirror neuron system, respectively) and gives specific guidelines you need to parent your unique child.

Throughout the book, nature concepts (neurological, genetic, and biological) are intertwined with nurture concepts (environmental impacts, learned behavior, and modern culture). Like the two sides of the yin-yang symbol, they are inextricably juxtaposed throughout a child's life. In addition, *Wired and Connected* is based on a child being raised in a "good enough" environment.[1] What's good enough starts with a child's secure, loving, and trusting attachment to his or her primary caregivers. This emotional security must be matched with adequate food, shelter, physical/emotional safety, schooling, and health care.

To reinforce this wisdom and a "good enough" environment, I often reflect on Dr. Russell Barkley's profound presentation at the 1997 annual CHADD (Children and Adults with Attention Deficit/ Hyperactivity Disorder) Conference. He began by discussing the plethora of research on how inadequate environments (not "good enough") can stunt a child's ability to reach their genetic potential and that hardly any research exists on how "super parenting" can positively enhance a child's genetic potential. Barkley boldly stated, "Parents can't engineer their child." Rather than seeing themselves as engineers, Barkley went on to say that "parents should be shepherds who watch over their children and lead them to greener pastures."[2] In other words, keep your kids safe from the big predators, lead them to open fields, and give them plenty of freedom to roam and make choices about who they will be as they develop their behavioral, emotional, and social abilities and grow to their unique potential.

From a "good enough" nurture foundation, the book explores the brain's changes at various ages, as well as the small, but significant, differences between boys' and girls' brains. Each chapter contains numerous lessons and exercises designed to nurture children in distinct ways to help them realize the full potential of their social nature and the Brain Activities at the end of each chapter are designed as fun activities for the whole family.

INTRODUCTION

AWARENESS OF YOUR CHILD'S UNIQUE BRAIN CONFIGURATION

"When I approach a child, he invokes two sentiments in me;
tenderness for what he is, and respect for what he may become."
~Louis Pasteur

Nearly every day for the past thirty-eight years, I've had the joy of teaching and observing children as they socialize and play. Some children instinctively join in, manage their behavior, and utilize empathy while negotiating the ups and downs of social conflict. These interactions end on a positive note and flow into the next social engagement. Other children, however, struggle with understanding and making connections, handling their emotions, noticing the emotions of others, and modulating their behavior. These children's play experiences end on a negative note, and before long, they are left isolated from their peer groups.

Take Tommy, for instance, a bright, athletic fifth grade boy who enrolled in my emotional and social development group therapy program. His parents were concerned about his intense emotional reactions and his lack of empathy for the kids with whom he was in conflict. After describing the program, I asked him why he was interested in joining our group. With the saddest of expressions, he looked at me and said, "I haven't been invited to a birthday party since first grade." My heart sank for him. He continued, "I used to think it was everyone else's fault for not inviting me, but now I know it's because of me." Confidently, I looked at him and said, "The kids and I are going to get you invited to a party!"

The confidence in my statement came from two sources. First, while not yet being conscious of the sophisticated neural network in his brain that pushed him toward connection with others, Tommy hadn't given up hope on his desire for friends.[1] Second, Tommy was becoming aware that his own emotional and behavioral responses had something to do with his social isolation. It was the self-awareness that helped me map out goals for him and his parents related to his impulsive responsiveness, his persistent arguing, and his failure to read and integrate the thoughts and emotions of those around him. It's this kind of awareness that I believe *Wired and Connected* will help you develop in relation to your child's social functioning, and that you, in turn, can teach to your child. By understanding three simple brain areas that make up your child's "social brain"—the frontal lobe (President), the limbic system (Factory), and the mirror neuron system (Mirror)—you can help your social butterfly soar higher or help your struggling child thrive with targeted solutions, which are offered for each unique social brain configuration.

A child's self-control helps determine who they become.

Increased social success is crucial for your child's future. *Who a child becomes is determined primarily by how well a child exercises self-control, manages his or her emotions, and socializes with others.* Like every other species, human beings are wired for survival, and the human brain is programmed to ensure our continued existence through interactions with others. Decades of psychological and sociological research, and my own work with thousands of children individually—in small social skills groups and in the classroom— illustrate that children who can connect, work, and play well with others lead healthier, more successful lives and develop strong, enduring interpersonal relationships. These children, according to best-selling author Michael Thompson are responsible for meeting the "moral demands of group life."[2]

These children also have what author Michele Borba calls the Empathy Advantage in her book *UnSelfie: Why Empathetic Kids Succeed in Our All-About-Me World.* This advantage, she notes, results in many positive outcomes, such as promoting "kindness, prosocial behaviors, and moral courage, and it is an effective antidote to bullying, aggression, prejudice, and racism. Empathy is also a positive predictor of children's reading and math test scores and critical thinking skills, prepares kids for the global world, and gives them a job market boost."[3] But sadly, our modern culture seems to be taking children in the opposite direction as "teens are now 40 percent lower in empathy levels than three decades ago, and . . . narcissism has increased 58 percent."[4]

Fortunately, the evolution of the human brain means that children's brains are naturally wired to become mature, socially *connected* members of society.[5] Harry Reis, a professor of psychology at the University of Rochester who researches the positive impact from performing acts of kindness, says, "Humans are wired to give. We are a cooperative species, and there are mechanisms in us that promote social behavior."[6] While parents, teachers, and clinicians play a crucial role in social development, it's the interplay and awareness of the three key brain areas that ensures this maturation process. Becoming conscious of their powerful social brain allows children to learn to regulate their brain-based behavior and take an active role in their social development.[7]

While a neuroscientist would find this to be a very simplified approach to brain functioning, these concepts and terms (President, Factory, and Mirror) are intentionally designed for easy use. After thirty-eight years of work in the field, I have observed that we all *yearn for understandable concepts that increase children's self-awareness and motivate successful behavioral change. That self-awareness and behavioral change leads to a child's sense of self-confidence.*

The strategies discussed in this book are rooted in three fundamental driving forces in a child's life. *The first is to master themselves and master their environment.* When children control their internal or external world, they beam with pride. That glow gives way to a fundamentally important second drive: *Attaining respect and approval from parents and teachers.* Early in life, children are dependent upon their adult caregivers for meeting their physical and emotional needs. Each day as they get older, we as parents want to help them "expand their base of dependency" by relying on other adults and peers. While we want our children to talk to us about their emotions, we also need to teach them to share their joys, successes, worries, and sorrows with others. *Remember, parents are not the only contributors to a child's behavioral and emotional well-being.* When these two foundational drives are established, they allow for the third drive: *Peer Respect.* As adolescence approaches, respect from one's peers becomes increasingly important.

It is the combined respect from parents, teachers, and peers that provides the foundation for a child's sense of self-respect. While I still enjoy hearing my ninety-three-year-old mother telling me how proud she is of me and most certainly enjoy recognition from my peers, it is self-respect that helps all of us persevere through stress and adversity. A social personality based on self-confidence and self-respect allows children to honestly address their own shortcomings and navigate the obstacles that prevent them from mastering their internal and external worlds. In his book *Emotional Intelligence: Why It Can Matter More Than IQ*, Daniel Goleman summarizes why a child's self-confidence and the functions of the President, Factory, and Mirror are important: "Helping children improve their self-awareness and confidence, manage their disturbing emotions and impulses, and increase their empathy pays off not just in improved behavior but in measurable academic achievement."[8] These are the important ingredients for your child's future.

As you read and understand more about your child's brain, you must accept the distinct brain configuration with which your child has been blessed. Accepting a child's unique makeup also requires us to affirm and support diversity in all our children. The goal is not to make every peg fit but to help each diverse peg reach its potential. One size doesn't fit all, and we must look beyond the parenting books that offer five or six general solutions for specific child development problems that are supposed to work for all children. In other words, we must approach each child in a personal way in our roles as parents, teachers, or clinicians.

Many academic professionals are also looking at the need to implement more individualized instruction based on a student's strengths and needs. When discussing the deficiencies of core academic standards, cookie-cutter curricula, and the homogenization of individual talents and creative abilities, education specialist Yong Zhao tells us:

> When students come to school, they may be otherwise talented in other areas. That could be very valuable but now you want to fix them so they can read before they could do something else. If we did the same thing to Michael Phelps, the great swimmer, if you want him to be able to read before he could swim—he was kind of ADHD—he would still be hooked on phonics in some basement.[9]

Individuality equals diversity, and as any biologist says, when a species lacks sufficient diversity, it ceases to exist. After reading this book, I hope you will gain a deeper understanding of each child and empower yourself to guide his or her social success.

Finally, you must remember that social brain development is something you can't rush.

The fast-paced, materialistic, impulse-driven society in which most Americans live makes these interventions more crucial than ever. From humankind's earliest days of survival on the African plains, our brains have slowly adapted over tens of thousands of years. The recent changes in our culture and lifestyle, however, have occurred at a lightning fast pace. Simply put, we have ancient brains that are trying to survive in and adapt to a brave a new world.

In addition, your child's growth goes through many unique phases, and those phases require adjustments to your approach. My hope is that the strategies contained in this book will help you be the best parent, teacher, and counselor you can be and for each child to learn how to be the best friend he or she can be. As for our friend Tommy, his first birthday invitation came from another group member. All the boys recalled the event being fun and successful. After about six months, he joyfully shared with the group that he had received an invitation to a classmate's birthday party and had a great time!

In closing, I'd like to share a meditation I read from Marian Wright Edelman's book *Guide My Feet*. As you'll read in the following pages, I've had to deal with some tragic situations during my professional career. The following meditation has sustained me through the toughest of times and continues to keep me grounded as a therapist and parent. All of us need some form of inspiration through tough times:

> When God wants an important thing done in this world
> or a wrong righted, He goes about it in a very singular way.
> He doesn't release thunderbolts or stir up earthquakes. God

simply has a tiny baby born, perhaps of a very humble home, perhaps of a very humble mother. And God puts the idea or purpose into the mother's heart. And she puts it in the baby's mind, and then—God waits. The great events of this world are not battles and elections and earthquakes and thunderbolts. The great events are babies, for each child comes with the message that God is not yet discouraged with humanity, but is still expecting goodwill to become incarnate in each human life.[10]

SECTION I

BRAIN BASICS

"Man masters nature not by force but by understanding."
~Jacob Bronowski

"For the group, as well as for the species, what gives an individual his genetic value is not the quality of his genes. It is the fact that he does not have the same collection of genes as anyone else. It's the fact that he is unique. The success of the human species is due notably to its biological diversity. Its potential lies in this diversity."
~François Jacob

Biological diversity means that humans have the ability to adapt and evolve in ever-changing environments. It also means that as nature and nurture forces interact, every child's brain functioning is unique in relation to that interaction. To understand how this plays out in your child's social brain, it helps to have a simple understanding of brain cells, or neurons, and how they work and communicate. The chapters in section I also look at how inherited genetics play out in a child's placement on the Spectrum of Presidential Functioning. Presidential gender differences are also explored. The parent-child activities focus on how to increase your child's understanding and ownership of how their brains work.

CHAPTER 1

BRAIN-BASED FOUNDATIONAL PRINCIPLES

Early on in my kindergarten classes each year, I talk about the importance of wearing a helmet to protect the front of the brain. After asking the kindergartners to knock on their foreheads, I draw a picture depicting how the brain floats in cerebrospinal fluid inside the skull. I then explain how a sudden stop at a high speed—falling off your bike, for example—could cause the brain to impact the skull, causing a concussion.

I then explain how the frontal lobe, or prefrontal cortex, governs self-control and decision-making. I tell them to think of the frontal lobe as "your President," since it is commander-in-chief of emotions and behavior. The executive functioning of the frontal lobe is like the executive branch of our government, with the final say in all decisions. While they might not yet fully understand the sophisticated nature of their brain systems, the students begin to understand the inner workings of their brain, not only its functions, but the importance of protecting it.

THE VALUE OF UNDERSTANDING BRAIN-BASED BEHAVIOR

The key for all children to expand their ownership and understanding of the brain is to have caring parents and adults who *also* understand the developing brain and own this information in their parenting and teaching styles. A brain-based approach simply makes sense to children as we help them navigate their social,

1

emotional, and academic worlds. It places control of a child's behavior into his or her own hands and encourages maturation. Children who fail to internalize and take responsibility for their own behavioral choices externalize blame later in life, finding fault in others when they can't bear the consequences of their own actions.

Living in a successful, caring community requires that adults and children take responsibility for their social and moral choices, which results in self-trust and trust in others as we navigate our day-to-day functioning.

In addition to sound parenting strategies, understanding a child's behavior from a brain-based perspective dramatically increases your ability to be patient during particularly difficult times. As a parent and educator, I often have to take a deep breath and think about what is going on in a child's brain before I respond. I've often heard, "It was an accident!" to which I like to reply, "No, it wasn't an accident. You failed to use your President and analyze the potential consequences of your choice." In other phases of a child's life, it might actually be true when a child says, "I don't know why I did it." Parents and teachers often complain about a behavior without considering the root causes that emerge from the child's developing brain areas.

My son once had a mood swing when he was just beginning fifth grade. Quickly before school, I reminded him to do a chore. Uncharacteristically, he refused. Unfortunately, I didn't control my emotional response and started in on a loud reprimand. He seemed visibly upset, looked down, but then complied. On our way to school fifteen minutes later, it dawned on me what had happened. My son had experienced his first puberty-driven mood swing. As we drove, I apologized for losing my temper but reminded him that we both need to do our chores before heading out for the day. He acknowledged his mistake, forgave my response, and we moved on.

Later that day, the fifth grade teachers sent a letter home to all the parents about the mood swings of the pre-teen and how parents must remain calm and not overreact. I chuckled at the timeliness of the letter and thought to myself, "What a fool I am. I failed on my first moody pre-teen moment, and I'm the school counselor!" Needless to say, I've tried to practice patience ever since. After all, we must remember that if our children didn't act like children, then they would be adults!

The patience that comes with self-awareness and an understanding of the brain can be particularly helpful for children as well. Recent research out of Stanford University demonstrated that young teens were more resilient in dealing with peer stress when they understood that they and their classmates were in a temporary phase of social development.[1] Every brain system has developmental phases. Like the toddler potty training phase, these growth spurts are rarely precise and tidy.

FIFTEEN FOUNDATIONAL PRINCIPLES

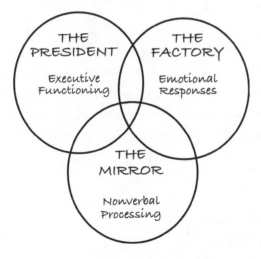

To help parents, educators, and children create self-awareness and a better understanding of social brain development, this book explores three major areas: the frontal lobe (the President, section II); the limbic system (the Emotional Factory, section III); and the nonverbal system (the Mirror spectrum, section IV). The last section (section V) explains how the interplay between these three systems shapes a child's personality and subsequent social functioning. Recognizing how a child is wired in these three areas can help us create environments that will maximize each child's gifts and talents. **In this regard, one philosophy of parenting or teaching does not fit all.** Here are some points to keep in mind:

Adapt your approach

Adults who understand a child's makeup in the three social brain areas can provide support where it is needed. Like a good business manager, we need to adapt our approach to each child's individual personality.

Consider biological diversity

Biological diversity means that humans can adapt and evolve in ever-changing environments. It also means that as nature and nurture forces interact, every child's social brain functioning is unique in relation to those interactions. To understand how this plays out in your child's brain, it helps to have a simple understanding of cells, or neurons, and how they work and communicate. This facilitates an understanding of additional brain processes in each of the three main areas (chapters 2 and 3).

What does the President do?

Your child's frontal lobe, which I term the "President" (section II), is the master control system for the rest of the brain. The President's executive functioning abilities help your child manage academic endeavors, initiate tasks, and shift to new strategies when needed. For the development of emotional control and successful social skills, the President's management of your child's impulses is paramount.

How well does your child hold on to happiness?

Children are born with genetically programmed temperaments (their emotional "Factories") that factor into their emotional output and stability (section III). Some children are naturally better than others at regulating their emotional reactions in adverse situations. Fortunately, parents can teach their children how to temper their responses by utilizing the President to slow down or stop the Factory's impulsive, erratic emotions.[2]

Read social cues

As children interact with others, they are activating and developing a complex neural network that allows them to understand others' thoughts and emotions. It is this ability to read social cues (or nonverbal communication) that helps them coexist with others, and most importantly, empathize. The mirror neuron system (section IV) guides this process as children differ in their nonverbal abilities. Some children do this with ease, while others struggle as they enter into social engagements.

Approach each child's development uniquely

Parents must approach their child's overall social brain development by understanding the three major brain areas and how these three interact together to create different needs for different children (section V). A child with low Presidential abilities, an angry or anxious temperament, and low Mirror processing is going to need a much different approach than a child with high Presidential abilities, an easy-going temperament, and high Mirror processing.

Understand your own brain functioning

Examine your own tendencies in the three areas. In most cases, "The apple didn't fall far from the tree" is an appropriate metaphor. If you are frustrated by your child's emotional volatility, but he or she watches you get upset during a traffic jam, it's going to be hard to sell anger management. If you are concerned about your child's distractibility and impulsivity, but they observe you constantly taking phone calls or texting while driving, it will be difficult to provide them with what they need for learning self-control.

Parent for independence

To be direct, you aren't going to be around forever, and your child needs to learn how to survive without you. Start early on with letting your children make and learn from their mistakes. If you get involved too early or too often, you will slow down their development of self-respect. Remember the mantra from the Little Train, "I think I can. I think I can. I did!" as a way of building self-confidence and self-respect. A study by Neil Montgomery of Keene State College in New Hampshire found that freshmen in college who had helicopter parents were more anxious, less open to taking new action or new ideas, and were more dependent than their peers who were not monitored constantly by their parents and given responsibility instead.[3]

Develop empathy

In *UnSelfie*, Michele Borba describes how overdependent children may someday lack the moral courage to do the right thing: "Instead of boosting confidence, our micromanaging lowers our children's self-esteem and reduces their moral courage to step in or speak up to help. It's also why overprotective parenting can be disastrous at producing empathetic leaders."[4] Today's smaller families can lead to this type of obsessive parenting.[5] Next time your child calls you with a reasonably small problem, try saying: "I have confidence that you can figure that out yourself."

The three Cs of good parenting

I first found the three Cs (calm, consistent, and concrete) in Ross Campbell's book *How to Really Love Your Child*. Working backward, first, being concrete means being very clear and specific with your rules and consequences. Look in your child's classroom, and you'll see many posters that clearly identify and graphically illustrate the marching orders. Second, being consistent means that these rules will be followed every day. While no one is immune to stress or the special circumstances that may arise in family life, you want to keep life as consistent as possible. Third, stay calm as you follow your clearly laid-out standards and impart them to your children. If you get too shaken up when managing your children, your kids will learn one of two things: that the rules will be up for grabs if they can get you worked up enough (for example, they will learn that if they irritate you enough, you might just give in out of frustration), or they will focus on your irritability and won't understand why you created the structure in the first place. Michael Thompson echoes this advice by saying that 50 percent of behavior management is taken care of by being crystal clear.[6]

Utilize your community

I'm also a true believer in the proverb *It takes a village to raise a child*. If you aren't able to modify your parenting in a particular area, inform your child. By admitting this vulnerability, you become a model of how self-awareness promotes success in family and community living. Then, find others who can support you in these situations.

Create a safe environment

While the brain has amazing abilities to form and reshape its neural pathways throughout life, it can't be overemphasized how important it is to protect your child's brain and create the right environment for brain development the first time around. As for social brain development, international brain expert, Russell Barkley puts it this way: "There are neurological (brain) factors that contribute to self-control and willpower, along with learning and upbringing. And when these brain systems are functioning improperly or become damaged, normal levels of self-control and will power are impossible."[7] In other words, brain development will not be optimal unless a child's environment, like a newer hotel designed to meet modern needs with comfort and style, is designed to accommodate the rapid neurological changes taking place. A safe and stimulating environment allows your child to flourish.

You can't microwave brain development

Each area of the social brain goes through phases of development and growth. To expect children and teens to have complex social brain skills is just as unfair as expecting first graders to understand calculus or Shakespeare. They have not yet reached that level of social brain development. While we come pre-wired for many of these abilities, growth and maturity depends on a nurturing environment.[8]

Gender differences in the brain

The development of the social brain is impacted by gender. These gender differences are partly the result of a twelve- to eighteen-month Presidential development differential between boys and girls.[9] While the timing of Presidential development in boys lags behind their female counterparts early in school, the male's President kicks in during the mid-elementary years. However, the developmental disparity reappears during adolescence and young adulthood in all areas of social functioning.[10] It is truly amazing that kindergarten and middle school teachers in mixed-gender classrooms survive the year, let alone the day.

Stages and changes

Finally, remember that children are constantly changing and developing. Each stage of brain development they go through brings joy, along with angst and uncertainty. Accept the joy and embrace the challenges of each stage and etch all of it into your memory.

BRAIN ACTIVITY: CONCUSSIONS

As an interactive way of teaching young children about concussions, I use a rectangular plastic container that contains two white seals floating on an ocean of blue fluid. Both figures are also encased in white fluid. We pretend that the seals are just floating along happily in their calm fluid. I then move the container slightly and we see how the floating seals become more active inside the container. When I shake the container more vigorously, we see the seals floating out to the edges of the container while still being cushioned by the white fluid that surrounds them. I explain that this is the equivalent of running in PE. Finally, I give the gadget an intense shake. We listen to the seals clicking against the walls of the container and observe how they ricochet from front to back to front again. I explain how the battered and twisted seals are similar to what happens to brain tissue during a concussion.

Protect Your Brain!

This activity is a great way to explain how a helmet only works if it is properly fitted and fastened. The lining absorbs much of the energy that takes place during a collision and reduces the impact of the brain hitting the skull.

1. *First, help your child understand the damage that concussions inflict on the President. Brain trauma compromises executive functioning (section II), and the effects of a brain injury can be permanent and life-changing. Because children have weaker necks and their head-to-body ratio is four times greater than adults, that means an impact can cause more rapid head movements.*[11]

2. *Let your child know that no physical activity is without risk; however, contact sports pose a greater threat to brain health.*

3. *Share the latest research with your child that demonstrates how just a few concussions over the course of a lifetime can raise the risk of developing diseases such as Parkinson's, Alzheimer's, Cranial Traumatic Encephalopathy (CTE), and Amyotrophic Lateral Sclerosis (ALS).*[12] *All of these diseases are fatal.*

4. *Helmets during sporting activities and bike rides are a "no-brainer." Make sure your children take every precaution to maintain the health and safety of their brains. If you are going to allow your child to play tackle football, wait until at least the age of fourteen. Neurologist Robert Cantu put it this way, "If you have to take hits to the head at all, you're better off taking them at later ages."*[13]

CHAPTER 2

OUR THREE BRAINS
AND A HEADLESS CHICKEN

In my brain-based curriculum, the entire fourth grade year focuses on the specifics of how brain development occurs and how the development of our human brain structure separates us from many other species. The curriculum begins with the story of Mike the Headless Chicken. Even the most disinterested students participate when we explore this tale of the automatic brain structure (especially since it took place in Colorado.)

It was 1945 in the small farming town of Fruita, Colorado. Farmer Lloyd Olsen was getting ready for a special occasion. His mother-in-law was visiting from out of town, so Lloyd decided to prepare a chicken dinner. He grabbed his axe, went into his yard, and selected a five-month-old Wyandotte chicken named Mike. Knowing that his mother-in-law favored the neck portion of the fowl, Lloyd lined up his axe, brought it down and severed the chicken's head right at the top of its neck. While his detached, bleeding head lay lifeless on the chopping block, Mike staggered around in circles like any other beheaded chicken would. However, rather than falling over dead, the headless chicken regained his composure and returned to the chicken pen and walked among his cockerel brethren. Like the other chickens, Mike continued to peck for food and preened himself with his neck, albeit futilely.

Amazed that Mike was still alive, Lloyd decided to use an eye-dropper to nourish the chicken by dropping grains and water directly into his esophagus. As long as Mike was watered and fed, he seemed as healthy as any other chicken. Realizing the money-making potential, Lloyd saved the head and began taking "The Headless Wonder Chicken" to nearby carnivals, where spectators could view this amazing chicken and his lifeless head for twenty-five cents. A short time later, Lloyd, his wife, and his new manager took Mike on a national tour. Unfortunately, after becoming a national celebrity and the subject of several newspaper and magazine features, Mike's life ended after he choked on a piece of grain at a motel in Arizona. Local legend has it that Lloyd bought a new truck with the money he made exhibiting Headless Mike. His legacy lives on in Fruita, where they hold an annual Mike the Headless Chicken Festival.

THE AUTOMATIC, EMOTIONAL, AND THINKING BRAINS

My first question to students is this: How did Mike survive without a head? First, the University of Utah concluded that Lloyd's precision axe swing missed Mike's jugular vein and carotid artery, and a blood clot formed, which prevented Mike from bleeding to death.[1] Second, and most importantly for Mike and for my students' beginning understanding of the brain, Mike's extra long neck still contained his brain stem. The brain stem (or the automatic brain) houses the autonomic nervous system, which controls involuntary, basic functions such as breathing, heart rate, and digestion. So, even without his head, Mike not only survived, he thrived and grew from two-and-a-half to eight pounds over the course of his eighteen-month life. No animal can live without a functioning brain stem, which is our "First Brain."[2] You'll find some fun activities at the end of this chapter to help your kids understand how this automatic brain works on a subconscious level.

Life would be pretty boring if humans only had a brain stem. Fortunately, humans, as well as many other animals, have a "Second

Brain," which generates a host of emotions. Wrapped around the automatic brain like a donut, the Second Brain or the limbic system, which I like to call the "Emotional Factory," can turn the heat up or down when we need to respond.[3] Starting with the amygdala, which sits next to the brain stem and collects information from all our senses, via the thalamus, species are able to engage the fight, flight, or freeze response when overcome with fear.[4] This basic fight or flight response of the amygdala is sometimes considered to be part of the First Brain response system; however, for the purposes of this book, we will look at it as part of the larger emotional/limbic system of the Second Brain (further explained in section III). If you've ever seen a rabbit freeze and then take off running when you get closer or heard a dog bark and growl when it perceives something unfriendly is nearby, then you've witnessed responses from the amygdala. Prehistoric man had to deal with many predatory threats living in the wild and must have had a highly developed amygdala to survive and carry on the human race.

In addition to this basic amygdala response, nature has endowed humans with complex feeling brains. Besides fear, we experience scores of emotions: love, compassion, jealousy, loneliness, greed, disgust, happiness, sadness, and surprise, to name a few. These emotions fill our lives with zest and passion and plant the seeds of human achievement in disciplines such as art, music, theatre, and literature. However, this blessing carries with it the burden of integrating a volatile stew of complex emotions. Unless we want to merely survive like cavemen, children and adolescents need to learn how to manage these emotions in a productive manner. A lack of emotional control leads to social, cognitive, and physical maladies.[5] Additionally, runaway emotions are obstacles that stand in the way of establishing and sustaining social relationships.

Remarkably, the brains of humans and other mammals have evolved a "Third Brain" known as the neocortex.[6] Imagine living a life in which you couldn't think abstractly or learn and process information in complex ways. What if you had emotions and impulses but lacked the ability to stop yourself from acting on them in the heat of the moment? Life would be even more violent and chaotic if the neurological foundations for empathy (the ability to understand and feel the thoughts and emotions of others) weren't pre-installed in an infant's brain. Fortunately, the neocortex gives our species the ability to more creatively adapt to ever-changing environments and solve the many complex problems that can arise as we work and live in community with each other.

During smart board lessons with students, I refer to the neocortex as the "thinking brain" and draw it as a big, watermelon-shaped area sitting above our first two brains. I then load it up with lots of light bulbs in the main section and create the all-important President sitting in front.

While all of human functioning emerges from these three "brains," it is the President, Factory, and Mirror, or the mirror neuron system (located within the neocortex and limbic system), that play crucial roles in our social/emotional development and success.[7] Working together, the combined functions of the President, Factory, and Mirror—that creates our ability to read the emotions/ intentions of others—will determine how effectively a child will interact with the rest of the world. Some children will have positive functioning in all three areas, while others will struggle in one, two, or all three. When you understand your child, you can then implement cognitive and behavioral strategies for greater success (sections II–V).

Some additional basic brain functioning concepts will help you and your child more fully understand his or her unique social brain. Your own patience and survival as the parent of a preschooler hinges on understanding that the human brain has evolved from bottom to top (automatic to emotional to thinking) over hundreds of thousands of years and develops in the same order inside a newborn's brain. In younger children, you can see basic survival skills and emotional reactions but little self-control or reasoning skills. Go to any grocery store and you'll see a younger child crying in the buggy when his or her demands for a cookie aren't met.

As the brain develops, it also goes through sensitive phases where successful development is crucial.[8] The President, for instance, goes through many changes in preschool and again in adolescence. There is even an old proverb that says, **Your child at three and four is how they will be at thirteen and fourteen.** Obviously, an adequately structured and nurturing environment is vital during these sensitive periods. If you aren't keeping watch over your preschool or adolescent kids, you may be risking their very survival.

THE KAYAK ANALOGY FOR HOW THE BRAIN COMMUNICATES

It's also important to understand how the brain works and communicates with itself. The highlight of my fourth grade curriculum every year is when Dr. Kerry Brega and Dr. Daniel Craig from the University of Colorado Denver bring their "bucket of brains" for a class visit. With a mix of excitement and anxiety, students line up to hold an actual human brain and explore the outside structure with their eyes and hands. It's pretty easy to tell which students might be future medical students by the looks on their faces when they hold a brain. In addition to exploring the outside of a brain, students examine a variety of cross sections of the brain. Right before their eyes, students can see the two basic structures of the brain: the gray matter and the white matter. To appreciate this image more clearly, first imagine a gray scoop of ice cream. Now imagine that the scoop has long, thick strands of ribbonlike white marshmallow between layers of the gray ice cream. The white matter isn't random, but looks as if the ice cream scooper had sculpted this mix with perfect precision and replicated it billions of times. The inside of a brain looks something like this multi-colored, perfectly crafted scoop of ice cream.

The adult brain is made up of approximately 100 billion brain neurons, (just about the same number of neurons as an infant brain).[9] The gray matter is made up of the neuron's dendrites and central body. The 100,000 dendrites for each neuron are like a

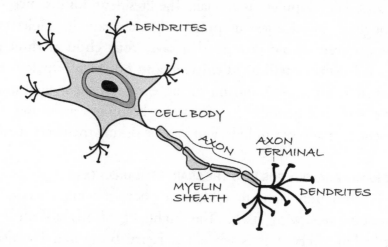

branching bush. Their job is to collect input from thousands of other neurons and transmit that data to the central body.[10] The white matter is made up of axons (each neuron has one axon), the arm-like extensions that branch out from the central body and run deep into the nervous system.[11] These white arms transmit the information processed by the neurons within the gray matter. If you look at the white matter under a microscope, you can identify the long axons that branch and send signals to other neurons.

Visually, you might imagine a community of 100 billion tele-phone poles, with each pole receiving information and connecting up to 100,000 other poles.[12] The limitless potential of the connections within this network is mind-boggling. Or, as I like to tell students, "Brain cells love to make friends with a lot of other brain cells." The main structural difference between the abilities of the adult brain and the child brain is found in the prodigious axon branching off that single axon (think of a tree branch with other branches coming off of it); the pruning process takes place during development to establish these networks and connections that the brain needs to function properly.[13]

Unlike the old-fashioned telephone or hard-wired computer network, our brains have a wireless component as well. When a neuron's message reaches the end of its white matter, it spreads out like little fingers (axon terminal). A small gap, or synapse, sits between the sending cell and the cell it's trying to communicate with. So how does the neuron's message jump the gap? A burst of electricity triggers chemicals, known as neurotransmitters, to carry its message from its axon terminal over to the receiver neuron, whose terminals are called dendrites. When docking on this neuron's dendrite, the neurotransmitter affects the electrical balance of the receiver neuron and causes it to fire. On and on the message is communicated electrochemically down the pathway for whatever we are processing (body functions, emotions, thoughts, or movements to name a few) at a given time.

When explaining this process to a child, I use this story: "Imagine that you are taking a package from your house to a friend's house. Unfortunately, your houses are separated by a river. So, you walk from your backyard down to your dock. Getting into your kayak, you paddle across the river and tie up to your friend's dock. He is there to greet you and accept your package. Gleefully, he runs the package up to his house (where he will decide where to send it next) while you paddle your kayak back to your dock and get prepared for another package. If you paddle to this friend's house thousands of times, the pathway becomes so engrained that you can follow it in your sleep."

I like to tell students that when they learn new concepts, such as pre-algebra and geometry, their brains just created a new pathway.

However, that is only half the process, since the pathway will all but disappear if they don't reinforce that learning. The more frequently a particular pathway of neurons is followed, the more deeply this pathway etches itself in our memories (neurons that fire together stay together).[14] This pathway concept is significant when talking to students about the importance of daily reading and their summer reading and math practice. Like a short cut that creates a well-worn dirt path, the grass will grow back if we don't keep walking on it. And, like a brain cell's friend connection with other brain cells, if you don't stay in touch with your friends, you'll start to lose your bond.

While there are hundreds of different types of neurochemicals in our brains (the kayaks and packages in the example above), later chapters will focus on a few neurotransmitters that are crucial to understanding social brain functioning. During the transition from childhood into adulthood, we need to remember that the speed of the messages travelling in the brain circuits also radically changes. In the elementary years, a child's brain fires at the relative speed of a paddleboat (2 mph), while a mature adult's brain is more like an Indy car (200 mph).[15] This increase in firing speed increases through late childhood and adolescence as each neuron's axon becomes coated with myelin. Myelin is a substance that insulates the axon for the electrical impulses, much like the plastic coating on an electrical wire, enabling turbocharged brain speed.[16]

BRAIN ACTIVITY: HAVING FUN WITH OUR THREE BRAINS

Some morning, as you say goodbye to your children on the way to school, say, "Don't forget to breathe today!" This seemingly obvious statement is a great way to get them to roll their eyes as well as get them thinking about their automatic brain. In explaining "automatic" or "subconscious," your children can understand that they don't have to think about breathing in order to breathe throughout the day. If you want them to be conscious of breathing, challenge them to a hold-your-breath contest. While the thinking brain initially commands breathing, it isn't too long before the automatic brain takes over and everyone thankfully exhales.

Now challenge your children to a staring contest—the first one to blink loses. Even the best "starers" eventually succumb to the automatic brain's need to blink. Once again, you can think about blinking if you want, but you don't need to think about blinking in order to keep your eyes moist throughout the day.

Finally, tell your children to intentionally have their hearts beat tomorrow. It's ridiculously subconscious. Do some brainstorming with your children on how they could experience their heart rates on a conscious level. Then, run in place together for thirty seconds so that each of you can feel your heart beat. Now, sit down, cross your legs, and take some deep yoga breaths. You both will feel your heart beat and your breathing change within a minute.

Thankfully, like Mike the Headless Chicken, there are many processes we don't have to think about in order to survive the school or work day. Have some fun brainstorming and Googling other functions that our automatic brains perform. Also highlight how we can be conscious of these automatic functions and use that consciousness for more positive outcomes. Next time your children are upset, model how taking three deep breaths can turn down the heat in the Emotional Factory. In particular, the President, Factory, and Mirror function much better when we are more aware of how we are using them.

CHAPTER 3

THE BRAIN ADAPTS TO AN EVER-CHANGING WORLD

As we increase our understanding of brain development in our species, think about our earliest ancestors. A functional, robust automatic brain and a basic emotional brain system were adequate for the basic survival, protection, and procreation of our early predecessors.

Yet, as humans evolved and adapted to their ever-changing environment, it became advantageous to live in community with other humans. Living in groups made it easier to hunt larger prey, raise children, and protect each other. It also helped groups problem solve and adapt to harsher, new environments as humans migrated into climates like Northern Europe.

This sort of community survival required our ancestors to develop a more thoughtful and socially sophisticated brain better suited for solving complex problems. Fortunately, our brains have the amazing ability to transform learned behavior into longer-term genetic changes for future generations. This new brain, the neocortex, gave our ancestors these skills.[1] The President allowed our ancestors to begin controlling their impulses and stay focused on longer-term goals which, in turn, helped the entire community to survive.

THE ORIGINS OF OUR "NEW BRAIN"

Evolutionary biologists believe that the development of our President, for instance, accelerated when humans added farming to their traditional hunter-gatherer methods of food procurement. In Thomas Hartmann's *Attention Deficit Disorder: A Different Perception,* he discusses the origins of our more primitive ancestors' instincts, which worked well in a hunter-gatherer society.[2] He then examines the traits of successful farmers and how a higher functioning President helped agrarian cultures survive. Hartmann then theorizes that those who were more impulsive would have fared quite well with our hunter-gatherer ancestors where life was more from moment to moment and based on the availability of food sources. The people who survived in this early society were those who were distracted by sights or sounds and then followed with a quick throw of a spear. These same traits would make coexisting with modern day agrarian societies much more difficult. In a farming world, crops are planted and decisions are made over a spring-to-fall harvest schedule. This mode of farming, or keeping one's eye on the prize and driving daily behavior to accomplish longer-term goals, favors those with less impulsivity and stronger Presidents.

With so many different responsibilities, our President must be a sophisticated, finely tuned machine. Attaining optimum Presidential functioning takes time. In fact, the President does not operate at full capacity until approximately age twenty-five for females, and for males can take several years longer.[3] The brain continues to speed up into our mid-thirties. During my lectures, these surprising facts of the ages when we reach full neurological maturity usually elicit gasps from the parents of middle school and high school students. As they would say in farming communities, "That's a long row to hoe!"

Decades before full brain maturity, preschool children are just beginning to develop their Presidential abilities. Prior to this, parents are the primary "brakes" for their children's emotions and impulses. By age three or four, we begin to see girls moving up the Spectrum of Presidential Functioning. On average, approximately eighteen months later, we begin to see boys exerting more behavioral and emotional control as their Presidents come online, as well.[4] By the early elementary years, neural-typical students have a functioning frontal lobe that helps them sit still, stay focused, and control their emotions throughout the day. For instance, children at this age have Presidential reminders about exercising emotional control when they hear adults say, "Remember, you get what you get and you don't pitch a fit." If a child doesn't use the President to control emotions for those issues, which other children consider to be small or trivial, he or she might receive the classic peer response: "Stop being a crybaby!" It's amazing how the fear of embarrassment can motivate children to use their Presidents before reacting emotionally.

GENETICS AND SOCIAL BRAIN DEVELOPMENT

The development of the President and our farmer brain as a whole was reflected in our genetic instructions. Of the estimated 100,000 genes it takes to design a human, it's estimated that 30,000 to 50,000 of these genes are dedicated to the brain.[5] Our ancestors began to pass on these new brains to each generation.[6] Generation after generation of humans followed their parents' "genetic instructions" and added to these genetic instructions as they encountered new environments and solved more complex problems.[7] While this evolution took place for our entire species, those with

SPECTRUM OF
PRESIDENTIAL FUNCTIONING

LOW   HIGH

higher brain capacities thrived, enabling them to survive, reproduce, and pass on these instructions.

Within our species, each family passes on different instructions. Depending on the mix of genes from one's parents, the outcome can vary from child to child. For instance, one child might receive advanced Presidential abilities, another might be in the mid-range for Presidential functioning, while a third might have more significant struggles with executive functioning.[8] When given tests or when rated by parents and teachers, children who fall approximately in the bottom 10 percent on the Presidential spectrum are considered to have attention deficit hyperactivity disorder (ADHD).

When I meet with parents early on in therapy, I frequently explore a child's genetic history by asking about the parents' own behavior in school, with friends, and in family settings. When I ask where their son or daughter falls on the spectrum, the response is predictable: a parent's own perception of where he or she falls on the spectrum often mirrors the child's. This is especially true for parents who were also diagnosed with ADHD: If one parent has been diagnosed, there is a 57 percent chance of the child having ADHD.[9] Research indicates that there is also a connection between the symptoms and severity of a father's ADHD and his offspring.[10]

Sadly, this genetic component is amplified among adopted children. Research suggests that 46 percent of adopted children have ADHD compared with up to 8 percent of school-age children in our country.[11]

When looking at a family's genetic heritage, it's also important to consider a child's gender since there are gender-specific genetic differences in social brain development.

When it comes to Presidential functioning,[12] geneticists have known for years that the main genetic blueprints for building the President sit on the X chromosome. Remember high school biology? A female embryo has two X chromosomes while the male embryo has one X and one Y chromosome. From a blueprint standpoint, it's like the foreman has two copies of the design for the Presidents of girls, and only one set for the Presidents of boys. While there are many boys on the high end of the Spectrum of Presidential Functioning, we tend to see more girls on the high end of the spectrum due to that extra blueprint, and we see more boys in the middle and toward the low end.[13]

As mentioned earlier, the development of boys' Presidents lags behind the girls' and that their ultimate destination on the spectrum (in mid-elementary school and into adulthood), on average, will be lower than girls. Any third or fourth grade teacher will tell you that more of the boys struggle with sustained attention, organization, homework completion, and behavioral control. Eighty percent of high school dropouts are boys, and boys are more than three times as likely to receive disciplinary suspensions compared to girls.[14] Boys also score lower on many standardized tests, and they are more likely to be retained. Currently, only 42 percent of American college students are males.[15] If I counted the number of times I utter the phrase, "Focus please," while teaching a class, I would find that many more of these comments are directed at boys.

WHY ARE BOYS LOWER ON THE SPECTRUM?

Why have boys evolved a President that is lower on the spectrum compared to their female counterparts? Wouldn't it make sense for both boys and girls to have high Presidential functioning? Think of how well all children—regardless of gender—would perform in a school environment where consistent focus and self-control are highly valued.

Evolutionary biologists believe the reason for this disparity traces back to our ancient ancestors.[16] We might consider how mettle and risk-taking are prerequisites for hunting big game and heading into battle. If infantry soldiers in the seventeenth and eighteenth centuries had paused to contemplate the horror that awaited them, it would have been difficult to heed the commander when he cried out, "Charge!"

I first heard this concept from Dr. Randi Hagerman, who was then head of the Fragile X Clinic at Colorado's Children's Hospital. She is now medical director of the MIND Institute at the University of California, Davis, which is one of the world's leading autism research clinics. She asked us to think about the traditional roles for men and women during ancient times and the harsh environments in which they lived, such as the Plains Indians who inhabited Eastern Colorado centuries ago. The men walked or rode great distances each day as they hunted game and protected their lands from intruders. If you have ever hunted before, you know that you need to be able to quickly divert your focus when you hear a twig break or see the slightest movement. Boys notice movement more effectively, have better night vision, and can read smaller fine print, while girls are able to discern colors more accurately and have wider peripheral vision.[17]

The women might be at the camp taking care of the young, preparing yesterday's catch for the harsh winter to come, or going out to gather water and food. These tasks require someone with a formidable attention span (toddlers have a way of wandering off easily) who notices the tiniest of berries. Female eyes are better suited for identifying bright colors, and their precise, gradual movements, and impulse control allows them to collect those well-hidden berries.[18]

The equilibrium between the genders ensured the whole tribe's survival. It would be pretty difficult for a pregnant woman or a woman with young infants to keep up with a buffalo chase. In addition to protecting a mother or future tribe member, the tribe also needed members to care for those who might not be able to speak or couldn't care for themselves: the elderly and injured. As will be explored in section IV, this caring for others was also aided by a female's greater ability to notice the facial expressions, and hence, the emotions of others.

Having these particular skills and abilities doesn't mean that one gender is better than the other; rather, it emphasizes how differing environmental demands require these skills for continued existence. When highlighting this point, I encourage my fourth graders to consider what would happen if all tribe members had uniformly high Presidential functioning. I then have them imagine that we are all Native Americans sitting around the campfire, weaving baskets as we listen to a storyteller. I ask the kids, "What might happen?" We brainstorm and decide that it wouldn't be too long before a predator, like a mountain lion, might sneak up and snatch one of the tribe members while the rest of us were focused on the story. I then explain that if half our tribe members are more distractible and impulsive than the rest, they would notice movement in the grass and throw their spears. The tribe member who saves us from the lion would be declared the hero of the evening.

While these complementary genetic traits made sense for our ancestors, our modern world and school environments don't always support the executive functioning of boys. There just aren't many wild lions roaming our school hallways that demand a quick response. Fortunately, many schools now recognize the natural needs of boys and integrate them into their teaching approach.

BOYS IN SCHOOL

Thanks to the work of Michael Gurian and the Gurian Institute, tens of thousands of teachers have learned and implemented techniques, which help make school a better fit for boys.[19] Gurian's books and lectures explore how gender-based learning differences affect a child's fit with contemporary school environments and note how boys are more likely to engage in hands-on roughhousing and competitive play (discussed further in section IV). Along with competition, most boys like bright lights and raucous sounds for pushing their Presidential concentration to higher levels. Girls, on the other hand, usually prefer quieter, softer settings and cooperative activities for maximizing their Presidential functioning.[20]

Modern schools are frontal lobe intense: **The classroom consists of lots of listening, contains throngs of kids who create many distractions, and has little hands-on action and adventure.** Gurian notes how schools and classroom delivery methods are typically designed by adults who learned well in these environments.[21] In other words, school designs currently favor males and females who are higher up on the Spectrum of Presidential Functioning.

However, students who struggle with ADHD have an even more difficult experience than males in traditional schools. Some individuals' chromosomes have small gene variations that are associated with poorer executive functioning and differences in frontal lobe development. These genetic differences mean that these students will be on the lowest end of the Spectrum of Presidential Functioning (approximately three boys for every girl).[22] Can you imagine how difficult school is for these students? Despite having adequate cognitive skills, these children receive more behavioral referrals, lower grades, and have higher drop-out rates (32 percent) when compared with other students.[23]

It's important to remember that much of the genetics we have been talking about relate to statistical averages. A person's genetic makeup is as unique as his or her environmental circumstances. Where do you think your child is on the Presidential spectrum? The environment you provide your child needs to match his or her executive functioning.

We must also appreciate the strengths and contributions of children who don't fit the statistical norm. All species need to have genetic diversity in order to be able to adapt to ever-changing environments. The marshmallow experiment offers a fun and important look at how children fall on the spectrum.

BRAIN ACTIVITY: CAN YOU RESIST THE MARSHMALLOW?

The Stanford marshmallow experiment was first conducted in the late 1960s and early 1970s.[24] *If you search Google or YouTube, you can find a contemporary version of the experiment titled "The Marshmallow Experiment—Instant Gratification." In the experiment, a researcher laid out a marshmallow on the table in front of a four- to six-year-old child. The child was then told that he or she could eat the treat now or wait fifteen minutes and then receive an additional marshmallow to eat. When testing each child, scientists found that a portion of the children ate the marshmallow immediately. Some ate it even before the researcher left the room. Another portion tried to wait the full fifteen minutes but eventually caved in and ate the treat after an average of seven minutes. Watching these children try to not eat the treat was comical as they squirmed and squiggled, touched and licked the treat, and stared at it and sat on their hands before finally eating it. However, a third of the children were able to sit patiently in their seats. They looked around the room and waited the entire fifteen minutes in order to receive their reward.*

In the results, researchers found that the four-year-olds were more likely to eat the treat immediately. As we will explore in the following chapters, there is a huge difference in the development of the prefrontal cortex for a four-year-old compared with that of a six-year-old.

The researchers then wanted to know why the children who waited the entire fifteen minutes (the waiting group) were able to resist the whole time. The answer was obvious from watching the children who tried to wait but couldn't (the tried-to-wait group). Can you or your child guess what the researchers observed? Like the first group of children who ate the snack immediately (the immediate group), these children in the tried-to-wait group weren't able to resist temptation because they were focused on the treat. While they waited longer than the immediate group, they continued to think about the treat for the seven-minute average. Because they were obsessing about the treat, they couldn't control their impulse to consume it.

During interviews with children in the waiting group, the researchers discovered their secret for success. Instead of focusing on the treat, they distracted themselves during the wait period. They looked about the room, fidgeted with their outfits and thought about what they would be doing afterward. They weren't thinking about the treat. Unlike the immediate group and the tried-to-wait group, who both lacked the impulse to achieve a greater, longer-term goal, the waiting group was able to halt their impulses and then apply a strategy for sustaining their will and overcoming the desire for immediate gratification. These distraction techniques can also help the President control a child's emotions when he or she is afraid of a bee or upset over not getting a cookie.

The researchers then wanted to look at how the children in each of these groups developed over time. This part of the research took years to study and, in fact, is still being researched today. The researchers wondered if a child's impulse control grouping at age four to six could correlate to possible life outcomes many years later. What do you and your child think the researchers found when they looked at these kids in their twenties?

Yes, the marshmallow experiment from early childhood had predictable results at age twenty! Those children who couldn't wait and immediately consumed the treat were more likely to have lower levels of overall life satisfaction, lower levels of academic attainment, lower income levels, and higher incarceration levels. They were constantly following their impulses and couldn't sustain their motivation for longer-term goals and payoffs.

The group of children who could wait, however, were more likely to be content with their lives, had attained advanced degrees, and earned a higher average income. They also had the lowest levels of legal problems and other behaviors associated with young adults. The kids who could control their impulses for the immediate treat at age four grew into adults who could resist other immediate desires (perhaps not going out to a party when homework has to be done) in order to obtain longer-term goals and rewards.

What about the children in the tried-to-wait group? Their results on the surveys were right in the middle. They were doing better than the immediate group but not as well as the waiting group. They could fight their immediate impulses at first but couldn't sustain their motivation for longer time periods.

So, it seems that one's impulse control level as a preschooler might be a predictor for impulse control and Presidential functioning later in life. In fact, these results might also apply to middle age and beyond. Years later, follow-up research with these same children found that additional health consequences were showing up later in life. Adults in the immediate group had the highest levels of obesity, heart disease, and diabetes. On the other hand, adults in the waiting group enjoyed greater health and physical fitness.

A forty-year study in New Zealand also supports Stanford's marshmallow experiment results. Following 1,037 children who were born in the same twelve-month period, the study revealed that "childhood self-control strongly predicts adult success, in people of high or low intelligence, in rich or poor."[25] It also showed that those children who showed signs of self-regulation early on were less likely to commit a crime or develop later addictions. In addition, as adults, they were healthier and wealthier than their peers who were more impulsive.[26] In fact, a child's ability to self-regulate is a better predictor for academic achievement than IQ.[27]

Instructions for Can You Resist the Marshmallow?

The marshmallow test isn't a standardized test of future behavior, and failing it doesn't ensure a negative outcome for your child. The test is simply an indicator that impulse control might be challenging, but it is a skill that you can help your child develop.

1. *Grab a handful of marshmallows or whatever sweet treat your child enjoys.*

2. *Have your child sit at the kitchen table and place one of the treats on the table in front of him or her.*

3. *Explain that you are going to play a game of choice. Your child can eat the treat right away. Or, if he or she can wait fifteen minutes without eating it, you will give out two more treats at the end.*

4. *Remind your child to remain seated in the chair. Set the timer, and then leave the room.*

5. *When time runs out, come back into the room and have a good laugh while you either offer two more treats if your child could wait, or acknowledge that your child already enjoyed the one treat. (Note: This waiting should be relatively easy for your elementary aged child but more challenging for a four-year-old).*

6. *Imagine for a moment that you were trying this experiment with a group of four-year-olds. Brainstorm with your child about what they think would happen. Then tell them the story of the real experiment and the lessons behind it.*

7. *For future reinforcement, simply say the word "marshmallow" when your child is upset about an unfulfilled impulse.*

SECTION II

USE YOUR PRESIDENT!

"You don't know what you've got 'till it's gone."
-Joni Mitchell

The frontal lobe provides the master control system for the rest of the brain. These executive functions, which I describe as a child's President, help him or her manage academic endeavors, control impulses, initiate tasks, shift to a new strategy when needed, and develop successful social skills. Important Presidential skills (and the neurotransmitter dopamine) help your child master these tasks. Like the rest of the body, however, a child's President needs to be optimized internally and externally for maximum performance.

CHAPTER 4

THE PRESIDENT
MEETS A TAMPING IRON

Nothing captivates elementary aged children like another gross brain story. The amazing tale of Phineas Gage holds serious implications for our brain functioning.

In 1848, Phineas was the foreman of a railroad track construction gang that was blasting through granite bedrock. Phineas possessed uncommon physical strength but ascended to foreman of the crew because of his strong character and sharply focused mind. He was an organized leader who wasn't impulsive or emotional. In the field, he had a keen eye for detail and a unique ability to coordinate and direct his men and their various tasks simultaneously. Off the job site, he was known for having good manners and treating women respectfully. Phineas also avoided the impulsive behavior that was so characteristic of other workers, such as drinking excessively, gambling, and fighting.

The process of blasting granite was quite dangerous, so having a foreman who possessed self-control was paramount. After a hole was drilled and filled with gun powder and sand on top, Phineas had the most dangerous job of placing a long iron tamping rod into the hole. Using a sledge hammer, he would then pack the sand that was sitting on top of the gunpowder. One particular day, however, there was no sand on top of the gunpowder when Phineas' tamping iron descended into the hole. The gunpowder exploded, sending the tamping iron back out of the hole at lightning speed. The iron pierced Phineas just below the left cheek. Given the force of the blast, the three-foot rod shot completely through the top of his forehead and landed some thirty feet away. Phineas was thrown to his back as blood, bone, and brain matter—propelled by the tamping iron—erupted from the gaping hole in his head.

Expecting to find him dead, Phineas' crew members rushed over to his body. Collective shock rippled through the group when Phineas sat up, fully conscious, and talked calmly about the explosion. The workmen placed Phineas in a cart and took him into town. His men took him to a hotel, where they summoned the town doctor. A short time later, Dr. John Harlow arrived to clean Phineas' wound and gently place larger pieces of his skull back into place. Dr. Harlow also pulled over the remaining skin tissue and stitched it to cover the hole and placed Phineas in bed. Miraculously, some ten weeks later, Phineas' doctor declared him "fully recovered."[1]

Phineas could function just as he did before the accident, but soon others noticed something different about him. Since a portion of his brain, or his prefrontal cortex, was now missing, Phineas' behavior began to change.

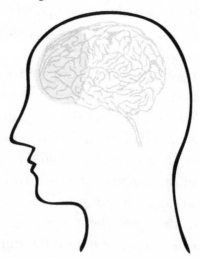

Thanks to Phineas (the rest of his story is at the end of this chapter) and the many advances in techniques for exploring our brains, we now have a full understanding of what functions occur in the frontal lobe. The President's tasks are too numerous to list, so we will focus on the six essential executive function skills: attention, organization, working memory, time management, movement, and emotional/impulse control.

As discussed in chapter 3, children have different levels of Presidential functioning just like the quality of water, music, and light varies among fountain shows around the world. While children have a general overall placement on the Spectrum of Presidential Functioning, their abilities with any given executive function can vary. Some children might struggle with one or two of these functions while another child might struggle with all of them. Over the years, I've seen children who struggle with attention and organization but not impulse control or movement activity. Others struggle with impulse control and/or hyperactivity but don't have problems with attention.

SIX ESSENTIAL PRESIDENTIAL SKILLS

Attention

Attention refers to our ability to orient ourselves to either internal or external incoming stimuli. Think of your average student sitting in an elementary school class. The teacher asks the class to get out their math books and turn to page 16, problem 3. In this situation, the President hears the message and motivates the student to sit down, pull out the text, and begin working on the project. The President should then sustain attention and focus by reminding the student to stay on the task until it is completed. Successful completion also involves messages to avoid distractions emanating from other stimuli. These distractible stimuli could be external, such as the mower going past the classroom window. The source of these stimuli can also be internal. Thoughts related to hunger, such as when lunch will be served, is an example of internal stimuli.

Unless the President identifies these internal and external stimuli as an emergency, its job in these situations is to "close the gate" on stimuli trying to enter our train of consciousness. Imagine trying to carry on a conversation in a room full of people where your ears can discern several other conversations. The President effectively filters out this irrelevant background information. If some of the internal or external stimuli are deemed to be important for a later time, the President will line these thoughts up at the gate and prioritize them until it is their turn to enter the conscious mind.

In addition to paying attention and avoiding distractions, the President's job is to help the child shift attention to other tasks when the time is necessary. For instance, at some point, the teacher will ask the students to close their math books and pull out their spelling work. This skill is important for transitioning to new tasks and being able to keep up with the demands of the changing schedules around which most schools function. Your family's morning and evening schedule is also greatly impacted when your child needs to shift focus from one task in order to complete another. Many a morning has begun with distress when a child fails to keep moving along before the school bus arrives.

Organization

The ability to stay on top of a teacher's requests in the classroom requires a degree of organization. Have the students brought back the math book from last night's homework, for instance? Can they find their books in their lockers or desks? Do they have writing utensils, and have they been sharpened from the last assignment? Do the math books get placed back in the desks in an organized fashion prior to starting the spelling work?

Some students seem to be naturally organized and have no trouble remembering all of life's details. Others fail to keep track of their supplies and are always running behind schedule. At homework time, these are the students who forget their assignment planner, leave the worksheets at school, and don't know where the field trip permission slip is or can't seem to find that overdue book in their rooms.

Another aspect of Presidential organization is the ability to think about future demands and then plan ahead. While this skill is obviously essential for academic and work success, it's also helpful for one's relationship success. The husband who waits until Valentine's Day to make dinner reservations doesn't make a favorable impression on his spouse. On a basic biological level, the child who doesn't plan a bathroom break before class can be faced with an embarrassing emergency.

Planning ahead and organizing is particularly important for academic success. One parent of a second grade girl recently told me about his daughter forgetting to bring home her spelling work. Immediately driving back to school, the child ran into the building to retrieve the work from her teacher. A short time later, she ran back to the car, happily waving her worksheet. Arriving back home, Dad looked over the worksheet and realized that the actual spelling word list was on a second page. "Oh, I forgot to get that one," she said. A trip back to school not only resulted in the embarrassment of her having to face the teacher again but also in a consequence of deducting from her allowance to cover the extra gas.

Working memory

Working memory is the ability to hold on to information for a brief period of time and then discard that memory upon completing a task. It's a bit like an Etch A Sketch, which allows people to make drawings that then quickly disappear. This information has no long-term relevance. Rather, working memory is a set of instructions that will help you accomplish your current task. Imagine how full our brains would become if we remembered every detail ever given to us. Like turning the pages on a newspaper article, you don't need to remember the jump page number once you are reading the story again.

For your child, mental math entails remembering one number while you execute a function (addition, multiplication, etc.) with another number. If they forget the first number, you have to start all over again. Switching tasks entails remembering specific details for just a moment. For instance, when the teacher says, "Put your math book away and then get out your spelling book and turn to lesson 23," that means holding on to page 23 while changing books.

Working memory also impacts social functioning. Is your child constantly forgetting to take an assignment or project to school even though you reminded them right before they were getting ready to leave? As children move into upper elementary, where group projects become more common, the other students quickly learn who they can and can't rely on for remembering their tasks and getting them turned in.

Time management

When the teacher gives out a math assignment, the student usually understands how much time will be allotted for that day's lesson. When initially scanning over the problem, the President's job is to determine how long the problem will take given a child's acuity in a particular subject and inherent processing speed. I knew, for instance, that I was one of the fastest math students. I could effortlessly whip through my math problems with time to spare. However, I was one of the slowest readers in the class, so I knew that I needed to use all of the allotted time and read as fast as I could. As the student progresses through the lesson, the President helps initiate, track, and manage task completion related to the remaining time.

While part of time management is being able to read a clock, it's also the ability to internally estimate how quickly time is passing without looking at a clock. Think of a great athlete who perfectly times a last-second shot. As a child's ability to estimate time increases with age, the increments for time management become smaller and smaller. While driving with my son at the age of four, for instance, he would ask how long it would take to drive somewhere. I would estimate the time in twenty-minute increments because that was the same length of one of his preschool videos. "Two videos," I'd say if the drive was about forty minutes. I could then watch him think and give me a confirming nod that he understood how long it would take. As my son got older, his ability to estimate chunks of time became more sophisticated.

At home, you as a parent can quickly assess your child's placement on the Spectrum of Presidential Functioning when you say, "We have to leave in five minutes." Higher end children realize that they still need to put on their shoes, grab their equipment bag, and fill up their water bottle. They then speed up their pace to accomplish the tasks. Lower end children may start out to get their shoes, but then might find a misplaced figurine. When you see your child sitting shoeless on the floor lost in imaginative play, you'll know where they reside on the spectrum.

Movement control

On the top of the frontal lobe in the middle sits a small finger-like area called the pre-motor cortex, which is the center for our movement control. In school terms, it's the ability to sit still throughout the lesson. Kindergartners will often be spinning around, laying on each other, and flinging their arms and legs when playing or while trying to sit at circle time.

While children in pre-K have a hard time sitting quietly for very long, the length of time for body control should expand as the child gets older. By early elementary, most students can sit and attend adequately for twenty minutes. As the years pass, that time expands to thirty and forty-five minutes. While high school classes often reach ninety minutes, we need to acknowledge that it is sometimes difficult for adult brains to control our bodies for that long. Ironically, it is regular movement and activity throughout the day that helps children control their bodies when it is time to sit still.

Impulse/emotional control

For physical and social survival's sake, one of the most important Presidential abilities is **the capacity to stop our immediate impulses and think about potential outcomes to our proposed behaviors.** At home, when your child turns to chase a ball across the street, it's the President's job to say "Stop!" when they reach the curb. If the ball ends up on the roof, the President helps your child to consider the possible consequences of shimming up the gutters before trying to retrieve it.

In the math example above, imagine that another student loudly passes gas in the middle of class while everyone else is trying to work on their math assignments. The impulse is to laugh. It's the President's job to stop the laughter and then evaluate circumstances, such as the teacher's temperament, the level of one's social connection with the child who passed gas, the duration that laughter would be appropriate, and the decibel level of one's laugh.

While the situation above relates to short-term goal achievement, the President also helps us stop impulses when we are working on longer-term projects. As children start on book reports, for instance, they must control their impulses to go and play when they are faced with the day's tasks for that longer-term project. Being able to control one's impulses in order to complete long-term goals is crucial for academic and social success. Impulsive children are unable to control their desires in order to obtain greater rewards. They are literally prisoners of the moment.

A good example of seeking immediate gratification can be found at the local arcade, where children crank their tokens into the chance games and cheer themselves on as the game spits out long strands of coveted tickets. Once the tickets are in their hands, only but a few children can resist running over to the prize counter and immediately spending them versus saving them up for a much bigger prize on a future visit. Many children, at home and school, need larger tasks broken down into manageable chunks and positive reinforcements for accomplishments along the way.

CAN YOU GUESS WHAT BECAME OF PHINEAS?

Phineas took a little time off to visit his mom before going back to work for the railroad. While he was physically strong again and possessed his same verbal and analytical skills, Phineas' co-workers noticed some changes in his behavior. According to some accounts, he was now quick-tempered, lacked the solid judgment he was known for, changed his mind frequently, and began using the foulest of language with his workers and with women. Dr. Harlow later wrote, "He is fitful, irreverent, indulging at times in the grossest profanity (which was not previously his custom), manifesting but little deference for his fellows, impatient of restraint or advice when it conflicts with his desires."[2] Sadly, the changes in his personality were so severe that the railroad decided to let him go.

After surviving an accident that took much of his frontal lobe, Phineas became a curiosity among the mid-nineteenth-century medical community while visiting the Harvard Medical School. This group was thrilled to have a living patient who had sustained damage to his prefrontal cortex in their company. For the first time, due to his postaccident personality changes, doctors understood how the prefrontal cortex governs self-control. One doctor stated: "We have been informed by the best authority that after the man recovered, and while recovering, he was grossly profane, coarse, and vulgar, to such a degree that his society was intolerable to decent people."[3]

After leaving Harvard, Phineas worked a variety of jobs, including a stint at P. T. Barnum's American Museum in New York where he was displayed with the predictable moniker, "The Man with a Hole in His Head." Phineas liked excitement and adventure, and after his stretch in the circus, he went on to be a stage coach driver in South America, which is not exactly the easiest or safest of jobs.

Unfortunately, due to the accident, Phineas developed seizures and moved back to his mother's. The seizures grew more frequent and ultimately took his life in 1860 at age thirty-six (eleven and a half years after the accident). Fortunately for science, Phineas donated his skull to the Harvard Medical School.

PROVIDING THE STRUCTURE YOUR CHILD NEEDS

When working with children on the lower end of the Spectrum of Presidential Functioning, an earlier point of Phineas' story—one that is often hard for younger students to grasp—is essential. Phineas still possessed his basic intelligence in math, reading, and writing after the accident. It was his impulse control that was diminished. In other words, a person who suffers damage to the prefrontal cortex could retain his or her intelligence but still struggle with Presidential functioning. Like a comic strip's light bulb that represents an idea, the front part of the brain's job is simply to orchestrate the many light bulbs with the changing demands of any situation. The President does this by telling which bulbs to turn off and which ones to turn on with perfect timing and intensity. The President's function is similar to the computer that controls the light, water, and music show at the Bellagio Resort in Las Vegas. Each element has to be controlled perfectly, and all three elements must be precisely coordinated.

As amazing as the Bellagio show is, it pales in comparison to the intricate choreography the President plans and deftly executes every day. For instance, when your child arrives at school, the President must call out its commands: "Keep working, hurry up, ignore the kid who farted, get ready to finish, or move on to spelling after organizing your math book." This elaborate neurological dance occurs throughout the day until the President rests with a good night's sleep.

Depending on your child's Presidential functioning, it's important to remember one of the most basic concepts of successful parenting: *The less internal control your child has, the more external control they need.* Children on the lower end need clear rules and expectations spelled out before, during, and after a given activity. I told a group of students before our upcoming trip to a water park that they were going to be like horses in a corral. As I drew a picture of a corral and listed the rules and boundaries for the trip, I explained that they would be fenced in like horses so we wouldn't lose anybody. I then explained that if the rules were followed, we could expand the corral for the afternoon. If not, then the corral would become smaller. One insightful boy said, "I don't need a fence; I need a brick wall!" This boy knew where he was on the Presidential spectrum.

In fact, this young man was on the lower end of Presidential functioning, having been diagnosed with ADHD. He had chronic problems with numerous Presidential functions, which affected his behavior at home and at school. In addition, students with ADHD have much higher rates of academic, emotional, and social problems. Researcher William E. Pelham, now with Florida International

University, found that 80 percent of children with ADHD have social skill deficits, compared to 7 percent of all children.[4] Once again, it's not that these children aren't smart, it's just that they can't manage all of their light bulbs and balance those Presidential functions. This deficit can irritate or alienate others.

Years ago, I was delightfully surprised by a student who was paying attention to my class and wasn't exercising his impulses for fun and stimulation. I had just explained how some children are on the lower end of the scale and that this is called having ADHD. The young man jumped up on top of his chair and cheerfully exclaimed, "I have that!" I recalled how several years earlier it was reported that he had stacked up several trash cans to retrieve a football from the roof, evidence of the boy's tendency to act impulsively without regard to safety.

The less internal control your child has, the more external control they need.

From a basic survival standpoint, it's critical for adults to understand children's approximate locations on the Presidential spectrum and remind them of the importance of thinking about using their Presidents. Too frequently I've seen children and teens make poor choices that resulted in injury or property loss to themselves or others.

Unfortunately, with low Presidential functioning as an ADHD hallmark, children who suffer from ADHD face many of the same challenges as Phineas did after his accident. The good news is that unlike Phineas, with treatment, careful monitoring, and interventions, children with ADHD have the opportunity to increase their Presidential functioning. At my office, we offer parent coaching, individual/family therapy and social/emotional development group therapy for ADHD families. We also refer children to executive functioning classes/camps and often recommend home-based tutors to help with specific learning issues, organization, and homework support. For children whose ADHD has a major impact on their academic and behavioral functioning, we also refer families for a medication evaluation. Obviously, families can't implement all these options at once. My standard advice to parents is: You have to balance your time, money, energy, and the needs of your ADHD children as you walk this path.

Remember, with consistent support, any child who suffers from executive dysfunction can learn to use his or her President and manage impulses before they result in life-changing decisions. Like building a great stone wall one brick at a time, gradual improvement—both socially and academically—will cultivate a track record of success that boosts a child's self-worth and carries into adulthood. Finally, given the importance of impulse control, I'd like to offer the following strategies.

FIVE WAYS TO STRENGTHEN YOUR CHILD'S IMPULSE CONTROL

The 1-2-3 behavior system

I highly recommend Thomas Phelan's behavior system from his book, *1-2-3 Magic*, which also contains a wealth of parenting tips.[5] Dr. Phelan is the parent of two boys with attention deficit hyperactivity disorder and developed his concepts around his own parenting. His 1-2-3 approach is similar to what our grandmothers used. If your children start misbehaving, then start counting. The number one serves as a warning and number two is the reminder of the impending consequence. If you get to number three, the consequence is immediately enforced. Phelan's book and video is particularly good for cutting down negotiations with your child. As I look back to my own childhood, my father utilized this same sort of system when my brother and I misbehaved in the basement. While he read his evening paper, we'd first hear his voice telling us to calm down. If later we heard the arm on his La-Z-Boy chair go down, we knew we had to quiet down fast. If we heard the sound of the arm going back up, we knew we were OK, but if we heard his feet hit the ground, we knew that he was coming to the basement door and that our playtime was over.

"Knipp" it in the bud

Follow the old adage, "Nip it in the bud." One of the best compliments I ever received was from a mom who said, "Around our house, we just 'Knipp' it in the bud!" In addition to the fun play on my nickname, I was thrilled that she understood the importance of cutting off temper tantrums and overly rowdy behavior with her three young children. Like a freight train, it's a lot easier to stop one when it's just starting up than when it's running full steam. When your child starts acting up, don't wait too long before you say one of the following statements:

- That's one (if you like the 1-2-3 behavior system approach).
- Stop now, or you will have to _____.
  (Insert the consequence you find most useful.)
- Settle down, kids.
- Take that behavior outside. (My mom's favorite.)

For younger children, a positive sticker chart for calming oneself down in a prudent fashion can also be very motivating.

Besides helping your child manage their emotions and energy more effectively, you'll find that you as the parent will remain calmer. When you are upset and yelling, it's a pretty good sign that you waited too long to intervene. To quote one of my favorite child authors (Ross Campbell, author of *How to Really Love Your Child*), parents should be "pleasant but firm." When you "Knipp" it in the bud, you'll have a much better chance of achieving that goal.

Coordinate school and home systems for behavior management

Don't be afraid to use your village of teachers to support your efforts. Schools have great systems for behavior management so try using the system from school at home. To survive the structure-free summer after first grade with my son, I utilized the same Green, Yellow, and Red card system they had at school. In addition, don't be afraid to work with your child's teacher for a little extra support for before-school and after-school behavior. Since I had become very tired of yelling at my child every morning to hustle up and get ready, I took him into his teacher's classroom after school one day and explained that I was just going to wait patiently for him to be ready in the mornings in order to decrease all the tension. I asked the teacher, "If he is late, could you hold him out of recess for every minute he is late to school?" She replied, "I'd be happy to." We were never late to school the rest of the year, and I was able to enjoy my coffee and newspaper every morning.

Ask neighbors and other parents to use the same structure

In addition to school support, empower neighbors and other parents to support your structure. Before an upcoming play date or activity, let your children know that they are expected to adjust to the standards of where they are going. Then let the adult in charge know about your home system should any problems arise. For instance, if you are using the 1-2-3 behavior system, let the other adults, instructors, and babysitters know that they can start counting to three if your child misbehaves. Your child is likely to stop inappropriate behavior if they know that number three will carry a consequence back at home. Other parents in our community felt free to discipline my brothers and me when we were growing up or send us home if social conflicts weren't corrected. If we were running around outside and got out of hand, we knew that our elderly neighbor was always looking out her window and was

more than happy to call our mother about the Knippenberg boys'
behavior.

Build awareness that your child can relate to

I worked with a seven-year-old boy who was coming to my
office due to impulse control behaviors at home and school. While
he often lacked a filter related to silliness, inappropriate language,
and roughhousing, he was amazingly controlled when it came to
playing the card game Uno with me. Each time it was his turn, he
would thoughtfully analyze his cards and the potential consequence
of his playing options before making his selection. He took great
joy in beating me soundly over the course of five or six sessions. I
told him, "You know, social situations are just like playing Uno.
You just have to slow down and go over the potential consequence
of all your options before you make a choice." Then he was able
to understand his impulse control in a completely different way.
A Denver-based nonprofit also uses chess to teach teens how to
control their impulses and utilize decision-making strategy in real
life: "That's our motto," director Phillip Douglas says, "make your
next move your best move."[6]

In her sessions with younger children, my therapist wife has
several different posters and drawings for reinforcing impulse
control. Phrases such as, "Stop and think," "Make good choices,"
"Filter please," and "Is that just right or too much?" are often used by
her and the child's parents at home. When it comes to great books
for younger elementary students on the subject of self-control, my
two favorites are David Shannon's *David Goes to School* and Bruce
Hale's *Clark the Shark*.[7]

BRAIN ACTIVITY: WHEN WILL WE GET THERE?

Time management, or the ability to perceive how quickly time is passing in relationship to current and upcoming demands, is essential for success in a variety of areas. Late assignments and the lack of accurate time perception that often causes them are a chronic problem for students on the lower end of the Spectrum of Presidential Functioning. Think about the emotional toll it takes when you're constantly running behind. It's the same feeling your child has when they receive another missing or late assignment notice. Developing these time management skills for your child in a novel and fun way is easy to do.

At the conclusion of my class on time management, I give the students an exercise for their homework during the upcoming week. Before they are to begin their homework assignment for each night, they have to write down the estimated time they think it will take to complete their assignment. Then, they are to utilize a clock or stopwatch to track the actual time it takes. The students should compare their total time estimates to the amount of time they actually spent on the assignments for that evening and throughout the week.

Given that this lesson falls mid-year in fourth grade, many of the students' estimates are fairly accurate since they are familiar with their homework routine. However, several other students significantly underestimated how long these tasks would take. I can't imagine the conflicts that might be happening nightly in these households with such discrepancies.

At home, you may wish to have your children use the time estimations for homework throughout the entire year. Again, emphasize that it is not the amount of actual time that matters, but the ability to accurately predict how long a given activity will take.

In addition to this activity, try having some time estimation fun in other areas. For instance, try time estimation in the car. When my son was young, I would ask him to estimate how long it would take us to drive home from school that afternoon. While the drive typically averaged eight minutes, the estimations involved thinking about factors such as the time of day, road construction, and any weather that could get in the way. After your child makes their estimate, check your electronic navigation system to see how they compare.

On longer car trips, have fun with helping your child understand time instead of being hostage to questions such as When will we get there? My family uses time management to estimate how long the day's journey might take us. These longer estimations include factors such as rest stops, food needs, and how long our dog can ride in the back of the SUV before she needs to walk and take care of her business. These trip games also involve a lot of great math practice as we learn how to estimate map mileages and average travel speed. For younger children, chunk the trip out into predictable distances.

Finally, kitchen timers work great for helping your child complete tasks while also learning to think about time. There is a wonderful clock at www.timetimer.com used by many parents and teachers that helps children see exactly how much time is passing as they are completing a task. You set the clock for the desired amount of time, which is indicated by the color red. As the clock ticks away, the red disappears so that the child can see exactly how quickly time is passing. There are also many great watches on the market today that allow your child to set multiple alarm settings as reminders for what tasks need to be accomplished. Wearing a simple digital wrist watch really helped our daughter be more mindful of time when she was in fifth grade.

CHAPTER 5

DOPAMINE: THE "FRANCHISE PLAYER" OF YOUR PRESIDENT'S EXECUTIVE TEAM

Every year the NFL draft offers the long-suffering fans of beleaguered franchises hope that this could be the year they land the next Tom Brady or Aaron Rodgers. Perhaps this will be the year they pick a quarterback that will make the team a contender for the next ten to fifteen years. If not, even the most capable receivers, tight ends, and offensive linemen won't reach their full potential. Those other players, talented as they might be, are completely dependent on the physical skill and timely decision-making of their quarterback.

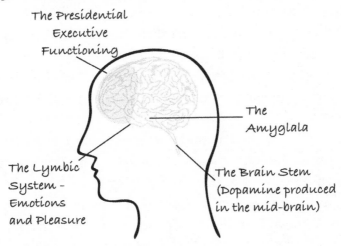

DOPAMINE HIGHWAY

Effective Presidential functioning within the brain isn't so different than the formula for a winning football team. There are many neurotransmitters our brains use to communicate a variety of messages. Dopamine, however, is the superstar quarterback, or the Peyton Manning of neurotransmitters. While norepinephrine and other chemicals are also vital, dopamine, which "touches the ball on every play," is the field general of executive functioning.

There are two areas of the brain that produce dopamine. For our purposes, we will look at the dopamine system, which starts in the ventral tegmental area in the mid-brain.[1] Like pathways through a forest, one string of neurons wraps through the emotional area of the brain, while another pathway runs up through the President. Dopamine pathways are also responsible for maintaining automatic brain functioning. The variable speeds at which our dopamine levels rise and activate our brains in the morning can be observed in your own family. Some wake up bright eyed and bushy tailed while others take longer to shake off their early morning grogginess.

As their dopamine levels rise into the range I call the sweet spot, your child deploys their President on a variety of morning tasks: getting dressed, making the bed, eating breakfast, brushing teeth, and combing hair. The President also helps to kick off the school day by assisting in the organization of class materials and turning in homework.

If we were to look at a child's neurons using our earlier kayak analogy, we would find that the message of paying attention is being taken down to that dock and getting loaded into the kayak (the dopamine kayak in this case). Quickly and efficiently, the messenger in the dopamine kayak paddles across the stream, docks, and passes off the message to his friend waiting on the other side. The messenger turns the kayak around and heads back to the original dock and prepares for the President's next message.

A baseline of dopamine is different for each person. Your child's brain has its own unique chemical composition.[2] What if, for instance, a child suffers from low dopamine levels? The kayak isn't waiting at the dock when the messenger runs down with the message. In addition, your child's brain uniqueness is also responsible for the number of dopamine receptors, or docks, your child has.[3] What if the dock on the other side is missing? Or, what if the dock on the other side is damaged in some way and the kayak has a hard time docking? Some kayaks turn around too quickly before reaching the other side or stay at the new dock too long and don't return home to receive a new message. Even a slight disruption of this rhythm can affect brain functioning.[4]

As we will explore in chapter 6, a child's dopamine levels are impacted by nutrition, sleep, and exercise throughout the day. In addition, if a child doesn't like a particular topic, their dopamine levels might decline slightly. When a child encounters a boring or distasteful task, it takes extra effort to keep the President functioning. Children higher up on the Spectrum of Presidential Functioning are able to maintain Presidential functioning through adversity, while others find it virtually impossible. If their dopamine levels drop below the sweet spot, you'll observe them drifting off into daydreaming or seeking the dopamine enhancing act of horsing around with a friend.

When the material is particularly interesting, their dopamine levels will rise slightly higher. Novelty also increases the President's attentiveness. It makes sense that our ancestors would be a little more focused when encountering a new situation, such as meeting new people or traveling to a new place.

THE PLEASURE SIDE OF DOPAMINE

Too High	*Hyper-focus: Other functions diminished*
Just Right	*All functions*
Too Low	*Under-aroused functions*

In addition to Presidential functioning, the dopamine system also has a relationship with the brain's pleasure circuit.[5] This means that a child's interests and motivation affect the President's dopamine process as well. If a child likes a particular subject or enjoys an activity, this system works more efficiently. In these cases, dopamine levels slightly increase. Like an adult who prefers enjoyable activities to difficult or monotonous tasks, a child's President works more effectively when the task at hand is stimulating. For struggling readers, new research shows that when students choose books based on their interests, their pleasure connection with reading increases.[6] The extra dopamine onboard helps the reader stay more focused and feel pleasure with the task of reading.

At the same time, it can be hard for children to keep their Presidents focused on the task at hand when other incoming stimuli seem so tempting and fun. Even children at the high end of the Spectrum of Presidential Functioning may find it hard not to laugh when another child blurts out a joke. Many parents have also received the following admonishment from teachers and administrators: "Constant chatting with peers is slowing your child's progress." For kids who crave the pleasure of social connection, the urge to chitchat overrides their President's messages to stay on task.

A child's pleasure system can be utilized to help them get motivated with school and homework. Some children can easily get ready for the task at hand because they take joy in pleasing their teachers or parents by getting the work done. These children seem to embody the well-known saying, *Don't put off till tomorrow what you can do today*. For many children, the school day is a minute-to-minute battle to stay motivated and on task. Unless they are doing something they like, teacher feedback can indicate that a child has "low will power," is "unmotivated," or even "lazy." When it comes to homework, they can give you a long list of avoidance techniques and argumentative strategies. Rather than using character-defect adjectives, it's important for teachers and parents to remember that these students are merely struggling to keep their dopamine systems up and running and then utilize strategies to increase their motivation.

FIVE WAYS TO INCREASE YOUR CHILD'S MOTIVATION

Save the most pleasurable activity for last

Positive reinforcement is one way that humans motivate themselves. (For instance, if I follow the rules of the road, my insurance company will send me a rebate on my premium.) One way to help children complete tasks is to help them build insight into what is most motivating. You can design strategies for finishing homework or chores that use high motivating tasks, which will reinforce getting the low motivating tasks done. For example, your child might choose to work on spelling words first and then do the more pleasurable reading homework afterward. Some of my son's most productive homework sessions took place with his best friend. I'd set the boys up at the kitchen counter for homework time. The carrot for staying on task was their much-anticipated free play afterward.

Implement consequences for non-compliance

In addition to being motivated by positive reinforcement, humans can be motivated in order to avoid a negative consequence. (For instance, I won't speed to avoid getting a ticket.) Some children will increase their motivation when they know a consequence will be coming for noncompliance. If your child responds more effectively to consequences, be very clear about what future activity won't be taking place unless their tasks are completed. If arguing or manipulations ensue, make sure that you are firm and very clear about what needs to happen. Then walk away and let your child rise to the occasion.

When it comes to utilizing negative reinforcement, remember that if you stay engaged in the argument, you're likely to become even more stressed and start increasing the consequences. Later, you'll realize that being grounded for a month is too harsh a consequence and not possible to reinforce.

Encourage creativity to combat boredom

Since a child's dopamine levels are highly variable, every parent should be aware of their child's need for stimulation. Children become bored easily and that usually means a lot of complaining. For example, after snowshoeing for hours to get to our favorite mountain hut, my then ten-year-old son yelled out from inside the hut, "I'm bored!" just as I was sitting down for a cold beer after the long hike in. I quickly responded by saying, "That's great. I don't ever get to be bored. I bet you'll find something to do." His creativity kicked in, and when I returned to the hut an hour later, I found him playing in his newly designed army fort with camouflaged netting and sleeping bags strung up around the bunk beds. The increase in his dopamine levels saved the day.

But don't immediately substitute electronics for an added dopamine kick. Pediatrics professor Michael Rich, founder of the

Center on Media and Child Health at Harvard Medical School, believes that electronics block a child's creative process: "Boredom is where creativity and imagination take place. . . . A phone fills that gap."[7] It's better to promote thoughtful, Presidential-rich activities such as bracelet making, knitting, or model building. The next time your child complains that they are bored, try using my mother's standard response, "Find something to do, or I'll find something for you to do."

Add a time frame to complete an activity

For children who like challenges, try adding a time frame for an unpleasant homework task. You might say, "Let's see if you can finish those five problems in the next fifteen minutes." For younger children, you can also add in a positive reward such as a shared activity together or time in the yard when the task is completed. For older students, help them decide what might be a fun break activity in between each assignment. Some ideas include playing with the dog, working on a Rubik's Cube, or jumping on the trampoline.

Let your child follow their motivations

For some children, especially those with high Presidential functioning, doing homework is a naturally pleasing activity. They love and embrace learning and might even ask the teacher for more homework. In addition, some children might be tapping into a third motivation for humans: altruism. (For instance, I drive the speed limit because I want my community to be safe for others.) These children complete their tasks so they can be the best student they can be and a good role model for the rest of the class. At home, they are driven to complete chores because they care about family harmony.

Even if your child isn't motivated by schoolwork or home chores, they still need to follow their passions. Many children find their passion in hobbies, athletics, and artistic endeavors. I once worked with a student who had dyslexia and was passionate about dance. Her mother asked if she should have her drop dance in order to take on additional tutoring. "Absolutely not!" I replied. She ended up dancing all the way through high school.

DOPAMINE AND HYPER-FOCUS: A TWO-EDGED SWORD

Humans have many habits that we find inherently pleasurable, including our natural craving for calorie-rich sugars and other sweets. Even though we might regret that extra slice of pie or scoop of ice cream now, we also have the desire to repeat that behavior again as we anticipate the pleasure of the dopamine reward.[8]

Ironically, at these higher levels of dopamine, the President loses many of its other functions. Have you ever been so engrossed in something that you completely lost track of time? When I first began playing the computer version of the game Risk, I felt such joy. Transfixed by the game, I would lose track of time and play it for hours on end. I stopped playing cold turkey after about three months of sleep deprivation. During these activities that induce extreme pleasure, the President moves into a space known as hyper-focus and finds it difficult to manage the other messages it needs to communicate, such as "It's time to go to bed" or " I'm about to pee in my pants." At this point the dopamine dock is loaded with messages such as "stay focused on this task," which vastly outnumber more sensible messages like "I need to stop now" or "Bedtime."[9]

Children can become so absorbed in their Legos, iPads, or television programs that they find it difficult to pull away and get washed up for dinner or start their homework.

First-person shooter video games in particular increase dopamine sixteen-fold.[10] This spike is roughly equivalent to the dopamine surge one experiences when using marijuana.[11] This hyper-focus and extreme pleasure circuit created by dopamine makes it difficult to wrestle a child away from a screen and parents might hear excuses such as, "But I just started playing!" or "I have to finish this level before I can save it!"

The other problem with hyper-focused states is the crash that occurs after a dopamine surge.[12] When they sink lower than the sweet spot, or optimal dopamine level, children experience several neurological side effects. On an emotional level, parents see the effects when their children are moody and agitated for an hour or so after the dopamine is released. Teachers see the day-after effects on a child's homework. Instead of being focused on the homework, the student's brain is focused on consolidating the memories from the video game they were playing right before starting on their studies. For our ancestors, memory consolidation was ideal for remembering where in the woods a predator is living. However, remembering gaming strategies won't prepare your child for a school day.

Hyper-focused states, however, can have their benefits. The brain relaxes when we focus on one thing versus juggling multiple tasks throughout the day. As we will explore in the brain activities on breath work and visualization (chapters 8 and 11), single-mindedness takes high levels of focus in order for the brain to relax. Brilliant artists, writers, musicians, and athletes also achieve great feats during these highly enjoyable, high-level dopamine periods.[13] In his book, *Ninety Percent Mental*, retired all-star baseball pitcher Bob Tewksbury comments on players getting into a zone: "When (former Giants pitcher) Matt Cain threw a perfect game, he said he didn't even know what he had until the eighth inning. When people are in a zone like that, they don't think about anything and just compete. But those times are not often."[14] While it can be beneficial, the problem with hyper-focus is that it is impossible to sustain. Busy schedules, not dopamine levels, dictate how we spend the majority of our time. It's hard to be a functioning parent or student the next day if you have been hyper-focused all night on your next creation or next gaming victory.

BRAIN ACTIVITY: ORGANIZATION

Use a planner

I'm a big believer in students writing everything down that they need to do in their school planners. At home, you can help your child create a list of what they need to do and when it needs to be completed.

It's easy to go online and search for organizational strategies and tools for children. At our house, heavy emphasis and reinforcement is placed on my daughter filling out her school planner. Before her final year of elementary school, she also went to a two-week organizational day camp. The students learned and practiced all sorts of strategies and even used them to plan out fun afternoon activities and trips. For younger children, make sure to reinforce the teacher's method for organizational demands. If it's a note that was sent home in the assignment folder or in an email, sit down with your child and read it together. Then help your child brainstorm what they will need and how they will accomplish the tasks.

Organize on a daily basis and declutter

Younger elementary students usually have a home folder in their backpack. It's good practice to sit down and go through this with your child on a daily or weekly basis. Then, make sure your child puts it back in their pack.

If your older elementary child struggles with the advanced organizational demands at school, there are all sorts of locker organizers on the market. My daughter prefers color-coding book covers that match the folders for each subject. At home, make sure you have daily chore lists and then organize your child's room so that everything has its place. Pack an equipment bag in the order of how your child will use those materials. As my son and I learned with scuba diving, we now pack our gear bag in the order of when we will put it on. If we pack our masks, snorkels, and fins at the top of the bag, we learned that they will fall off a rolling boat while we are digging for our wet suits. You can also organize your child's chest of drawers in the order of how they will get dressed.

If your child likes to collect things, you will have to help them deep purge on a regular basis. The decluttering and reorganization needs to happen weekly with your child's backpack, locker, and desk.

Let's review that you have everything

Before leaving for school or any other activity, make sure you stop before opening the door and say, "Let's review that you have everything." Teach your children to act like they are checking out of a hotel room when transitioning between spaces. They should always look around for their missing blankie, stuffie, or clothes before you let that room door close behind you.

BRAIN ACTIVITY: A PLAN FOR HOMEWORK

1. *Have a healthy snack and a glass of water as the two of you chat about your day. Then, take a fifteen-minute exercise break before you begin working on homework—walk the dog, shoot some hoops, or go for a jog. Lastly, for younger elementary students, implement the following routine for organizing the work they have:*

   • *Estimate how much time each assignment will take. Go over the list of assignments and help your children estimate how much time each will take or which assignments will be more difficult. For motivation purposes, I suggest that students start with either the longest or the hardest assignment first. Once they get those done, everything seems much easier.*

- *Stack the assignments and work in fifteen-minute increments. After making these decisions, stack up the assignments in order on the left side of the desk. As your child gets started on the first one, let them know you will check back in with them in fifteen minutes (also tell them to stack the finished work on the right side of the table). If they get stuck, tell them to put a check by the problem and move on to the next one. You should then go about your own tasks. At the break, take five minutes to review what has been completed and review any questions your child has checked off. Repeat this process until your child approaches the last fifteen-minute segment. When they have finished, do one final review and help them organize the completed work into their assignment planner and backpack.*

2. *Keep using this homework routine as your child moves into upper elementary. As each month goes by, encourage your children to use this system on their own and minimize your direct involvement. While some children will get right to their work on their own, others will need this consistent structure. While most parents start this homework routine at the kitchen table, children will mature into wanting to do their work in their room. Depending on your child's Presidential application abilities, you may need to have them leave the door open to ensure they are staying on task.*

3. *An "ask and show" process is helpful for reviewing homework when your child is able to finish the assignments on his or her own. Instead of checking the online portal or approaching your children about what's been completed, get into the habit of having your children come to you. Let them show you the online portal and their completed homework. When it comes to reviewing the accuracy of the work, try to avoid immediately identifying what the mistakes are. The goal is for your child to review and find them. Try and make a game out of it by saying something like, "I noticed three things that need to be corrected. See if you can find them." This same approach can be used when going over the chore list or checking to see how clean their room actually is.*

Other things to keep in mind

- *If your child goes to an after-school or study hall program, it's not a bad idea to ask the staff to promote this homework routine and keep a watchful eye if your child tends to get distracted.*
- *If your child has after-school sports and arts practices, you'll need to help them break down the assignments into the various times they have available for homework.*
- *Children do well with a color-coded block schedule to help them visualize when they will be doing assignments.*

CHAPTER 6

THE CARE AND FEEDING
OF THE PRESIDENT

The more we use the muscles in our arms and legs, the stronger they get. The same can be said for Presidential abilities. Educational consultant Jim Wright suggests self-management techniques for students that have been proven to be effective by a variety of researchers over the past two decades.[1] One involves a timer and an attention checklist. Each child is given a check sheet and a timer is placed on the child's desk, which is set to buzz silently every two minutes. When the timer goes off, the student simply needs to place a check under one of the two headings: "I was paying attention" or "I wasn't paying attention." Students who use a timer and check sheet are better able to maintain their focus.[2] In other words, deliberate, conscious thought about using your President improves its functionality.

This research into self-management techniques has implications for improving Presidential functioning. Rather than demanding that students pay attention, I find it more productive to remind them to use their President. While the intended effect of these differing approaches is the same, teaching students about their President places them in control of their own brains instead of mindlessly following the demands of the teacher. A great example of this is a mindfulness strategy where you simply ask, "Where is your attention?"[3] This question promotes reflection on the part of the child. If your children are daydreaming while cleaning their rooms or completing school work, a simple "focus please" can trigger them to get back on task. I also like to utilize both of these phrases when I observe students who are about to do something foolish or dangerous. When they make a bad decision, it is valuable to have a follow-up discussion on how they could have used their Presidents to greater effect and exercised better judgment.

Teachers can increase attentional awareness by setting up a rating system from 1 (high) to 3 (low). At the end of class, the teacher rates the student and the student rates him or herself and then they share their ratings. The goal is to see if the ratings match.

I also encourage students who struggle with focus to draw a picture on an index card or sticky note as a visual reminder to use their President. Some students sketch a picture of an eye to help them remember to look at the teacher or look at their work, which is particularly effective since we usually pay closer attention to what we are looking at. Students who tend to blurt out answers might draw a raised hand to remind them to raise their hand prior to talking. Students with organizational issues might make a to-do list for steps they regularly forget, such as writing their names and dates on their papers. And children who might need to pause and think if their comment or question is on the topic before speaking could write out the word "Topic?" to remind them. Prompts with visual and auditory reminders help children who are working to improve their executive functioning.

THE BIG FOUR PRESIDENTIAL OPTIMIZERS

In addition to understanding the daily consciousness of Presidential functioning, it's extremely important to integrate into your child's daily routines the Big Four Presidential optimizers: water, nutrition, exercise, and sleep.

Water

If you've ever had a headache in your forehead, chances are you're dehydrated and just need to drink a big glass of water. For years, doctors have told us that it's important to drink plenty of water throughout the day. Not just when we exercise, but also when we are hard at study. Our brains need plenty of water for optimal neurotransmission. Among other things, water helps remove waste products, keeps our brains from overheating, and keeps brain transmissions flowing.[4] Not having enough water actually shrinks gray matter and makes it harder to think.[5] By the time your children feel thirsty, they may have lost up to 2 percent of their body weight from water loss, and their cognitive ability may decline by 10 percent.[6] Fortunately, schools today are much better at allowing children to have water bottles at their desks or take frequent breaks to the drinking fountain. As I like to tell my fourth graders, you know you're properly hydrated when your pee has just a hint of yellow!

Nutrition

Proper nutrition, both before school and at regular times during the day, keeps our President functioning well. Have you ever eaten only a donut or other simple carbohydrate for breakfast? Soon after, you begin to feel tired and hungry. Remember that the President is one of the most fragile parts of our brain. When it lacks adequate amounts of glucose, we start to struggle with focused attention and mental sharpness. Remember all the connections your neurons are making? The cells can't generate new axon arms if they aren't properly fed. This is especially true for children as their busily connecting brains consume twice the amount of glucose as adults.[7]

What's the best thing for your child to eat before the start of the school day? Either complex carbohydrates or protein, preferably both. Both of these provide more sustained energy over the longer period of time your body takes to make glucose from complex carbs and protein. When you eat more protein, your blood glucose levels stay higher for longer.[8]

In addition, it's important for your child to consume good fats such as omega-3 oils from fish, nuts, seeds, and dark leafy greens. We know that 60 percent of a child's solid brain matter is made up of fatty membranes, and these fats help maintain flexible, dynamic membranes that are able to transmit and receive information and sustain other cell functions such as energy production and water storage.[9]

Given all the research, it's a good idea to pack protein, complex carbs, or whole fruit in your child's snack container. Fortunately, taking former First Lady Michelle Obama's lead, parents are now pushing schools to provide healthier lunches for their children. As mentioned in the Brain Activity: A Plan for Homework in chapter 5, a glass of water and a healthy snack of protein, complex carbs, or a piece of fruit is great for an afternoon snack.

Exercise

It's also a good idea to keep the oxygen flowing with a little bit of exercise. A few years ago, just as I was walking in to a classroom to do a presentation, I was greeted by all of the students who were walking out. The assistant was teaching that day, and I thought that she must have forgotten about my presentation. I asked the teacher about the departing students, and she replied that they were really unfocused that afternoon and needed to take a break and go move their bodies. If you've ever tried teaching students in the afternoon, you know that the assessment of her students' physical and neurochemical needs was accurate.

Our hunter-gatherer ancestors were used to walking long distances every day in the search for food. This type of physical activity increases blood flow to the brain. The blood flow in turn, improves executive functioning and overall thinking as it transports glucose for energy and oxygen that soaks up the toxic electrons left over from all that neurochemical processing.[10] In fact, our brains are so large that the oxygen from every fourth breath a child takes is needed just to feed his or her brain.[11] Exercise also stimulates proteins that promote connections between neurons.[12] In humans, aerobic exercise has been shown to reduce symptoms of depression and anxiety as well as improve attention, planning, decision-making, and memory. Even better, exercise suppresses the release of the stress hormone, cortisol (which will be discussed further in section III).[13] Exercise can also stimulate creative ideas. In *A User's Guide to the Brain*, John Ratey notes how the brain areas that are used to coordinate physical movement also coordinate the movement of thought in the brain. This, he observes, may help us find a solution or generate a creative idea.[14] Some of my most creative thoughts happen in the lap lanes of the pool.

Perhaps the best book about the importance of exercise for optimal Presidential functioning is *Spark: The Revolutionary New Science of Exercise and the Brain*, also by Ratey, who elaborates on how exercise affects our brains and our thinking. For the President, exercise increases dopamine levels 400 percent and has a fairly long-lasting effect. Caffeine increases our dopamine levels about the same amount but wears off more quickly and causes many people's energy levels to crash.[15]

Ratey also outlines a research-based model for whole-school student exercise. Hopefully, the days of cutting student PE and recess are over, and we will see a return of these invaluable curriculum components. Teachers currently implement all sorts of brain break activities and exercises designed to get students moving. We now know that movement increases blood flow and offers opportunities to utilize different parts of the brain after long study periods. In fact, the Centers for Disease Control and Prevention found that physical activity not only positively affects grades, test scores, and academic achievement, it also affects children's classroom behavior and concentration.[16]

Sleep

Perhaps the most important Presidential maintenance activity is a good night's sleep. And the quality of the sleep is just as important as the quantity. Prolonged exposure to light during sleep undermines the brain, just as light directed at a flowering plant during the night hinders its development. The brain is extremely active during the time a child is sleeping and works to consolidate all of the information taken in during the day. Children's brains are busy building connections and deciding which experiences should be committed to longer-term memory. They are also solving problems as they sleep by digging into past memories of successful problems solved and then devising new approaches for the current problem.[17]

Every parent knows the consequences of hosting a slumber party. After staying up late and waking up early to excitedly play with their friends, the President struggles to stay awake for the remainder of the next day. One of its important Presidential functions is to control our emotions. A tired President means that these emotions come right out with no filter. I can still hear my mother saying sarcastically, "Someone didn't get enough sleep last night," after one of my sleepovers. "I did too!" I would yell back, immediately reinforcing that she was right.

This lack of emotional control also affects the process of falling asleep. As the higher regions of the brain begin to power down, the emotional centers are still quite active. Childhood fears, such as monsters for preschoolers or robbers for third graders, begin to creep into a child's conscious thought. Throughout the day, the President is focused on completing tasks, not these nighttime phobias. When the President starts to shut down at bedtime, these worries creep into the semiconscious mind and bring with them fear-based questions. **The worst thing a parent can do at this moment is to entertain these questions with long, detailed explanations.** Giving your child's current brain state, you are only going to provoke more questions. The best thing you can say at this point is, "Your President is shut off right now, let's talk about that in the morning when your President is working again."

A tired President can also result in extremely agitated motor behavior in a child. This kind of hyperkinetic activity has a completely different feel to it, which can help us quickly realize that a child is simply trying to stay awake. Since the brain is ready to shut down, children must constantly move about in order to keep it from completely shutting down. When sitting through a boring lecture, fidgeting is the only way for some kids to keep themselves stimulated and awake.

Researchers have found that 25 to 50 percent of children with ADHD also have co-occurring sleep disorders.[18] While the direction of cause and effect is not known, it's easy to understand how a lack of sleep compounds ADHD. Researchers found that on average, children with ADHD who were given 3 to 6 milligrams of melatonin—the brain's sleep hormone—before bed fell asleep seventeen minutes sooner and slept a half hour per night longer than children given a placebo.[19]

Make sure to practice good sleep hygiene for yourself and model it for your kids. Researchers have found that spending time with screens before bed leads to not only less sleep, but sleep that is less restful, and later bedtimes for children.[20] This means no screen time (computer, TV, or video games) at least thirty to forty-five minutes before bed. The blue light from the screen activates our visual cortex and stimulates the brain to wake up at the very time we are trying to fall asleep. This is particularly true for children as their eyes have larger pupils and more transparent lenses. That means your child is absorbing more blue light when looking at a screen before bed.[21] While a person might fall asleep watching TV, this habit interferes with the deeper sleep states the President needs for its nighttime work as well as for optimal functioning the next day.

Dr. Michael Rich, founder of the Center on Media and Child Health at Harvard Medical School, points out how late-night electronics causes disruption in their stage 4, or REM, sleep. This is the stage of sleep that takes the days' experiences in school and with friends and then decides what to take from short-term memory and transfer it to learning centers in the brain. Basically, this disruption means that "the cycle isn't complete with the learning centers."[22] It's also important to have a consistent bedtime and practice pre-bedtime rituals, which help soothe your child emotionally and promote a good night's sleep for their overworked President.

Fortunately, for those who do need to work closer to bedtime, many new electronic products have tools for changing the screen's light spectrums from daytime blue light to softer, evening yellow light (some now have a red light setting as well). While an action game or movie will still activate the brain, the yellow or red light helps induce melatonin as the brain believes nighttime is approaching.[23] This blocking of electronic blue light was highlighted by team Cannondale at the 2016 Le Tour de France. They designed blue light-blocking sunglasses for their riders to wear in the evening so that they could manage their social media without losing important sleep. One study involving female basketball players found that red light illumination positively affected sleep quality and performance.[24]

BEING CREATIVE

After you teach and reinforce the Big Four of Presidential care and maintenance to your children, seek out teachers and other parents with creative approaches to help improve executive functioning. One teacher stuck Velcro on the bottom side of a student's desk so that he could have kinesthetic stimulation from rubbing the soft material. It was quiet and didn't involve any movements that could result in a chair tipping over or another child getting hurt by a flying object.

Fidgeting can help children with sustained focus. The trick is to find ways to move that don't irritate the teacher or fellow students. I tell students that I don't mind them fidgeting as long as it doesn't make noise and that their eye contact remains on me. During first grade, my daughter's teacher tied three-inch pieces of material onto a girl's hair band and she was allowed to wear this on her wrist and play with the strings of material while she did her work. There was no way she could sit still, so using her fidget was far better than having her find a lose thread on her sock and slowly unravel them. Being inconspicuous with these movements is the key.

Physical movement during academic tasks, as it turns out, does not hinder student learning. It actually increases focus. According to a University of Central Florida study by psychology professor Mark Rapport, fidgeting helps stimulate areas in the brain that control working memory networks.[25] As kids become more aware of their President's needs, an individual child doesn't stand out anymore for having a band around the legs of a chair (used for students who struggle with leg movements when sitting), sitting on a yoga ball instead of a chair, or wearing noise cancelling headphones. The yoga ball helps children focus more since they have to increase their neural motor activity to keep themselves from rolling over. The headphones help children who are easily distracted by noises during silent work time. Distracted students may work better in a front row corner seat that's away from the windows or with a three-sided desk cardboard blinder.

Remember that when it comes to finding creative solutions, children can find ways to misuse them or make them counterproductive. Thinking putty seemed like a great tool until it ended up in the carpet or in a child's hair. If your children were part of the 2017 fidget spinner craze, you and your child's teacher quickly realized that the spinners were more of a distraction than a focusing tool. Experts believe that's because the spinners do not require much physical activity as compared with actual fidgeting. The spinner, it seems, does all the activity.[26] Most schools around the country banned them for the 2017-18 school year after watching students balance them on their noses, compare tricks with each other, and have battles with them.[27]

BRAIN ACTIVITY: WHAT'S YOUR FAMILY BEHAVIORAL PLAN?

GOAL	Clean the house for two hours this weekend
GOAL	Pack lunch at least three times this week
GOAL	Take out the trash after school each day
GOAL	Turn in all homework on time this week

Now that we've completed our understanding of the President,
it's time to set some goals for Presidential development within the

whole family. Parents are most often concerned about their child's attention and impulse control, but I find that kids are much more receptive to working on their own goals after seeing Mom and Dad take responsibility for their weak areas.

My son and I set up a money jar system aimed at increasing our impulse control when it came to using inappropriate language when we were frustrated. We started a list of words that were unacceptable, such as hate, crazy, stupid, and various cuss words. If he used these words, he had to place a quarter from his allowance into the jar. If I had a linguistic lapse in judgment, I would have to put a dollar into the jar. At the end of each month, we donated the money to our church. While neither of us had a huge problem with inappropriate language, the act of donating money was a good reminder for our Presidents not to slip, and to exert more control when we were frustrated. Too much of any emotion can overwhelm even the best of Presidents, however. I'm passionate about Colorado University football, so my frustrations with a poorly played game once resulted in a twelve-dollar tab for the jar. If I had saved all the money from swearing over the gridiron misfortunes of my Buffs during the past decade, I could have funded my son's CU college tuition!

Together as a family, take stock of the areas in which each of you need to improve. You can then set up a family goal sheet or individual goal sheets for tracking your progress and then apply either positive or negative consequences. In terms of reinforcements, one of the questions I'm most often asked is what reward system should be used for home systems. "Whatever is meaningful to your child" is my standard response. You see, what works for one child in a family may not work for another. The reinforcements you select must fit the motivations of each individual child.

For instance, my wife loves to tell the story of how she needed to do things differently for her two children. Being sent to her room was an extremely motivating negative consequence for my wife's daughter because of her zealous, social nature, and getting to go out with friends was a positive motivator. My wife's son, however, loved spending time alone and would happily fill the time with his many books, so being sent to his room served as a positive reinforcement. The key to any reward system is being aware that kids are motivated by a wide array of social and intellectual interests.

I also emphasize the importance of utilizing more positive reinforcements over negative ones in any reward system. Did you know that most dogs like getting praise from their owners just as much as they like getting food?[28] And research has found that children who receive more positive feedback have more focus in school.[29] Numerous studies have looked at the ideal positive-to-negative ratio for motivating a child to want to change their behavior. They found the ratio was 80:20.[30] That means using praise, hugs, compliments, and earned privileges motivated children to change their behavior 80 percent of the time, and negative comments or consequences only worked 20 percent of the time. The research also showed that when using negatives, you need to be "prudent" in deciding which behavior warrants the negative reinforcement and how intense the consequence should be.[31] I can't tell you how many times I have had parents in an audience who gasped at this research and said, "At home we are 80 percent negative!"

When setting up a behavior plan or sticker chart (which younger ones love), it's effective to use a combination of positive and negative consequences and to devise a tiered system of reinforcements. Please keep in mind that the younger the child, the more frequent the positive reinforcements should be. I remember helping a young girl who had huge emotional outbursts when she was frustrated. It wouldn't matter where she was in the house; she would kick and scream and refuse to go to her room to calm down. Once her Emotional Factory took over, she would try anything to keep her parents engaged and then argue her way toward what she wanted. Given this behavior and her desired outcome, it was clear that her President was not in charge of her emotions, and it was also imperative that she needed to learn how to disengage from her parents.

A positive sticker chart was set up and the first rule was that if she got upset, her parents would request that she try and calm down. If not, then her parents would leave the room. If she didn't follow them out of the room, she would receive a sticker. If she earned twenty stickers, then she would get to go to Target to use five dollars of her allowance. On the other hand, if she followed her parents out of the room, she would lose an upcoming play date, missing out on perhaps her favorite activity. Her parents also used the 1-2-3 system by Thomas Phelan so she knew that when Mom or Dad started counting, the consequence would come quickly.[32]

This worked fairly well and the young lady earned her trip to Target in about a week. Next, they moved the goal to fifty stickers for a trip to a local amusement venue. To earn a sticker, she needed to leave the room and go to her bedroom when asked. The negative play date consequence still applied, but an additional negative had to be implemented for her new I'll-slam-my-door behavior. If the door was slammed, her parents would remove it from the hinges for a week. They also decided that she could earn an extra sticker if she could go to her room without storming out, yelling, or rolling her eyes. While this fifty-sticker goal and higher-level expectations took longer, she eventually reached it.

Finally, a goal of one hundred stickers was set for earning a trip to the Mermaid show at the local aquarium, a significant incentive for an eight-year-old girl. The same rules were kept in place, but an extra bonus was added: if she could stop her emotions in the moment, talk quietly about them, and accept her parent's decisions, she could earn two stickers. About six weeks later, she earned that trip. More importantly, she was now quite proud of how she could use her President to stay calm and solve her problems.

While we will look at additional behavior management strategies later on in section V, I wanted to end this brain activity about making a family plan with a few brief thoughts about using behavior management systems. First, a systematic approach only works when used consistently. Raising a child isn't much different than training a dog. Behavioral changes simply require consistent follow through. So, make it easy on yourself; after you create a weekly chart, make several copies. Then put the chart where you and your child will see it every day, such as on a kitchen cabinet door or the refrigerator. It's also a good idea to have all the stickers in a drawer or a container right next to the chart. The quicker you get the stickers up after the desired behavior, the better. It not only helps to immediately reinforce the desired behavior for your child, it also helps you from forgetting to do the stickers. Also remember that each child is different, and for some children, especially when they are younger, it is important to start with very reasonable and reachable goals (maybe only three, five, or ten stickers to start.) Some kids may also need to stay at a small number of stickers for a few cycles to keep them motivated before increasing the requirement for the next, larger motivating reward.

Second, always remember the importance of building your child's insight into how they are managing their President. Even if your children blow it, give them an unexpected sticker if they sincerely talk about how they didn't use their President and what else they could have done. In the evening, when you are reviewing the day with your children, start by asking, "How do you think your chart went today?" Then, have them bring the chart to you and explain what is on it. Ask them to describe any difficulties to you. If their story matches that of the teacher, other parent, or supervising adult, they can still get a bonus sticker for simply acknowledging what really happened.

CHILD SUPPORT SYSTEM
Presidential Reference Guide

Children with High Presidential Self-Control
- Decreased structure
- Positive reinforcement for good choices
- Promote self-problem-solving

Children with Lower Presidential Self-Control
- Increased structure
- Clear guidelines and rules
- Reinforce "Stop"
- Increased adult consistency and communication at home and school
- Emphasize Presidential awareness and responsibility taking
- Positive behavioral reinforcement for impulse control, self-regulation and use of President
- Model strong Presidential functioning

HOW DOES YOUR CHILD RESPOND EMOTIONALLY?

"Oh, bother."

~Winnie the Pooh

How well does your child hold on to happiness? Children are born with genetically programmed temperaments that factor into their emotional stability. Some children are naturally better than others at regulating their emotional reactions in adverse situations. Parents can teach children how to temper their responses and turn off their emotional output. Once emotions are turned down, the thinking-feeling brain turns on to help your child navigate social dynamics and frustrations with a thoughtful and emotionally balanced response.

CHAPTER 7

HOLDING ON TO HAPPINESS: YOUR CHILD'S EMOTIONAL TEMPERAMENT

When I first began doing this work, I knew that I needed a way to explain differing mood types to students. How do children with diverse temperaments react emotionally to the same stressful experiences? Like the President, a child's emotional reactions also have a genetic component. Kimberly Saudino from Boston University explores research on child temperaments in her paper "Behavioral Genetics and Child Temperament," and explains that differences in activity level, emotionality, and attention are often linked to genetics.[1]

While adults may understand somewhat how genetics work, it doesn't make much sense to children. What might make more sense is a story with different characters that portray different temperaments or moods. So, I decided to write a story based on the dispositions of six characters. The story illustrates the different ways in which people react to adversity. In my story, the characters individually set out to go on a hike through the forest and trip over the same rock in their path. When I tell the story, I ask the students to note the differing emotional reactions each character has to stumbling over the rock, which demonstrates their emotional makeup. Then I ask if the students might be able to identify those traits in themselves.

Olivia the Optimist was packed and ready to see her friends. It was a sunny day, and Olivia's heart warmed at the prospect of meeting them for a hike in the woods. She shoveled Skittles into her mouth as she tromped through the forest to the meeting place without a care in the world. With her focus divided between a mouthful of candy and the clean mountain air, Optimistic Olivia didn't notice the rock in her path. She tripped and landed awkwardly, kicking up a heap of dirt. At first, she was dazed and a bit frustrated, but then she rolled over to see the sunlight peeking through the canopy of conifer trees. She said, "Wow, a rock!" Olivia collected herself, stood up, and dusted off. She grinned broadly and exclaimed, "It's still a great day for a walk!" She then went happily along her way.

Minutes later Paralysis-by-Analysis Pete embarked upon the same path to meet his friends for the hike. He had a scarf wrapped around his neck for extra warmth and skipped through the woods happily anticipating the adventure, but with an air of hesitation as he considered the possibility of being injured or lost. He tripped over the same rock Olivia did, hitting the ground with a thud. "Oh my," Pete said, "I b-b-better get back home before I fall again. There could be more rocks. I could get hurt!" Paralyzed by fear and anxiety, Pete scurried home.

Controlling Connie left for the hike only after her bedroom was tidy and organized. Her moderate happiness (Connie preferred order and routine over unconditional happiness) didn't last long as the same rock that downed Olivia and Pete claimed another victim. In shock, Connie tumbled to the ground, soiling her immaculate outfit in the process. Enraged, she exclaimed, "Aahhh! Stupid rock! Why did you attack me?!" and got up and kicked the rock, which didn't budge. With her face now contorted into a mask of anger, Connie stormed down the path. "No stupid rock is going to ruin this hike for me!" As she furiously walked, she threw and kicked every rock she encountered.

Dejected Daryl never really wanted to go on a hike in the first place. It was no surprise to him when he tripped and fell headlong over the same rock. "Figures," he whined. He slumped over as he sat next to the offending rock on the verge of tears. "Not even the rocks want to be my friend." Gathering himself, Daryl plodded grimly along. Every rock from then on triggered his memory of sadness and rejection as he thought, "There is another rock that doesn't want to be my friend."

Making friends was never a problem for Excitable Ed, but he was already late when he remembered that he was supposed to meet them for a hike in the forest. "I'd better get there fast," he said. As he flipped and twisted down the trail, gaining speed with each maneuver, Ed was immersed in the joy of combining nature with his acrobatic dexterity. Unfortunately, he didn't see the rock in the path either and tripped like all the others. After several barrel rolls, he skidded to a stop. Rising to one knee, Ed briefly took an inventory of his bones and vital organs. Nothing seemed broken or punctured. "THAT WAS GREAT!" he exclaimed. "LET'S DO IT AGAIN!" Excitable Ed tore down the path with even more energy than before, making it a point to incorporate every large rock he could find into his route.

Before he set out for the hike Analytical Alex surveyed the weather. He had made precise preparations hours before the other children. "After all," he reflected, "it's wise to start early to prepare for every possible outcome. Disaster is only a flash flood, solar flare, or wildfire away. After all, the probability of unpleasant, unforeseen circumstances is 5 to 10 percent." Boldly striding down the path, Alex contemplated the statistical probability of enjoying a hike like this. Unfortunately, he hadn't considered the possibility of landing face first after tripping over a rock. Yes, Analytical Alex stumbled over the same rock that earlier had claimed his friends. He stood up almost brazenly, as if the incident hadn't happened. The rock was now loose on the ground from all the children who had tripped over it. Alex lifted the rock, examining it under a magnifier he used for mineral and rock identification. "Well, the composition is granite and quartz," Alex said, nodding as he put the rock back where he had found it. He looked up from the specimen and scanned the forest. "Hmm, interesting find. I wouldn't expect to find this combination of igneous rock in this part of the forest. It must be from the Paleolithic period." He found a smaller rock with the same composition and put it in his pocket it for further analysis. "I bet my friends would enjoy a lecture on the origin of this rock."

GENETICS OF TEMPERAMENT

Like the characters in this story, each child comes with a genetically influenced emotional temperament. Temperament refers to your child's emotional and behavioral tendencies that appear early on. Besides emotionality and activity level, these tendencies also include such things as attention, persistence, sociability, and reactivity (see chapter 8 regarding reactivity).[2] These tendencies are mostly considered to be genetically based, but research also shows us that the environment in which your child is raised plays a critical role in the expression of this temperament. It is estimated that parental DNA accounts for between 20 and 60 percent of temperamental variances, while the remaining 40 to 80 percent is attributed to environmental factors.[3] Think about the yin-yang symbol. The two sides are entwined and inextricably linked with each other.

For example, in his chapter, "Social Brain Circuitry and Behavior," Steven G. Feifer writes, "nurturing environments with consistent caregivers may have a profound impact on the behavioral manifestation of a particular temperament trait and, over time, actually alter one's brain circuitry."[4] These children handle stress better as they show less elevation of the stress hormone cortisol.[5]

Thanks to our expanded limbic system, your child has the capacity to experience the full range of human emotions (see chapter 8) as they go through life's trials and tribulations. While the environment you provide for them and guide them through will impact their emotional responses, you will see these general emotional temperaments day in and day out. You will also find that your child will revert to these defaults during times of stress.[6]

YOUR CHILD'S TEMPERAMENT

It's important for parents to understand which temperament or character they are raising and for teachers to understand the different characters in their classrooms. Each predisposition comes with its own blessings as well as diverse set of challenges and will require a different approach in helping children learn how to hold on to happiness as they walk down the path of life. In his poem "Three Stings," Shel Silverstein presents three children (George, Fred, and Lew) who have three different reactions after being stung by a bee. George concludes that he should have stayed in bed to avoid being stung, Fred thinks he's being punished, and Lew says, "I learned somethin' about bees today."[7]

Some children are like Lew in the Silverstein poem or Olivia the Optimist. They greet each day with joy and enthusiasm, but they aren't overcome by excitement. They experience life's frustrations but recover quickly from their bumps and bruises. They seem to possess innate cheerfulness, an easygoing disposition, and great reservoirs of resiliency. When discovering that a favorite ride at the amusement park is closed for repairs, these children think of the forty other rides they will get to enjoy.

Other children, like Silverstein's George, are generally happy but might struggle with the anxiety of Paralysis-by-Analysis Pete. Their anxious emotions are often anticipatory in nature and may keep them from engaging in new activities or play opportunities.

They often seem to sense the inherent danger in any situation and focus on the potential disaster rather than the joy or happiness with which they could be rewarded. They may actually know and desire the rewards, such as the prospect of making a new friend, but can't seem to move past their fears and anxieties to attain those rewards. When they see the repair sign on their favorite ride at the amusement park, these children worry they won't know which rides to ride or worry about what other rides might need repairs. Parenting the worry wart or wallflower can often be frustrating as you try to move Pete out of his anxious state. It's also important to note that some children with social anxiety may get more hyperactive as they run between people and activities. (Think of Pete swinging wildly at a bee!)

You might also have a Controlling Connie (or Silverstein's Fred) among your children. They might start out happy and enthusiastic, but quickly turn frustrated and angry when things don't go the way they had hoped. When participating in social activities, such as a game of tag, for instance, a Controlling Connie will feel slighted and upset when incidental contact occurs or opponents claim that they didn't feel the tag. Often typical parenting requests, such as turning off the electronics or cleaning your room, are met with anger and arguing. The nightly homework duty also can become a problem when frustration takes over. Some children's agitation can be felt throughout the day and creates a family or peer environment of walking on eggshells. These children become enraged at the park when they see their ride is closed and want to go home because "All the other rides stink!" While all children can turn into Connie after a sleepless slumber party, Connie's anger response and grumpy behavior are easily triggered. As one fourth grade boy

> Chronic agitation can have a family walking on eggshells.

said to me, "I guess I can be sort of a Connie when I play football." You could see the nods of his classmates as they recalled this young man's long string of arguments. I nodded internally as well, as I recalled the numerous conversations I had with his mother regarding his angry responses at home.

The child who is full of woe can be seen as Dejected Daryl. This child is consumed by melancholy and pessimism. A Daryl temperament can appear lackluster, unenthusiastic, and rarely motivated to join in on the fun. Milder forms of peer teasing and horseplay can be overinterpreted and taken personally, causing Dejected Daryl to retreat from further interaction. Something this child might hear is, "You can make a lot more friends with a smile than a frown." When parents ask what activities they might wish to participate in, a Daryl replies with "I don't know" and can't seem to find anything they might be interested in. Dejected Daryl and those who share his pessimism are risk averse when it comes to social interactions.

Other children inherently feel the enthusiasm and energy of Excitable Ed. They approach social interactions with great joy and see the rewards they might encounter along the way. Slights or teasing comments from others are taken as a signal to play. While the enthusiastic child gets things going, he or she can also struggle with taking things too far. The parental aphorism "It's all fun and games until someone gets hurt" was developed with this child in mind. They wake up like a hungry puppy ready to eat and play and go until they drop. At the amusement park, they are sure they will enjoy every ride and will set a lofty goal for the number of times they can ride the roller coaster. Reining this child in is a challenge. While they can be the life of the party, they can also wear on others as they get carried away with their comments and behavior. When describing Ed to fourth graders, it's common to see them perk up as they identify with his more positive traits.

Unlike Ed, some children seem emotionally neutral. They rarely express feelings and seem to lack emotional intuition. An Alex type doesn't possess the emotional expressiveness of his or her peers. Analytical Alex will often talk more about what they are thinking and enjoy activities that involve a high degree of mental processing. When asked how they are feeling, an Alex temperament will often reply, "I don't know." At an amusement park, Analytical Alex might wonder about the mechanical cause of the ride's malfunction instead of expressing disappointment over not being able to ride it. I've worked with a fifth grade girl like Analytical Alex. One day our group took their hard earned money from a bike-a-thon and donated it to the local animal shelter. As we toured the puppy and kitten nursery and saw the animals that had been selected for adoption, she had a smile on her face. Then the officer took us into the back room where we were shocked to see rows and rows of abused, neglected animals. We learned that these animals only had three days before they were to be euthanized. Stunned, we walked out into the parking lot. While the rest of the pre-teens actively discussed their emotional responses, I asked her how she felt. In a neutral tone, she replied with only one word, "mixed." It was clear that she was analyzing what she had seen in her head, but didn't have the emotional language to express it with deeper emotion.

While your child might neatly fit one of these emotional temperaments, it's just as likely that he or she is a mix of several of our characters. When I tell the "A Walk in the Forest" story to fourth graders, I begin by sharing what I was like at their age. I explain to them that I was a combination of Optimistic Olivia and Paralysis-by-Analysis Pete. My entire childhood I woke up every morning happy and often held on to that joy throughout the day. My brother even commented, "The entire Rocky Mountain range could fall down around him, and he wouldn't get upset." However, while I was generally more like Olivia, I sometimes felt Pete's anxiety.

It's also possible to see the traces of anxiety and obsessiveness that ran throughout my family tree, a genetic temperament. While my father considered himself to be a good German, the rest of us recognized his need to chill out.

I explain to students that I still possess these same basic dispositions today. I wake up happy, and when given enough time, I tend to make lemonade out of each of life's lemons. But my enthusiasm for life can also be too much at times when anticipation of a great reward, which never materializes, quickly turns into disappointment. In addition, I continue to have anxious feelings and might obsess about work or personal relationships at times or worry that things might not turn out according to my plan.

Quite frequently, children will identify as a Pete-Connie mix. They worry about their work to the point of perfectionism and then explode in frustration or tears when they can't figure out a problem or miss a couple of spelling words. While these children are driven to be successful students, they need to be reminded often to turn down their emotions.

Hyper-focused, moment-to-moment desires also characterize the Excitable Eds of the world. They become so engrossed in an exciting activity that engaging in it consumes their energy and Presidential functioning. They start countless collections, sports, and hobbies, all the time badgering their parents about going to the store to buy more of whatever they are wrapped up in. However, parents know that these passionate desires will pass as Ed moves on to the next preoccupation.

When I work with older students, I share how traumatic experiences can alter one's mood set.[8] Following the Columbine High School massacre, I struggled with secondary trauma (the side effects of working with those who experienced the trauma firsthand) for six months. I've subsequently had several bouts of depression and realize that my anxiety and fear can slide into hopelessness if

I'm not careful. My days of falling asleep naturally ended during that period of my life, and I know I will need to keep these Dejected Daryl tendencies in check for the rest of my life.

Fortunately, one's daily emotional responses can be turned on or off with a plethora of stress management techniques (see chapters 8, 9, and 11) that are available to us. In addition, one of the most exciting areas related to neuroplasticity and the brain is the idea that we can change our emotional temperaments over time. Through recent research with Buddhist monks, scientists are discovering that one's temperament can be reset after some ten thousand hours of meditation.[9] In other words, through the practice of meditation, these monks were able to turn down their emotions and become more Olivia-like. While most families don't have ten thousand hours to meditate, consistent relaxation and meditation on a smaller scale teaches children to turn down their emotional responses and amplify their self-awareness as well as their perception of others.

BRAIN ACTIVITY: UNDERSTANDING TEMPERAMENT

One of the best ways to help your children understand their basic emotional temperaments is to read the story at the beginning of the chapter. After finishing, explain that while we all have the emotions of the various characters at different times in our lives, most of us have one or two basic default emotions that we tend to experience as we go about our day (our emotional default), or which might last a little bit longer and be characterized as a mood. Some of these responses might help us hold on to feeling content or happy, while others make it hard for us to regain our previous level of happiness.

Parents should identify their own temperaments first. Are you Optimistic Olivia? Controlling Connie? Maybe a Paralysis-by-Analysis Pete-Dejected Daryl mix? Perhaps you are an Excitable Ed-Controlling Connie mix. For fun, ask your kids how they see you or identify other adults in their world. (Kids love to talk about the moods of the various teachers at school.) For a deeper understanding, talk about the temperaments of your extended family members. Perhaps there was a major worrier in the family or a grandparent who had anger issues or melancholy. You'll probably always find an Olivia in the extended family, not to mention one or two Eds among some of the uncles.

In addition, give personal examples of how your temperament and baseline emotions helped you in certain situations or made it harder in others. Which emotions do you try to guard against expressing in your own life? Remind your children that all emotions serve a purpose at some point but that sometimes those same emotions can be obstacles to solving life's problems. Anxiety, for instance, can help prepare us and keep us cautious and safe. However, it can also cause us to freeze up and panic. When directed at a moral wrong, anger is considered justified and a virtue for those who stand up to injustice. When talking with students, I mention that if they were to see a classmate bullying a preschool child and felt angry and stopped the bullying, they would be considered brave and heroic. However, there is no moral justification for the Connie-like explosive, irrational anger many children (and adults) feel. Playing with a nasty edge on the sporting field can propel an athlete to play harder, but too much anger results in mental errors and foolish penalties. Consistently anxious, angry, or gloomy dispositions erode happiness not only in ourselves, but they also have negative emotional impact on our friends, family, and anyone else we come into contact with.

Ask your children to identify their basic temperaments. You might be surprised at how accurately they can self-assess in the mid-elementary years. Remind them that although we all possess the full range of human emotions, each of us is uniquely predisposed to experience certain emotions more than others. Gently remind them of recent situations and how they might have responded. You can then look at how others in the family emotionally responded to the exact same situation. For example, I responded with great fear and anxiety at an old west show with a staged gunfight, while my siblings responded with joy and excitement. These comparisons aren't to be used to tease each other (the way siblings often do) but to help everyone understand his or her own unique responses. Looking at the family tree can also help children to not feel so different or embarrassed about their emotional responses when they understand that their basic temperament was most likely inherited.

Finish this exercise by exploring how people could work on being more Olivia-like when circumstances become difficult. Younger children prefer behavior charts filled with stickers to mark their success in managing their moods. For older children, a family feeling jar is ideal. Put a quarter in for each time a family member is able to utilize a strategy and guard against letting their mood or default emotional response take over a situation. If family members have a particular temperament, have a jar for that emotion. One student told me about her family's worry jar. If anyone was worrying too much, a quarter went in the jar. Later, when the jar is full, you can spend it on a family outing of some sort, like going for ice cream after a walk in the woods. (See chapter 15 for more family adventures.)

For my daughter's bee phobia, I read her the Shel Silverstein poem. She loved it, and it did help her fear. "You should put that in your book, Daddy" she said. We also made a copy of it to hang up in her room. She's going to try her hardest to be like Lew.

CHAPTER 8

YOUR CHILD'S EMOTIONAL FACTORY

My wife and I had just returned from a date night to find surprise visitors: a pair of snarling, salivating pit bulls throwing themselves into our front windows. The pair barked at our Golden Retriever inside the house, who was hysterically barking as well. My heart was in my throat as I considered our options. As my amygdala sprang into action, I grabbed a snow shovel that was leaning against the garage. My wife and I stepped on to the sidewalk and exchanged glances. Her eyes were as wide as saucers, and I'm sure mine were too. I could see our babysitter standing in the living room, paralyzed by fear.

That's when they attacked.

Instantly, a cascade of chemicals coursed through our bodies, causing our heart rates to soar. Blood rushed into our extremities so that we could prepare to run or fight.

"Get inside!" I yelled at my wife as I turned around with the shovel in my hands, prepared to defend the front door. The dogs, foaming at the mouth and barking hysterically, crept ever closer. My dopamine levels were now spiking, and I focused on the dogs with razor sharpness. My elevated cortisol and testosterone levels helped me memorize every detail of my predicament and triggered my muscles to react if necessary.

The bigger of the two dogs leapt toward me. I thrust out the shovel in front of me. The dog backed off but then circled to my right. Its companion now stood on my left, as if they were planning to assault me from either side. My hyper-focus seemed to slow down time, and I wondered if I could somehow make it to the front door before they ripped me to pieces. The same dog lunged again, and I used the shovel to create a barrier between us. As it turned back, I had time to make my escape into the safety of the house.

Once inside, my wife and I hugged and comforted the babysitter. Slowly, our oxytocin levels crept back up and our cortisol levels dropped after calling the police. While our state of high alert abated, our senses remained sharp as we safely returned the sitter home and were informed that the dogs had been located. However, we remained vigilant for several hours after our unnerving encounter as our chemical responses etched every detail of the intense encounter into our memories.[1] The core of our Emotional Factory, our amygdala—with its fight, flight, or freeze response—had saved us.[2]

THE FACTORY OR EMOTIONAL BRAIN

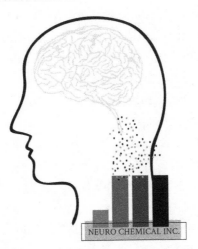

NEURO CHEMICAL INC.

Although the chemical interactions in our brains and our quick reactions might seem obvious given the situation, the human limbic system is extremely complex. In addition to the basic amygdala, it's comprised of several regions and carries out a diversity of brain functions. Sitting between the automatic brain and the neocortex, the limbic system is the epicenter of a variety of important functions.[3] Its primary task is emotional processing.[4]

In order to accomplish these emotional tasks within our brain, neurons and other cells within our bodies deploy a variety of neurotransmitters and hormones. The interaction of these chemicals within our bodies and brains determines our emotional states. Some of the key players are dopamine, serotonin, norepinephrine, oxytocin, cortisol, testosterone, and estrogen.

To help children understand this area of our brain, I ask them to visualize an emotional factory that pumps out chemicals that travel throughout our bodies and brains. These chemicals communicate a multitude of commands, such as telling our muscles to tense up or to relax depending on the demands of our environment. Let's imagine I am sitting on the back porch with my Golden Retriever on a warm autumn day. As a result, my brain and body are processing a great deal of serotonin, which helps me feel peaceful and happy. At the same time, my brain sends signals that connect with my muscle cells and tells those cells to relax. With increased blood flow to these relaxed muscles, my body temperature starts to rise and I feel a warm glow in my heart. As I pet my dog, both of our oxytocin levels rise, and we feel deeply connected. My cortisol levels drop as my stress melts away, resulting in a perfect chemical mixture for a beautiful day.

This interplay of environment and our sensitive emotional-chemical balance is played out every second of every day. It is estimated that each connection between the neurons transmits about one signal per second and that some specialized connections can transmit up to one thousand signals per second.[5] That speed of processing can trigger an emotional response in less than a quarter of a second.[6] While there are many factors at play, such as timing and the receptivity of dendrites, the Factories of some children may be genetically set to produce too much or not enough of these chemicals. For example, an overabundance of the neurotransmitter norepinephrine has been linked to higher levels of anxiety and panic. Conversely, low serotonin levels are associated with depression, and extremely high or low levels of serotonin have been linked to aggression.[7]

Our sophisticated emotional systems help us respond to all sorts of environmental situations. *Inside Out,* Disney's 2015 animated film, provides a great visual starting point for understanding these basic feelings. If you've ever seen Dr. Gloria Willcox's Feeling Wheel, however, you can see over a hundred more subtle feelings surrounding the six primary emotions of sad, mad, scared, joyful, powerful, and peaceful.[8] While younger children tend to understand these emotions in absolutes (good or bad or warm or fuzzy or cold or prickly), older children begin to learn that emotions are nuanced and complex. The key is to help children learn how to identify these emotions when they are small and then figure out how to appropriately express them.

I often speak of being mad as a secondary emotional state. Quite often, we feel embarrassed, left out, or confused. It's these feelings that often light the fuse of anger. If one can express these first feelings when they are smaller, they can turn off that anger fuse.

REGULATING EMOTIONS

With a vast range of human emotions, it's important to teach children that all feelings, at the right time and place, can serve a function for our survival and well-being.

Anxiety

Too much anxiety can paralyze a child. That's why it's important to help children find small ways to embrace and navigate the situation rather than avoiding it completely. For instance, anxiety can motivate children to put on a helmet or to stop before crossing the street after their kickball has sailed into the neighbor's front yard. It can also motivate them to take action like preparing more thoroughly for an exam or getting fired up for a sporting activity or a recital.[9]

Joy

Absolute joy is like watching little rays of sunshine dance around you on a walk through tree-covered trails in the fall. We often observe this emotion in children as they play and learn. While we want children to experience joy every day, we also need to help them manage the less desirable tasks as they go throughout the day.

Fear

Fear tells us that something could be dangerous, and we should avoid things like swatting a wasp's nest. Sometimes fear can become irrational and obsessive. My daughter used to have an obsessive fear of bee stings and shots when she was younger. Many picnic dinners were cut short in tears and hysteria. We encouraged her to not look directly at what was causing her fear—the bee or the needle—and to take deep breaths while saying to herself, "I'm OK, that's just my amygdala going off."[10]

Obsessive desires

Children may also need guidance and structure when their desires become obsessive. In first grade, my son was obsessed with the army and wanted to wear his camouflage clothing to school every day. One morning, his teacher caught me on campus and suggested we change up his outfit now and then. So we came up with Camo Friday.

Sadness

Sadness tells us that we need to be soothed and nurtured. A baby's cry will bring his or her parents to tend to the need. Researchers have found that human tears activate compassion in others.[11] In Disney's *Inside Out*, the character of sadness helps the main character (Riley) look more deeply into herself. Sadness also brings Riley's parents to her aid and causes them to come up with solutions for her.[12] Most importantly, the emotion of sadness teaches us to value relationships and keeps us connected with those we have lost.

Anger

Anger tells us that we have a problem that we need to think about and solve.[13] Sometimes these actions are reckless, while other times they can be heroic. Take the heart wrenching story of Mark Bingham. As a college student, he was arrested after angerly running onto the field of a college football game and tackling the Stanford mascot (a giant redwood tree). Years later this same intensity helped him to lead the charge down the aisle of United Flight 93 and prevent the plane from reaching its target on 9/11.[14]

Hate

Even extreme feelings such as hate can serve a useful purpose. I often tell my children that hating child abuse can motivate us to change it. Dedicating one's life to ridding the world of things we hate makes the whole world better. Many people who research cancer or plan fundraisers or drives have been motivated by their traumatic experiences with the disease.

THE SIZE AND VALIDATION OF EMOTIONS

Children often lack a full understanding of logic and cause and effect (see chapter 9), and can overestimate how tragic a situation is or might be.[15] In addition, the brain is wired such that nerve signals travel more readily from the amygdala to the upper regions of the brain rather than vice versa. This makes our intense amygdala harder to turn down.[16] Using a 1 to 10 scale is a great tool for children to assess the size of their response to a problem. Is it a mouse-sized problem or an elephant problem? I might ask, "What size is it?" and then pause before I follow up with, "Is it really a 10?" When the child thinks about it for a while, they often realize that the problem is more of a 2 or 3.

Validating a child's feelings can be therapeutic, even if those emotions are destructive. For instance, I met with a boy who had just experienced a violent crime scene and was struggling with the intensity of the emotions that resulted from that incident. "I'd feel that way, too," I said. "Now we have to figure out how to manage those feelings and then do something productive

Mouse or elephant-sized problem?

with them, so you don't think that this kind of thing will keep happening to you."

For younger children, I've found particular success with the Warm Fuzzy (emotions we like to have) and Cold Prickly (difficult emotions) concepts developed by psychotherapist Claude Steiner in his book *The Original Warm Fuzzy Tale*.[17] I explain to the children how their job is to learn how to make Warm Fuzzies bigger by sharing them with their friends. Cold Pricklies, on the other hand, can be shrunk down by surrounding them with Warm Fuzzies if we reach out to others, think about solutions, and have positive thoughts. A kindergarten girl came up with a third character named the Warm Pricklies that represented a mixed feeling about something. I quickly affirmed her creation by talking about how I had a Warm Fuzzy when I was in their classroom, but also had a Cold Prickly because it reminded me of when my own son was in elementary school, and how I missed him now that he is in medical school.

NOT ENOUGH, JUST RIGHT, OR TOO MUCH

Another aspect of temperament studied in infants has to do with intensity (high vs. low reactivity).[18] Like the Olivia's of the world, we might think that the perfect emotional trajectory would be to rise gradually, not get too intense, and then dip quickly. In terms of family life and social relationships, lower reactions and less intense emotions can make solving problems a whole lot easier. However, there really is no ideal response for every scenario in life. There are times when we need group members who rise up in anger or others whose worry reminds us to be more cautious. It's all about the right balance at the right time and place.

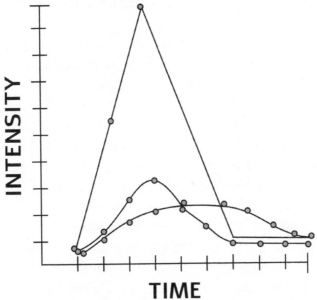

A great question for your child's emotional responses is, *"Is this not enough, just right, or too much?"* This is an important question to ask because considering the answer increases children's insight into their emotional worlds. Once you and your child begin to notice patterns that are interfering with emotional success, you can formulate specific goals to work on.

For children who love sports, I like to quote Peyton Manning, the great quarterback who was known for his emotional control during a game. Describing a technique that he learned from his father, he said something like, "It doesn't matter if I throw a touchdown [a 10 in excitement] or throw an interception [a 10 in frustration], I go back to zero on the very next play."[19] Or, as a dad who is a professional golfer taught me, "If it's a bad shot, think about it for five seconds and then move on to your next shot. If it's a good shot, think about it for ten seconds and then move on." That's great advice since so many of us stay focused on our mistakes for too long.

We can also help our children get to their "zero" in a more meditative way like the US Olympic alpine skier Mikaela Shiffrin at the 2018 Olympics. In PyeongChang, she won the race in which she wasn't favored, but finished fourth in the race where she was favored. After winning the first event, she needed to get back to "zero" and look at what was going through her mind and body that day in order to make a plan for her next event. Unfortunately, she wasn't able to. She told the *Wall Street Journal*, "It was such an emotional high. It was like I let myself feel too much."[20]

The same need for getting back to "zero" was true for 2018 Olympic snowboarder Shaun White. After his first run of the men's half-pipe finals, he threw his helmet into the crowd and celebrated what appeared to be a gold-medal winning run. He was at an emotional high. What he didn't expect was for Ayuma Hirano of Japan to post a higher score. White had to retrieve his helmet and try to regain his focus for his second run, where he fell. Despite the pressure and emotional high, in the end, he was able to get himself back to a place of "zero" and completed his final run in perfect form, winning the gold medal.

SCREEN ACTIVATION

While every parent hopes their child will never be in an emergency, the amygdala responds in a similar fashion to graphic pictures of violence or when playing first-person shooter games. While not firing at the same level as a real life emergency, the player's amygdala has this same response. Muscles tighten, the heart rate increases, and memory is dedicated to memorizing the environment and patterns for survival. This reaction will continue even after the player stops playing, and any new learning related to homework will be lost. Higher norepinephrine levels, which the amygdala uses to activate our brains during a crisis, also disrupt sleep patterns.

When the brain continues to have these perceived life or death crises through gaming, the amygdala continues to respond and thus creates a state of chronic stress. In a jungle or war zone this neurological state of hypersensitivity to danger could be the difference between life and death. In a safe environment, however, one doesn't need this hypersensitivity. Remember, the fight-or-flight system was only designed for an immediate response to a short-term danger. The ongoing production of adrenaline in chronic stress scars blood vessels that can cause a heart attack or stroke, while cortisol damages the cells of the hippocampus.[21] This, in turn, impacts your child's ability to learn and remember. Chronic stress causes dendrites in the President to atrophy and thus impacts executive functioning.[22] Playing violent video games, even just for one week, can cause decreased brain activity in the areas that regulate attention, concentration, and emotion.[23] Dr. Borba notes how much a child is exposed to virtual violence: "By the end of elementary school, the average child will witness 8,000 murders and, by age eighteen, 200,000 other vivid acts of violence, on all screens including video, television, and online streaming."[24] The BBC News cites studies from Canada's Brock University, which found that overexposing children to violent images slows down their moral growth and diminishes their capacity for empathy.[25] *In other words, children become desensitized to violence.*

> **Shooter games create chronic stress.**

POSITIVE PATHWAYS

Fortunately, this repetition of established pathways can also play out in a positive way as studies have shown. In one study, psychoanalysts John Bowlby and Renee Spitz studied premature and "failing to thrive" infants after WWII who were saved by being held and cuddled. This much needed touch increased the infants' oxytocin levels while decreasing the cortisol levels.[26] This particular study helped change a common hospital policy that forbade physical contact with premature babies.

Other studies have revealed how orphaned and neglected children have higher levels of the stress hormone cortisol and decreased serotonin levels. After placement in foster care or being adopted by a family, the positive impact on brain chemistry was demonstrated in these children as they showed a drop in cortisol levels and an increase in serotonin. The safety, structure, love, and attention they received had rewired their serotonin output.[27]

BRAIN ACTIVITY: BREATH WORK

When your child is particularly upset or anxious, their blood flow gets directed to their extremities and less of it reaches the brain (that's why thinking isn't always rational during a crisis). Deep breathing on the other hand is essential for changing the body's blood flow to your child's core so as to calm down their emotional responses.[28] This also supplies more blood to the brain where we can think through our problem. If you have ever experienced a tangled mess of fishing line (called a "nesting"), you know how important it is to stop, take a couple of deep breaths, and start studying the nesting in front of you before you begin pulling on the string.

When you were a child yourself, your parents probably tried to get you to take three deep breaths when you were upset. Just getting your child to take some deep breaths when they are extremely activated, however, isn't going to have the maximum benefit for long-term stress reduction. During a meltdown, asking your child to take three deep breaths usually results in a few shallow chest breaths followed by: "It's not working!"

For increased effectiveness, start a daily breathing session with your child. Find a nice, quiet space to lie down on a yoga mat. Teach your child to breathe in slowly and deeply while you count to two and then teach them how to take the air down into their belly (they can visualize themselves filling up like a balloon with their breath). Many kids know this as a "yoga breath," or making your tummy look like the Buddha. Then have them exhale slowly while you count to two again. As you practice this eight to ten times, speak in a calm voice about noticing the feeling of the air coming in and flowing out. You can also talk about breathing your stress away or bringing a warm breeze of air into the body.

For an even better mind-body connection, try roller-coaster breaths. Have your child hold up a hand with the palm facing them and their fingers spread out. Starting at the base of the thumb, have them use their pointer finger on the other hand to trace up and then down each digit. Have them breathe in as their finger moves up a digit and then exhale as their finger descends the same digit. Five breaths for five digits!

You can also help them create their own visual image while they breathe. I like to visualize people in a park enjoying the sunshine and the fresh spring air. More and more research continues to show how the combination of breathing and meditation is an effective tool for reducing stress (discussed further in chapter 11). Remember though, this is a process that needs to be practiced every day for your child to truly understand how they can feel their body relax as they learn to manage their emotions.

If your child is ever extremely agitated with anxiety or anger, you can also have them go into the bathroom and splash cold water over *their temple areas. This will flip on the vasoconstriction response which will direct blood flow back to the core and help turn off their emotional response. Even more effective, have them stick their face into a bowl full of ice water.[29] I worked with two boys who struggled with getting overly upset about football at recess, and they loved going into the bathroom and washing cold water over their faces. With their hair soaking wet, they would come back outside with huge smiles and exclaim, "That works great!"*

BRAIN ACTIVITY: OPTIMIZING STRESS

In this exercise have your child imagine a surfer paddling his arms as he anticipates a big wave coming in. Filled with excitement, nervous anticipation, and fear, the rider's dopamine, epinephrine, and cortisol levels begin to rise as the rolling water comes closer. After gaining speed, the rider pops up and gets into position. Each movement of the wave is transferred to the board, and the rider amends his position. Balanced by these ever-changing adjustments, the rider moves down into the pipeline as the huge wave starts to crest behind. The surfer glides across the water in what seems like an eternal moment of bliss. The stress of wiping out looms large, but the danger is part of the thrill. No matter the outcome, each moment will be later shared with friends as the rider's memory locks in every subtle detail of ecstatic, perfect interaction with the environment.

If all goes as planned, the surfer will ride out of the pipe and roll gently over the backside of the wave as the pipeline collapses behind. Bystanders on the beach will watch with cautious anticipation as the giant wave crashes into a cascade of white-capped, churning water pounding into the sand. The observers are relieved when the surfer emerges unscathed, but things could be different with one slip. With one simple mistake, he could disappear into the pipeline, where a torrent of sea water could consume the gasping rider and toss him in every direction. Without a sense of vertical orientation, the anxiety and fear of that moment must be overwhelming.

While the description of a surfer's crash demonstrates the negative consequences of stress, stress can also be productive. Throughout history, many sports teams have taken an opponent too lightly and ended up losing in a so-called upset. Feeling stress prior to the game would have encouraged the players to study their game plan, respect their opponent, and come out razor sharp. Like the surfer who takes nothing for granted, a certain amount of stress and anxiety is beneficial.

This same reasoning applies to your child's academic performance. If a child doesn't feel any stress about an upcoming test, they may blow off their study opportunities. They may then lack the motivation to study more and lack the preparation to correctly answer a surprise test question. In fact, children "develop their coping skills most effectively if they are exposed to a moderate amount of stress: high enough that they don't notice it, but low enough that they can handle it."[30] This level of stress is different for each child so being aware of their temperament and past reactions will be your best guide.[31]

Too much stress, however, can have disastrous consequences. Too much emotion can overwhelm the President's ability to stay focused and think clearly during study time and during the next day's test.

Tips for Managing Stress

- *A good night's sleep and proper nutrition are essential for Presidential functioning.*
- *Reflect on your child's response to stressful environments. Some children thrive on stress. They gear up their brains for the task at hand and actually learn better when an element of stress is added. For children who struggle with stressful situations, help them anticipate stress and take proactive measures.[32] For instance, ask the teacher to notify students ahead of time regarding a pop quiz. This will help them show what they truly know without having an emotional surprise. Also, letting students know about an upcoming fire drill can help them emotionally prepare for the loud, stressful alarm.*
- *Build insight by talking to your child about how their reaction is/was related to a given situation. Recently, one of our parents was so pleased when her daughter said, "I'm sorry for overreacting."*
- *Find out what your child's inherent motivational level is. Those dopamine pathways (discussed earlier in chapter 5) start deep in the brain and help turn on our motivation. The couch-potato child might need to ramp up his or her emotions for what's coming next. Yet, children who are driven to be high achievers may need constant reminders to dial down their stress levels. I often tell high performers, "If it goes too high, you'll tweak out."*
- *Discuss with your child how each of us have different reactions to stress. Mikaela Shiffrin's struggles with her pre-race anxiety were well documented in the 2018 Olympics. She is a great role model for children*

who become overly stressed. Her anxiety became so extreme at times that she was known for throwing up before races.[33] Instead of walking away from her stress, she practices deep breathing, visualization (see chapter 11), and an empowering pre-race mantra that starts with "I am . . ."

- *To increase your child's insight into his/her optimal level of stress, draw the stress scale pictured above. Then talk about how you feel and act when your stress is too low, when it's too high, and when it's just right. You can make a list of thoughts or behaviors your child could do to help get to "just right."*
- *Teach children to take deep breaths and remind themselves to relax. These children may need a set end time for studying followed by a warm bath or a soothing neck massage. Getting some exercise can also be extremely useful. In addition to increasing oxygen levels and blood flow to the President, recent research finds that it also helps the brain deal more effectively with anxiety.[34]*
- *Help your children learn how to "take a hit." Advanced preparation is an important component in handling stress. All the study time in the world won't prevent students from experiencing a test question to which they don't know the answer. Some will get stuck on the hard question rather than moving on and focusing on what they can do. You can teach them that if they miss one or two answers, they will still be OK in the long run. Another way to think of this is to "focus and execute." In the 2018 NCAA Football Championship game, Alabama did*

just this. Down by thirteen points at halftime, coach Nick Sabin took his frustrated players into the locker room and when they emerged, they pulled off an amazing final play to win in overtime. When asked what he said to his players, he responded: "Focus on executing . . . rather than thinking the other guy's going to determine the outcome."[35]

- *Use logic. Younger children have a harder time understanding coincidence vs. correlation, or cause and effect. Most of them begin to understand the difference a bit more when they learn the concept of fiction versus nonfiction. Work these terms into your discussions about various fears as you help your child think rationally about the situation. Every year in third grade, I discuss how many kids are afraid of creaking sounds in the ceiling as they fall asleep. They are sure that a robber is in the house. We then discuss the science of molecular expansion/decompression related to heat/cold throughout the day (see chapter 9, Logic and the Magic Hat).*

- *Ultimately, remember that chronic stress and worry is useless at some point. As the Dali Lama said: "When we face a problem, investigate the nature of the problem. If we can overcome the problem with efforts, there is no need to worry. If you think the problem cannot be overcome with efforts, there is no use to worry."*[36]

CHAPTER 9

EMOTIONAL BASKETBALL

Now that you have a better understanding of your child's Factory, it's time to look at the important relationship between it and your child's President. To explain this to parents and children, I like to use a basketball analogy.

Imagine that the emotions are coming down the court with the ball on a fast break. The ball in this case represents an emotional impulse that your child is feeling. On the other end of the court is your child's Presidential defense. The President's job is to simply slow down or stop the Factory's impulsive emotional attack.[1] Once that is accomplished, your child's defense can now listen to you, or the teacher's, coaching tips to set up an effective defensive strategy.

As an example, let's suppose that the teacher is giving a lesson when another student makes a joke. The student sitting next to this student feels the urge to laugh. Rather than just blurting it out, however, they stop themselves for just a brief second. Just then, the teacher reprimands the first student and reminds the entire class to stay focused for another five minutes before it's time for PE. The second student listens to this coaching advice and settles back down into listening. As we will see later in this chapter, the second student might also rely on their own past coaching memories and experiences of how to control oneself during work time.

This basic basketball analogy is played out all day long inside your child's brain. The outcome will depend on your child's age, their placement on the Presidential spectrum, and their unique

Factory make up. Preschool children, for example, want greater control over their lives but have limited abilities to appropriately express their emotions. In basketball, it's akin to having four tall, fast players exploding down the court. Unfortunately, a President in its initial developmental stage means that the only defender is one small, slow uncoordinated guy who is just learning how to play the game. We'll call that guy Bob. While Bob may get some support from his coach (that's you as the parent), that emotional, explosive offense that averages six foot seven has a good chance of slam dunking over Bob. Perhaps this quick score happens when you are trying to get your children dressed, get them into their car seats, or handling a grocery store tantrum. Your child's volatility is on a fast break, and Bob—the slow-to-react, plodding Presidential defender—helplessly watches this emotional slam dunk develop. Your only hope as the coach is to call a time-out, regroup the defense, and try to teach Bob a few fundamentals before sending him back on the court.

As with basketball, emotional maturity takes years of growth and disciplined practice to start slowing down those fast-paced attacks. Thankfully, the emotional volatility of the pre-K years give way to what experienced parents and teachers call the golden age of childhood.[2] Sigmund Freud dubbed the elementary years the latency period as he observed the energy that middle childhood children put into learning, athletics, and same gender social relationships.[3]

During the elementary years, children experience an emotional dampening as their defensive President steps up his/her game. In our basketball analogy, this means that two tall, reasonably quick players are coming down the court with the ball. However, two long, lithe players who listen to their coach anchor the President's defense. In addition, it's a home game. A chorus of teachers and friends, who remind them of the importance of emotional control, cheer them on. This developing Presidential defense is up to the task and steals the ball from the attacking emotions. When this happens, emotional maturity has arrived in your family arena.[4]

PARENT AS COACH

Before looking at the players on your court and their unique Presidential and Factory make-up, let's spend some time with you as the coach. Have you ever been to a little league sporting event and observed a coach who is yelling and getting upset with the players? While these efforts are attempting to motivate a player, when dealing with a child's emotional system, yelling isn't always the best approach. **The best thing you as a parent can do is provide positive support and praise your child's effort and willingness to take risks and make mistakes.** Stanford University's Positive Coaching Alliance program for youth sports emphasizes how important it is to use positive praise with your child during the learning process (further discussed in chapter 14).[5] Remember, caring relationships create the optimal environment for learning.[6] Even better, kindergarten students solve problems more quickly when they see a teacher they like.[7] Learning to solve problems is what we want our children to do in all aspects of their lives.

As a parent-coach, this new formula isn't perfect. Even children who have the emotional stability of an Olivia the Optimist can give up some quick points now and then. Any significant event—the death of a family's animal companion, an argument between parents, the loss of a close friend, or even the excitement of a birthday party (when things don't go as planned or a guest brings a disappointing gift)—can overwhelm even the best defense. Presidential fatigue or lapses in attention will result in easy baskets for the offense as well. As coach, you still need to intervene with time-outs at this age, although the defense now has some awareness of when the players themselves should call a time-out.

UNDERSTANDING YOUR PLAYERS

Turning to your players on the court, an optimistic child with higher Presidential functioning is going to keep the emotional score down and experience greater relationship success. He or she won't get too upset by their friends' or siblings' mistakes; instead, a player with this temperament will call a time-out and regroup.

Temperamental children will continue to cultivate a deep roster of fast, emotional players coming down the court. If they are blessed with a high Presidential functioning defense, it's going to be an intense game followed by a post-game locker room discussion. Kids who exert such great defensive effort to stop their emotions may feel great shame and disappointment for letting their emotions score, but they should actually feel proud of their effort. When evening approaches, they will be exhausted from their daylong battle and will need some time with the coach to prepare for tomorrow's game. The coach's supportive talk should focus on how to minimize their emotional reactions through deep breathing and the act of reminding themselves that they are masters of their emotions—not the other way around. Having a set phrase, such as "See if you can dial it down" or "Are you being just right?" can also be helpful.

Children who are less emotional but have low Presidential functioning for defense will give up a lot of impulsive, fast-break points. Coaches of these players will hear comments such as "It was an accident," "I forgot," or "I didn't mean to." Their defense is sloppy when playing a rather average opponent. This child needs extended guidance and a scaled-down, structured approach to the next game, much like my daughter's beginning league basketball games where the children wore colored wrist bands so they knew who to guard. No full-court fast-breaks were allowed and the periods were only six minutes long. In life, these children need more rules and shorter, unstructured play experiences if they are going to experience success.

This same slow-paced, well-devised game plan is going to be especially important for those children who have lots of emotional offense, but few Presidential defensive skills. Their games are going to be like the Harlem Globetrotters playing the local high school team. The emotions will be coming down the court everywhere and the discombobulated defense will have little chance of stopping them. The games will feel like they are going on forever, and even the most patient coaches will lose their composure.[8] The Child Support System (chapter 13) details the extra structure and limits these players will need.

LEARNING TO FAIL

Finally, even when they give their greatest efforts, the best of teams lose. Whether it is a board game, athletic event, or an academic test, children need to learn how to handle failure. What makes this difficult is that the section of the brain that helps kids manage the big emotions of losing is the last to develop.[9] In his article, "What if the Secret to Success is Failure?" author Paul Tough focuses on the notion that: 1) There are qualities and habits beyond a narrow definition of intelligence that lead to success; and 2) Challenge and failure are a necessary part of learning.[10] Next time your child fails or doesn't meet the expectations they had hoped for, try focusing on how they felt about their effort, what they learned, and what they can work on next time. Michael Kimmel, a sociologist at Stony Brook University says, "'Brush it off, forget about it' is bad advice. . . . Let them feel the pain, and then later explain that failure is both inevitable and necessary to learn and succeed."[11] Also remember that children want your respect. Your child might feel embarrassed or shame in letting you down with their failure. Let them know that you are proud of their effort and then free them from the burden of worrying about you.

There will also be times when a child's struggles may necessitate a change in schools, a change in sports divisions, or dropping an activity that he or she was insistent on being a part of. When I was in fourth grade, it gave me great relief when, after expressing how the little league football team I was on wasn't working so well (I had little natural talent and my small stature was often pounded upon as a lineman), my mother recognized my emotional agony and gave me permission to not see it through to the end of the season. When making these changes with your child, a good phrase or explanation is, "We want to find something that is a better fit for you."

Every year, I teach third graders about the importance of learning how to make mistakes and fail. I tell them, "If I had a magic wand and could wave it so that all of you would have straight A's and not have any problems in your lives, I wouldn't use it." At first, that statement evokes some anticipation, and then disappointment in the class. After that, we go on to look at how important mistakes and failure are in learning how to handle adult life. For one of the classes, I read through a list of inventions that were created by mistake.[12]

I will also share wisdom from the collection of quotes I have up on my office wall. One is from a first grader who was struggling with making mistakes in math. Another is from Albert Einstein: "A person who never made a mistake never tried anything new."[13] My favorite failure quote comes from basketball superstar, Michael Jordan: "I have missed more than 9,000 shots in my career. I have lost almost 3,000 games. On twenty-six occasions I have been entrusted to take the game winning shot . . . and I missed. I have failed over and over and over again in life. And that's precisely why I succeed."[14]

For those children who love to play basketball or baseball and struggle with getting down on themselves if they miss a shot or strike out, it's helpful to point to the big leaguers. When they are feeling down, I'll ask, "Do you know how many out of ten baskets you need to make to be considered a great basketball player?" Then I'll pause before I answer, "Three to four out of ten." This response usually brings a wide-eyed expression to the faces of kids who are sure that the pro players make all of their shots. It's the same for hitting a baseball.

COACHING OLDER ELEMENTARY STUDENTS

No matter what type of personality your child has, the older elementary years are crucial for player development before they grow into the game-changing start of puberty.[15] While your child's defense has been bulking up in the lower and mid-elementary years, it's important to know that the first step in this pre-puberty process for older elementary students involves an increase in the emotionally charged offensive players coming down the court. As the testosterone hormone level for boys and the estrogen hormone level for girls increase, so do the pre-teens' changing emotions. I received a call from a parent who had been surprised by her fifth grade son's emotional response that morning. This young man was a "boy's boy" who played football and would barely react to hits on the field or slights by his friends. Yet earlier that morning he had sat at the breakfast table and cried because they were out of his favorite cereal. "What do I do?" his mother asked. "Nothing," I said, "just stay calm and remember that he is having one of his first hormone surges."

On the female side of the equation, I'll never forget the response I had from a sixth grader with flawless deportment. As part of my curriculum each year, I ask the students to raise their hand if they have experienced an emotional outburst at home over a situation that would have seemed trivial when they were younger. Typically, 80 percent of the students raise their hands. One composed young lady raised her hand and said, "I can't remember why I got mad, but this summer I was so mad at my mom that I stormed up to my room and slammed the door, found our favorite picture of us at Girl Scout camp, and tore it in half. I then taped the half with just me on my door so that my mother would know she was no longer in my life!"

The start of puberty brings with it a flood of hormones and brain changes that can overwhelm even the best Presidents.[16] Like a thief in the night, puberty invades and overwhelms emotions. Later, when they are alone in their rooms, children will often feel guilty over their responses and won't understand what precipitated the explosive emotional reactions. The flood of emotions that overwhelms Presidential defenses can surge in all sorts of situations and reminds us of the famous song lyric: "It's my party, and I'll cry if I want to."[17]

Recently, I was asked to substitute as the leader for our school's middle school girls' lunch club. Trying to engage them in conversation, I posed the question, "How is a rose like a middle school girl?" I expected reflections about inner beauty and flowering into adulthood until one of the sixth grade girls blurted out with a huge smile on her face, "They fall apart easily!"

While Freud characterized the latency period as a time of low sexual interest, plenty of kids have those "special feelings" for a classmate that can ruin their judgment and disrupt their behavioral choices.[18] The Once-ler in Dr. Seuss's *The Lorax* put it this way: "Cause when a guy does something stupid once, well that's because he's a guy. But if he does the same stupid thing twice, that's usually to impress some girl."[19]

For older elementary students, these special feelings start to come online with greater frequency. Older students love to hear my story of foolish behavior inspired by my feelings for a girl. It happened on Valentine's Day when I was in fourth grade. I came walking down the hall with my bag of cards and a big heart-shaped sucker that I had bought with my own money and snuck inside my bag when I left for school that morning. As I approached the class door, I noticed one of my friends walking toward me holding the exact same kind of sucker. We soon realized that our special gifts were bound for the same girl. Impulsively, we both raced to the door to give her our suckers first. As we wrestled to the floor, our teacher picked us up and led us to the principal's office. In the office, our principal talked to us both about what we had done and then announced we would receive the standard consequence in those days for fighting: a paddling. Adding salt to my wounds, back in the room the young girl announced that she didn't like either of us because of our decision to fight over her. It was a very bad Valentine's Day, and as I like to tell the students, "It's really important to use your President with these feelings!"

If you have a fifth or sixth grade student, you have probably heard them whispering and giggling about the annual school puberty talk. Even if your child hasn't shown any interest in "special feelings" yet, all the kids have a bit of squirmy interest and embarrassment about the subject when I do my annual talks. One particular fun memory was when a sixth grade girl joined us for coed lunch club, and one of the boys asked her about the girls' talk. She told us, "It was awful, the doctor talked about the P word!" I asked, "The P word?" She responded, "You know . . . P plus *enis*?" We all had a great laugh.

> **The drumbeat of puberty is getting closer.**

Some kids will need support at this age when faced with locker room situations. While younger children will change in the stalls, this embarrassed-driven behavior can lead to negative feedback as they get older. An easy solution is to coach them on finding a corner locker. This zone gives them a little more protection while they suit up for PE. Many kids have learned how to disrobe and change with a wrapped towel around them.

It's also fairly common for prepubescent children to engage in same gender exploration.[20] This usually involves slumber party games like strip tease or truth or dare. It is recommended that you have security measures on electronics when your children are at this age as the intrigue of looking at pornography is pretty compelling.

In your parent talks, make sure to talk about your family values and emphasize the importance of respect for others, especially regarding friendships. Make the point that coercion or force are never part of any healthy relationship. **It's also never too early to start talking to your child about what giving consent means.**

In addition, talk to them about safety procedures if they are ever alone at the mall or approached by a stranger in the park. If a slumber party or game of truth or dare starts to go too far, tell your child that they can say simple phrases that cause a distraction such as, "I feel uncomfortable," "I hear my mom coming," or "We won't be able to have any more sleepovers if we get caught." In the book *UnSelfie,* Michele Borba mentions great techniques to help children stand up to coercive behavior.[21]

INTERNALIZING COACHING: THE BLENDER COMES TO THE RESCUE

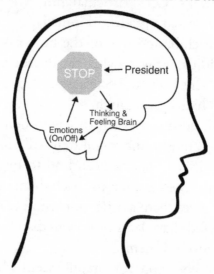

Nearly every day of my childhood, my mom would say to me, "How would you feel if" and then mention some behavior I was doing to someone else. Having insight (the ability to think about ourselves in relation to others) into our thoughts, feelings, and behavior is crucial for successful social interactions. This insight is brought into consciousness by your child's developing self-talk abilities. According to author John Ratey, "Self-talk is at the root of the empathy, understanding, cooperation, and rules that allow us to be successful beings."[22]

Fortunately, for the sake of social harmony, our brains also have a unique area that helps us process our thoughts and feelings— even ones as powerful as jealousy and the pain of rejection. The orbitofrontal cortex sits in the right hemisphere, just below the President and has connections to the limbic system.[23] Think of it as a Blender that mixes up higher level thoughts with one's emotions and nonverbal perceptions (discussed in section IV). The orbitofrontal cortex, or the Blender, has the ability to communicate back to our Factory and tell it to turn up, turn down, or turn on or off. It accomplishes this by reviewing our past emotional experiences and the many lessons we've learned about getting along with others. It also allows us to consider the positive and negative consequences of possible actions and how we, or others, might feel after we decide to respond in a particular way. Quite literally, it is the Blender's integration ability that guides our decision-making.

Imagine an eight-year-old girl who walks over to play with her best friend and sees this friend talking with a new girl. The two girls are making lanyards together and her best friend turns and energetically states, "I've just made a new best friend!" Instantly, our eight-year-old feels panic and jealousy. Her emotions tell her to storm off with a scowl on her face. Fortunately, in order to engage her Blender, her President springs into action and halts the emotional fast break. She activates her thinking-feeling brain and remembers that when she stormed off in the past, the situation actually got worse, and she received a consequence. She then remembers what her parents told her about always wearing a smile, even when she felt unsure. She immediately smiles and relaxes her body. She then thinks about how her friend made the new friend announcement. Did her friend make the declaration in order to intentionally hurt her? Was she trying to replace their friendship? Based on previous positive experiences, she gives her friend the benefit of the doubt. She determines that she doesn't need to feel jealous or threatened and tells her Factory to turn down. After reaching this conclusion, advice from her grandmother pops into her head: "Always leave room for another friend." Instantly, our eight-year-old girl says, "That's great. Can I join the two of you and make lanyards too?" Her emotional crisis has been successfully resolved. The defense now has the ball.

This is a simple example of how the Blender works in conjunction with the President, Factory, and Mirror throughout the day as your child plays and works with his/her peers.[24] However, remembering to stop and fully evaluate a particular situation isn't always so easy, especially when our amygdala gets triggered. Recently, one of the boys from my group stormed into the room and announced how much he hated his school principal for a recent policy decision. Without missing a beat, the boy next to him calmly said, "Well, I'm sure she is a better person than just that one decision." Even though he wasn't aware of Aristotle's teachings, the second boy had lived out Aristotle's words: "Anybody can become angry—that is easy; but to be angry with the right person and to the right degree and at the right time and for the right purpose and in the right way, that is not within everybody's power and is not easy."[25]

Finally, remember that emotional management skills and integrating one's Blender into the equation takes most children years to develop. As younger children try and use their words to handle their Factories, they can often try out negative, antisocial strategies as a way to gain control over what is upsetting them. Many pre-K children go through phases of hitting, spitting, biting, name calling, screaming, lying, and avoidance or withdrawal. These reactions often make them feel good because they gain some temporary control over the situation. What they are too young to realize is that while these strategies work in the moment, they backfire in the long run and leave the child feeling less in control. If these behaviors persist beyond six weeks or so, your child will develop a bad habit, which becomes more difficult to break. Given that the brain is wired more deeply through repetition, these antisocial behaviors become increasingly easy for a child to utilize. For lying, researcher Tali Sharot puts it this way, "The more we lie, the less likely we are to have an emotional response that accompanies it."[26] **The emotional response of shame and guilt have been downgraded in modern culture, but they serve an important role in a child's development of prosocial behavior.** Make sure to have a discussion with your child after they have failed to live up to your moral standards. See chapter 14 for strategies on helping your child express their emotions as well as numerous emotional and social stories and analogies.

GRANDMA'S RULES

You can't underestimate the power of your coaching and the shared wisdom that gets passed along from generation to generation. Phrases and stories that your parents or grandparents had, such as "Grandma's Rule—Work before play" hold many great lessons for your child's Blender. If you've had the pleasure of watching the 2017 movie *Paddington 2*, you see how the little bear navigates his new world by saying, "Aunt Lucy says." The parables, poems, and idioms that have been passed down for hundreds of years serve the same purpose. Wise sayings such as, "It all works out in the wash"; "Just say OK"; "You get what you get and don't pitch a fit"; "Turn lemons into lemonade"; "Look for the silver lining"; "The grass is always greener on the other side of the fence"; "Is that choice really going to help you feel in control?" and "The longer you avoid the problem, the worse your anxiety will become" can help children integrate past wisdom into their learning and development. Just like the Boy Scout and Girl Scout Laws, kids learn from these every day. Thanks to their Blender, they can pull these cognitions out when they need them (discussed further in chapter 14).

I still remember the morning my father came out to inspect his car, which I had just washed. Like any kid, I didn't notice that the bottom half of the car's sides had to be washed as well. His words were simple and straightforward: "Son, if you're going to do a job half-assed, don't do it at all." For a man who never cussed, I was struck by his language and demeanor. Rather than expressing anger, he simply expressed disappointment.[27] Needless to say, after feeling my father's disappointment, I went back and washed the car in a more thorough fashion.

Some of my father's other favorite sayings were: "There are two ways to do things: the right way and the wrong way." After a late-night sleepover, he would say, "You can't soar like an eagle if you've been hooting like an owl the night before." And when I was so worried about my first D in third grade handwriting, he simply said, "Don't worry about it, no one can read my handwriting either. Some day you will hire someone to do it for you." That brought me great relief!

BRAIN ACTIVITY: LOGIC AND THE MAGIC HAT

One of the joys of your child getting older is their increased ability to think logically about their fears and anxieties. In addition to being able to calm themselves with these emotional lessons, their emotional tool box gets even more diverse as they are able to incorporate scientific and mathematical concepts into their problem-solving and decision-making. As a five-year-old child, I looked at all the things stuffed under my bed and in my closet and logically thought that it wouldn't be possible for big monsters to be hiding there because it just wasn't big enough. Scientific logic can also help your child understand what causes thunder, why bees are needed in the environment, and how those scary creaks and cracks they hear at night are just the movement of wood molecules in the floor and ceiling joists. Thanks to Google and YouTube, you can look up just about any childhood fear and watch a cool video on it.

Besides lacking the size or ability to do much about many of their fears (kids love the Home Alone movies because they portray a child being able to stop the robbers), younger children also lack the ability to fully understand probability. When they hear about a bad thing happening, they fear it's going to happen to them as well. Fortunately, a fun math lesson and some basic media awareness can aid in rescuing your child from their anxieties.

Fifteen years ago I received a delightfully colorful, floppy hat, similar to what the Cat in the Hat wears, from our school librarian. After 9/11, I was trying to figure out how to reduce the students' anxieties about airplanes and elevators. While most adults were a bit unnerved when flying or riding in an elevator for the first time after the attacks, many of the children retained those fears for months. With so much graphic coverage of the event, their amygdala's were triggered and they lacked the logical ability to think about how rare the event was and that planes were not going to just start falling from the sky at any time. It was then that I came up with the Magic Hat Activity.

- *First, you'll need a hat or pillowcase and about six tubes of Starbursts (or a one-pound bag of individual pieces).*
- *Draw an X on one of the candies with a pen, and then dump all the candies into the hat or pillowcase.*
- *Have your child watch as you do this and then tell them that they will get to reach in and pull one out.*
- *If they pull out the candy with an X, they will get a*

*reward like an extra half hour of electronics. Watch
their eyes light up as they reach in, certain that they
will get the special X.*

- *If they happen to get it, give them the reward. Most
likely they won't. Then explain to them that while
they may be disappointed, they really didn't have
much of a chance of getting it. Then have them
look into the hat or pillow case and see all the other
candies.*

- *Have them replace the candy they just pulled out
and now repeat the experiment with a negative
consequence for getting the X. This one is just a
pretend scenario such as telling them they might
fall off their bike or scooter and need to go to the
doctor. As your child reaches in, ask, "What's the
chance of that happening to you?" Then explain that
of course it's possible, but not likely if they practice
their well-honed skills and safety precautions. Most
likely, they won't pull out the candy with an X and
like hundreds of previous times, they will have a safe
and fun ride.*

- *Now take this mathematical thinking a little
further. Put the one candy with an X on the table by
itself so they can see it and then ask them what could
change the chances of getting that X). For example,
if they didn't buckle their helmet (remove a handful
of candies and place them on the counter), or if their
shoes were untied (take out another handful), or if
they rode out into the street without looking first
(take out two handfuls). Now, return the candy with
an X to the hat or pillow case and help your child
notice the X is now among very few other candies.*

Have them reach in and try to pull it out again and
then discuss how their risk just went way up.

After enjoying several of the candies together, you can transition this lesson into whatever fear your child is currently struggling with. Maybe it's that pesky bee from Shel Silverstein's poem. Emphasize that if you wear shoes while running through the grass and don't go swatting at them when they are hovering around the flowers, there is a very little chance of getting stung. I actually had one class that calculated the number of times and number of kids that went out on the playground during the school day. We then multiplied that number by the number of days and divided it by fifteen (the average number of stings reported to the office each year). Assuming the four hundred and forty kids are on the playground for an average of four times a day that works out to approximately 17,500 Starbursts for every X. That's a pretty small chance and a very big pile of candy.

You can also use this logic to approach the bigger fears in a child's life. Shark attacks (prior to your beach vacation), robberies, child kidnappings, and school intrusions are frightening for children and parents alike, but using the Magic Hat activity serves as a rational, concrete counter to anxiety. During my class presentations, we have calculated all sorts of frightening events, and I have often asked children to imagine that the entire gym is filled with Starbursts and only one has an X. According to my fifth graders' calculations, the gym would actually hold 2 billion Starbursts, so the chance of someone reaching in and pulling the X out is really, really small.

However, you should be aware that there still is a chance that one of your children's greatest fears might come true, whether or not they pick the Starburst with the X. A sad but poignant reminder of this comes from a student who had done this activity with me when he was in third grade. When he was a middle school student he came to see me after the tragic death of his father and said, "I got the one with the X."

BRAIN ACTIVITY: FRIGHTENING NEWS

Another good activity to use with your kids is about media awareness. Help them understand that the majority of the time the news outlets use fear and controversy to boost ratings. Rarely do they cover the good that exists in the world every day of every year. I like to joke that we might read or hear a news lead about a house being robbed last night. But we won't ever see the headline: "1,999,000 Homes in Metro Denver Were Safe Last Night."

For older children, you can also talk to them about the link between viewership, advertising revenue, and sensational stories. Ask them if they need to know about some of these events. Then tell them that adults know the coverage is often overindulgent for the sake of ratings. My father used to say, "Must be sweeps week." Unfortunately, a child's logical brain and emotional responses don't fully understand this and can often get caught up in the sensationalism.

While I'm a big news junky and have many great conversations with my kids about all sorts of topics we hear on National Public Radio, I also encourage families to monitor the news when their kids are nearby. After all, it only takes one kid in the class with older siblings to hear about something horrible and fearful and then spread it around the playground. Rather than dealing with that scenario, follow the story yourself first and then sit down and have a chat with your child. It's better for them to hear it from you instead of other kids on the playground or seeing graphic newspaper photos and TV coverage.

At the end of your talk, remind them to feel free to ask questions or share their thoughts with you in case some of their classmates haven't heard about it yet. After a very tragic kidnapping and murder of a ten-year-old girl in Denver, a second grade girl came up to me before class. Her President was fully functioning as was her empathy for her classmates when she whispered, "Mr. Knippenberg, I know about that girl but thought I shouldn't bring it up in front of the whole class."

Since the Columbine shooting, I've used this probability activity after the numerous school shootings that have happened over the past two decades. I remind students that statistically, school is the safest place they can be. Far more child injuries occur at home and in the neighborhood. I tell them to think about how they are in a structured environment and are being watched all day by lots of adults. It doesn't mean that someone can't get hurt while at school, but the odds are much lower as long as they are acting in a reasonably safe manner.

CHILD SUPPORT SYSTEM
FACTORY REFERENCE GUIDE

Optimistic Temperament
- Positive reinforcement for flexibility and emotional recovery
- Increased unsupervised play

Anxious Temperament
- Plan ahead for potential anxieties
- Limit "content" discussion, focus on anxiety "process" (see chapter 13)
- Promote self-problem-solving
- Positive reinforcement for small steps and "letting it go"
- Limit expressed parental anxiety

Angry Temperament
- Reinforce "stop" and increased structure for negative behavior
- Limit content discussion and focus on anger process
- Increase adult consistency and communication
- Promote self-problem-solving
- Positive reinforcement for small steps and "letting it go"
- Consequences for aggressive behavior or refusal to try positive solutions

Sad Temperament
- Promote positive thoughts to combat negative thoughts
- Limits of negative self-talk and "victim" thinking
- Limit content discussion and focus on sad process
- Promote self-problem-solving
- Positive reinforcement for small steps and "letting it go"
- Extra TLC when needed and encourage gratitude

Excitable Temperament
- Embrace spontaneity but also self-regulation of behavior
- Increase structure if getting carried away or for constant demands
- Coaching for disappointment surrounding unfulfilled expectations

Analytical Temperament
- Encourage attachment of emotions to thoughts
- Encourage reflection on other's emotions
- Help with shortening long, detailed explanations

SECTION IV

MONKEY SEE, MONKEY DO

"Simon says:"
~Simon de Montfort

A children's game, Simon Says gives us a glimpse of how humans begin to imitate each other. As they play, children activate and develop a complex neural network, which allows them to move past simple mimicry to a more sophisticated understanding of others' thoughts and emotions. It is this ability to read nonverbal communication that helps us coexist, and more importantly, empathize. Some children seem to do this naturally, while others appear to struggle as they enter into social engagements. Refining one's nonverbal processing abilities requires repeated real world practice through unstructured play. Residing on the high end of the Spectrum of Mirror Functioning can be positive or negative in developing community with others.

CHAPTER 10

HOW DID YOU PICK YOUR SEAT?

WALKING INTO A CLASSROOM

Imagine yourself as a sixth grader. It's your first day of middle school, and you are a walking bundle of nerves. The halls are so vast, and they're full of more kids than you've ever seen . . . and they're enormous! This is nothing like elementary school, you reflect as you walk into your first class. The room is filled with two-person tables and this particular teacher allows for open seating. Just as you turn the corner and head into the room, you hear the teacher say, "Everyone take a seat." You have about two seconds to scan the room and head to your chosen seat. Think fast! What factors do you consider when picking the right seat for you?

For starters, it's obvious that you should select a chair that isn't occupied. While that task seems simple—you just look for a seat without a body in it—perhaps it's more complicated than you think. Did someone leave a pencil or a notepad on the desk before walking off to talk to a friend or head to the bathroom? Maybe there is a seat open, but a female classmate has pulled the second seat back and is looking around the room for someone. Is she saving it for someone? What would happen if you sat down next to her? Is she one of the more popular kids? Was she walking down the hall with that same girl? Does there appear to be kids sitting around her who are part of her group? What happened when she glanced past you standing at the door? Did she smile or just look away? Is she whispering to her friends? Are her friends turning and looking at you? Why are they giggling? Is it you? What do those smirks mean? Is that a mean look from one of the other girls? What about the boys roughhousing in the corner? What should you do?

Hopefully not all seat decisions are this complicated or potentially disastrous from a social and emotional perspective. *The thought process it takes to simply navigate the school can be overwhelming when a new sixth grade student is confronted with it.* When I give lectures on the social brain or talk to groups of students, I ask for their input on what goes into choosing a seat. Some of the most common responses are as follows:

- Did you do your homework?
- Do you see a friend?
- What if you see your friend, but know you will be tempted to talk to him/her and you have already been in trouble sitting next to that person before?
- Do you see an enemy or bully you should stay away from?
- Which kids are known for goofing around in class and playing pranks on others?
- Do you have a hard time hearing the teacher or seeing the board?
- Are you trying to make eye contact with a particular boy or girl?
- How did the teacher's voice sound when she asked you to take a seat? Was she happy and smiling or was she upset and demanding an immediate start to class?
- Who typically sits with whom in this particular class?
- What if you sit next to the kid who has a really low social standing?

- Is there a smart student in this class that you could sit with in case there is a group activity?

If these are the most common considerations, think about all the other possibilities for the average sixth grade student, such as one of my favorite responses from a sixth grade boy: "I always forget my pencil, and I know that Sandy always has extras."

Some students struggle with all these considerations.[1] A female college student responded by reflecting upon the behavior of other students: "I tend to ask a lot of questions to make sure I understand things, so I sit in the middle front of the class." I asked her if that was so she could make eye contact with the teacher and she replied, "No, it's so I don't have to see the faces of my classmates who are getting upset with me when I ask another question."

The most profound response was from another college student who shared that she had Asperger's Syndrome.[2] She sat on the far side of the room next to a window, tucked behind a support pillar with just enough of an angle that she could still make eye contact with me as the speaker.[3] She said, "I sat here because sitting next to others and looking at their faces is very hard for me and makes me feel uncomfortable. I can hide over here and also look out the window if I'm feeling overwhelmed by having people around me."

The directions are fairly simple: "Please take a seat." However, a student's consideration when deciding where to sit falls into the nonverbal category. They picked their seats based on a variety of internal and external factors not necessarily communicated with verbal or written words. Memories of seating positions and social dynamics from past classes as well as learned nonverbal cues informed their decisions.[4]

When examining why you would have selected a certain seat, think about how long your brain actually has to process that information and make a decision: two seconds, maybe five if you are lucky. If you stand and think too long, classmates might wonder what you are doing and make a snide remark. If you choose too quickly, you might make a disastrous decision. Not many students want to be the victim of pranks (remember the tack on the seat?) or have one of the popular kids look at you and sarcastically say, "What are you doing? Loser!"

So what is the difference between the kids who always seem to make the right social choices and those who always seem to get it wrong? Granted, not all kids care about where they sit in a room or don't worry too much about what others think. Some kids seem to have a good sense of self and don't worry too much about others' opinions. Others seem to be oblivious to what's going on around them or how others are jockeying for the seat they want. They might have the ability to read nonverbal cues but aren't paying attention to them, or they act impulsively in selecting their seat. Some kids seem to think about only one or two of those earlier seat considerations while others seem to process almost all of them. Like individual pieces of stained glass, these considerations hopefully blend into a larger stained glass picture of a chair, which results in both positive academic and social success.

In order to paint that ideal picture, you can help your children become aware of the nonverbal cues that people and animals use to communicate. Be intentional and encourage them to take time to scan situations and formulate hypotheses about what others are doing, thinking, and feeling.

Developing awareness of nonverbal cues involves slowing down a child's impulses and teaching them to use their President to stop and look. Yet some children simply read the cues more effectively than others. The social butterflies of the world seem to observe and interpret the cues in an effortless and efficient manner. Others try to process a social situation but can't quite put the pieces together. However, they can learn. For example, a fifth grade boy in one of my groups was struggling with reading body language and had been working on being aware of others' nonverbal cues for the previous three years in group. As we walked into the office after the group was finished playing in the park, he looked out to a young woman sitting on a park bench about one hundred yards away. Her head was down, her shoulders were slumped. He turned to me and said, "I wonder what she is feeling. I think she is sad or upset." In a few minutes, the young woman stood up and started marching toward the playground. As she got closer, a young man started walking toward her with a sorrowful expression on his face. The young woman stormed to the bench nearby. "I think she's mad," said my friend. "Me too," I replied.

Some of us can intuitively interpret nonverbal cues to paint a mental picture of what others are feeling. For others, making sense of facial expressions, vocal tones, and body language is a struggle.[5] In the next chapter we will look at how a team of neuroscientists discovered how the brain observes and processes this information in an area of the brain, which I've termed the Mirror.

BRAIN ACTIVITY: NONVERBAL OBSERVATIONS

When your children were infants, you no doubt spent plenty of time looking at them and mirroring their faces and emotions. As your child grows, you can keep mirroring each other. Younger elementary students love to play Simon Says. After performing the various complex movements the kids like to do, try adding in various facial expressions and emotions. For instance, you can say, "Simon Says: Make a happy face." Then move to more complex emotions: "Simon Says: Make a face like you were told that you couldn't join in on a game the other kids were playing." Or, "Simon Says: Make a face like you see in one of your friends standing alone on the playground."

Next time you are watching the Disney channel with your child, take advantage of the enhanced nonverbal expressions the actors use, and then talk about what is being communicated. The middle school themed shows are particularly good for explaining sarcasm. You can also explore the character's motives and who can and can't be trusted just by observing the nonverbal cues. You can also discuss how TV shows and movies use music that conveys the drama of a particular scene or parallels the plot structure, unlike in real life.

In particular, teach your children to look at others' eyes. Remember the phrase "The eyes are the window to the soul"? Now think about how your child's eyes light up when they are feeling pure joy. Evolutionary scientists also note how humans developed an upright forehead with flexible eyebrows about two hundred thousand years ago from their ancestors' backward sloping, bony bridge of a forehead. This, they believe, allowed humans to communicate subtle social gestures such as, "Hey!" "I'm angry," or "I'm not sure about what you are saying."[6]

As your kids get better at noticing the nonverbal communication around them, try watching a show with the sound off. You and your kids can talk about what you observed and take turns hypothesizing about what is taking place in the show. Now watch the scene again with the sound turned back on. It's pretty amazing what you can figure out without the sound on. One recent Sunday evening, we sat down with our daughter to watch the classic film, Charlotte's Web. To our surprise, it was being broadcast that evening in Spanish. The three of us were surprised at how well we could understand the film even though none of us speaks more than a couple of words of Spanish.

Your family's animal companions are also a great source for studying nonverbal behaviors. We know that animals utilize mirror neurons to observe and learn new behaviors.[7] At home, I recently gave our puppy an imitation bone. The pup put it in her mouth and then just dropped it with little or no interest. Later, her mother came running out and spied the new treat. She immediately picked up one end with her mouth and placed the other end between her front paws as she has hundreds of times before. As the pup watched her delight, he immediately wanted the bone. After he successfully grabbed the treat, he imitated his mother with the exact same paw hold.

Help your children observe how your animals utilized nonverbal cues to show curiosity, affection, friendship, anger, and sadness. Some animals seem to have an ability to express their emotions as well as notice our emotions and intentions. Author, veterinarian expert, and Asperger's Syndrome advocate Temple Grandin has written numerous books about animals' nonverbal abilities. In particular, she looks at how modern canines evolved from ancient wolves.

According to Grandin's book Animals Make Us Human, wolves have a complex set of social skills and possess sixteen important behaviors for managing conflictual relationships within a pack. Eight of these nonverbal signals, such as muzzle licks, looking away, or lying on their backs to expose the anogenital area are used to communicate submission. The other eight signals, like a raised back or gnarled teeth, are used to signal aggression and to tell the other wolves to back off. Wolves use these sixteen signals to navigate their relationships with each other and will even use a play bow as a way of saying "sorry" after a social mistake.[8] Recent research even found that if a wolf puppy doesn't apologize to the other pups and continues to express more aggressive behavior, the other pups will kick him out of the group.[9]

Our modern canine breeds demonstrate a mix of these nonverbal abilities. According to Grandin, Golden Retrievers have twelve of the sixteen behavioral abilities while Siberian Huskies have all *sixteen.*[10] *Both of these breeds are thus able to successfully navigate their conflicts with other dogs. On the other end of the spectrum, the French Bulldog only has four of these abilities while the Cavalier King Charles Spaniel only has two.*[11] *Additional research into the nonverbal abilities of canines also indicates that a dog will wag its tail more to the right if it immediately knows it wants to be friends. If the tail wags more to the left, it means that the dog is feeling unsure and anxious about the potential friend.*[12]

You can generalize these animal observations into specific social suggestions for your child. While we don't want them to play bow like a dog, we do want them to apologize when they go too far. Also help your kids see how dogs are constantly scanning humans and trying to read our thoughts and intentions. While the motivation for a dog's behavior is often in anticipation of receiving a treat or going for a walk, teach your children to stop and scan a room before entering. For younger children, focus on the obvious cues, such as level of motor activity, the volume level in the room, and the overall mood of the people in the room. After reviewing all these cues with them, gently remind them of the expected behaviors before going in. As your kids mature, help them notice more subtle cues, such as: Who seems to be in charge of the situation? Who should get to speak or sit down first? Who seems to be friends with whom? Who seems to be left out or shy? and Whom might you want to avoid?

You'll find that taking the time to review and practice these forms of nonverbal communication will help with the social and emotional development in your child.

CHAPTER 11

VITTORIO'S MONKEY AND THE SPECTRUM OF MIRROR NEURON FUNCTIONING

In his book *Mirroring People: The New Science of How We Connect with Others,* neuroscientist Marco Iacoboni tells a story about a group of Italian researchers and their accidental discovery involving macaque monkeys. Approximately twenty-five years ago, a team of neuroscientists studied an area of the brain associated with hand control and the act of grasping an object. The monkeys were implanted with electrodes, which measured the electrical output when a specific region of the brain is activated.

As the story goes, researcher Vittorio Gallese and a monkey were hanging out between experiments. Vittorio reached for an object and was surprised to hear sounds from the machine that was monitoring the monkey's brain activity. The monkey was sitting completely still yet his brain was firing the same motor cells the monkey would use for grasping an object. While the brain activity was below the threshold of causing the monkey's arm to move and grasp, the machine detected that the primate was mentally mimicking Vittorio's grasping action. Vittorio and his colleagues, surprised by what they had observed, began replicating the response with other objects, including ice cream and a peanut. The researchers noticed that when they grabbed the aforementioned snacks, it triggered the same pathway response in the monkey's motor brain areas as if the monkey had also grasped the ice cream and peanut.[1]

While Vittorio and his partners did not yet realize what they had stumbled upon, researchers around the world also noticed this phenomenon with monkeys and then with humans. *These combined studies led to the discovery of the mirror neuron system.* Mirror neurons, along with spindle neurons, do exactly what their names suggest. They mirror back what they see or hear by firing the same areas of the brain where the behavior being heard or observed takes place. Iacoboni goes on to theorize that when we see others' facial expressions, the mirror neurons send signals to our own facial muscles as well as signals to our emotional centers. So, when I see my friend looking happy, my mirror neurons are helping me reach a conclusion, such as "If I was making that face, I'd feel happy, therefore, my friend is feeling happy." Mirror neurons literally are our brain's mechanism for having empathy. Or, as Iacoboni writes: "Only after we feel these emotions internally are we able to explicitly recognize them in others."[2] In addition to imitating others' behavior, our mirror neurons' responses to our own movements can affect how we feel. The old phrases *Put a smile on your face,* or *Turn that frown upside down* actually work. Studies have shown that the physical act of smiling makes you feel instantly happier.[3]

Memories can also trigger the mirror neuron system. Additionally, the neurons generate an intense response when they anticipate or remember something that is particularly rewarding, like a sweet drink for a monkey or a marshmallow for a four-year-old.

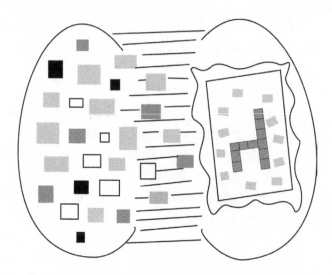

While the mirror and spindle neurons transition through different developmental phases and ultimately grow axons that stretch throughout our brains, *the basis for this empathy system is hard wired into your infant's brain.* By age twenty, the average brain is packed with about one hundred thousand miles of white matter tissue from all of the brain's various neuron types.[4] Do you remember smiling at your baby, who immediately smiled back? This indicates that the mirror neuron system is up and working. Research has found that babies as young as thirty-six hours old can discern facial expressions, and that seven-month-olds are able to match vocal expressions of emotion to their corresponding facial expressions.[5] By eighteen months of age, children start becoming aware of how others' emotions are different from their own.[6]

As the mirror neurons develop and the spindle cell axons grow longer and reach out to the emotional brain areas and the limbic system, your child's ability to fire a pathway related to social situations becomes increasingly sophisticated. By ages five or six, contagious yawning emerges more fully in children. Yawning is so contagious that even subjects who were told to suppress their yawns while watching someone else yawn, ended up yawning just as much as the subjects who were told to yawn freely.[7] At the same time yawning contagion is developing, children are also becoming more empathetic.[8] Individuals who demonstrate high levels of empathic behavior also tend to have stronger activations in the mirror neuron system for emotions.[9] In addition to understanding the emotional weight of a given social situation, by ages five or six your child will be able to reflect upon the past and envision future events, and imagine how he or she would feel if put in another's position and integrate these all together in the Blender (chapter 9).

You might recall the story in chapter 9 of the girl whose best friend wanted to introduce her to the new friend she had just made. What allowed the girl to make the positive choice of being happy for her friend and joining in on the fun was her ability to remember a similar past situation and think about what it might be like to be her friend, to be in her shoes. Viewing the situation from her friend's perspective allowed her to understand how her friend would feel and how she would want her best friend to react. That's a perfect picture of empathy in action.

Most of these mirror and spindle neurons sit in the right hemisphere and cross over to the left hemisphere via the corpus callosum. The corpus callosum runs perpendicular in the middle of the brain and connects the two hemispheres. Its 250 million axon fibers make up the thickest area of white matter in the human brain and serve as a transportation corridor for neuron activity.[10] The mirror neurons collect information and memories from various areas of our brain and then transfer them over to the right hemisphere.[11] Like the student in chapter 10 who is trying to figure out where to sit in the classroom and put the pieces of his stained glass chair or social window together, the right hemisphere assimilates the individual pieces into one overarching perception of a particular experience.

SPECTRUM OF MIRROR PROCESSING

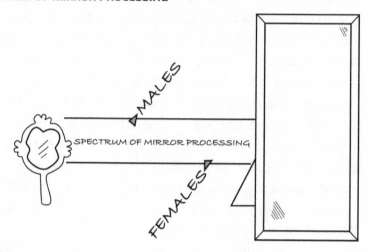

Observe any elementary school recess and you'll quickly notice that some students seem to naturally process the nonverbal cues going on around them. They notice who feels left out and perceive how their actions affect the feelings and behaviors of others. They are also able to read a myriad of social cues such as facial expressions, body language, and vocal tone among their peers. They are the social butterflies who float around the playground piecing together a huge stained glass window of social interaction. Others, however, appear awkward, struggle to fit in, have a difficult time resolving the many conflicts that arise in normal play, and often feel left out. It's as if they only see specific pieces of that social window and focus on one factor or dynamic in an interaction. These children just seem to be different and march to the beat of their own drum when it comes to socializing.

These differences, so easy to observe on the playground, exist in a laboratory setting as well. One cognitive test used to measure an individual's ability to understand what others are feeling by looking at pictures of people's eyes and eyebrows was developed by a professor at the University of Cambridge. Simon Baron-

Cohen and his team were interested in how adults with Asperger's Syndrome would score compared to the general adult population. As hypothesized, adults with Asperger's scored lower on his twenty-five-question test (16.3 average score) than adults from the general population (18.8 for men and 21.8 for women).[12] It is clear how children on the autism spectrum struggle to paint the big picture of life around them. Decoding nonverbal communication is arduous and they often confuse which pieces of glass correlate with that big picture and which pieces are irrelevant to the whole.

One of my strongest memories of this failed process is of taking a young man with more severe Autism up to the local grocery store to practice buying a soda pop. We walked along the sidewalk and then started cutting across the store's parking lot. Other shoppers were coming out of the store and heading to their cars. Not understanding why these other shoppers were coming toward us, the young man panicked and hurriedly ran back to my office. After calming him down, I realized what precipitated his anxiety: he didn't understand the correlation between the other shoppers walking in the lot and the cars parked nearby, so he concluded that they were walking toward him. He was frightened because they were strangers.

When we move up the social cognition spectrum from the autism spectrum disorder, we find people in the low-average range who often fit the classic example of the engineer or computer professional. They are quite good at their jobs because they are logical, pragmatic thinkers who can easily identify specific pieces of glass which make up the larger picture when it comes to writing code or drafting schematics. In his book *The Essential Difference: Male and Female Brains and the Truth About Autism*, Baron-Cohen refers to these people as being intelligent at analyzing, exploring, and understanding how things work (systemizing).[13]

When moving higher up on the Spectrum of Mirror Processing, we find people who are emotionally intelligent and who have a great capacity for empathy ("empathizers"). While we might hope that men would have the same sophisticated social processing abilities as women, experience and research demonstrate that this is simply not the case. In Baron-Cohen's research, adult females scored in the eighty-seventh percentile while adult males scored in the seventy-fifth percentile. However, remember that there are exceptions: there are many males who are proficient at recognizing others' emotions and nonverbal communication, as well as many females who excel at what Robert Sternberg calls "analytical intelligence" in understanding things.[14]

Baron-Cohen notes there are big differences between adult brains and a child's brain. This is especially the case when it comes to the mirror and spindle neuron systems. Both boys and girls show very early abilities to identify emotions, use expressive vocabulary, and make decisions based on relationships. For example, William Pollack, the author of *Real Boys*, points out that even as early as twenty-one months, boys can display feelings of empathy, including a wish to help people in pain.[15] In *The Female Brain*, author Louann Brizendine talks about girls' slightly higher abilities: "Girls as young as a year old are more responsive to the distress of other people, especially those who look sad or hurt."[16] She also notes that the verbal and emotional circuits for girls are enhanced by higher estrogen levels during the first two years of life.[17] Over time, boys and girls expand upon their own unique trajectories through the course of interactions with others.[18] While the differences between males and females become even more pronounced after puberty, it's important to encourage boys as much as possible to express their emotions and think about the emotions of others.

As puberty hits, however, we begin to see those gender differences that Baron-Cohen noted. Recent research at the University of Pennsylvania found that major wiring differences between boys and girls greatly expanded during adolescence and young adulthood.[19]

Young women had more connections between the two brain hemispheres (via an area called the corpus callosum) while men of the same age had more connective fiber within each hemisphere.[20]

These long strands of white matter between the hemispheres allow females to integrate more information into their perceptions of a social situation.

Comedian Jeff Foxworthy was neurologically accurate when he made a joke about the social functioning differences between men and women and the differences in their social processing: "Women have an eight-lane super highway and men have a little dirt path!"[21]

If we think like evolutionary biologists, we might wonder why men's and women's brains evolved differently. In our ancient traditional roles, women often cared for their young and had to rely more on nonverbal cues from their infants over the spoken word. Most mothers had to rely on pitch, tone, and facial expression to understand why their baby was crying. In fact, a woman's "gut feelings" have a lot to do with this enhanced ability to read nonverbal cues.[22]

These enhanced abilities were also crucial for navigating a female community where you had to trust other women to take care of your child while you went off to gather food. Given the many tasks that had to be carried out by women (including watching for predators), they had to form close-knit, interdependent groups. Higher Oxytocin (known as the bonding hormone) levels in women helped push them toward social relationships and deep bonding with other females.[23] The need for bonding with other females would obviously facilitate the development of these survival groups. This required a great deal of trust, but also a discerning, watchful eye in case other members in the group weren't acting in a trustful manner. How would you know that someone wasn't stealing extra berries for their family, or was envious of your baby, secretly interested in your mate, or trying to gain extra power and control? Vigilant nonverbal scanning and a keen sensitivity to the emotions and group dynamics around you were imperative for social and physical survival.

The interdependent social group dynamic for which the female brain is wired can be observed in today's hallways and playgrounds. Girls have an amazing ability to form deep, complex emotional relationships. As they learn to trust others, they also have a radar for who might spread rumors or gossip about them.

Girls will also play out relational aggression as they twist that fundamental, oxytocin-laden drive to be included into exclusionary behavior. I've had many in-class conversations about the classic "best friends" arguments and discussions with first and second grade girls. It's difficult behavior to change because there is much inherent anxiety around being rejected. This fear yields to controlling behavior and extreme jealousy should one's friend start making friends with another girl.

In comparison, the nonverbal processing and play behaviors of boys are more physical when it comes to attachment and bonding.[24] Our ancient male ancestors spent their time together training for competition and learning to work as a team. If you put any group of boys together, you'll see that they quickly resort to chasing each other, roughhousing, and engaging in competitions designed to measure one's prowess. When it's going well, boys roughhouse together, joke with each other, challenge each other, and make declarative statements such as, "I kicked your butt," or "I'm going to crush you next time." This behavior might seem extreme, but these are innocuous bonding gestures. **To be teased by one's friend is the highest compliment when boys are joking and competing with each other in this manner.** While it might appear to be raw aggression, boys are not trying to hurt each other physically or emotionally. Michael Gurian calls this behavior aggression nurturance.[25] What makes this bonding play hard to differentiate from intentional manipulative/bullying/controlling behavior is the poor Presidential functioning that often accompanies it. It doesn't take too long before someone gets hurt or something gets broken by an ill-considered maneuver or joke.

Like the characters in William Golding's *Lord of the Flies*, boys will also naturally bond into small groups and then compete with other groups besides their own. Because our ancestors needed to know that they could rely on the other guys during battle, this ability grouping often results in alienation for boys who display a visible weakness. As this dynamic progresses, boys can be foolishly loyal to the behavior of a group mate and unbelievably cruel to a boy from another group. At the same time, boys have to tune in to whether or not a group member's small behaviors are out of place. In a podcast interview, Ty Tashiro (author of *Awkward: The Science of Why We're Socially Awkward and Why That's Awesome*) acknowledges, "You didn't want to find out that Larry was stealing food from the storage shed when everybody is starving or that someone was going to betray you in a battle once you're involved in it."[26]

On the schoolyard, this male play can help all of the boys play harder and work together as a team. One physically adept and sensitive boy told me that when he was captain he would purposely pick the kids who weren't as good because he didn't want them to feel left out. Unfortunately, most captains aren't that considerate, which results in a group of children who never get the chance to play quarterback or receiver and are typically picked last. Two or three alpha boys can dominate the pickup games as they buddy up based on ability and manipulate the team selection process by declaring, "We are a package. If you pick me, you have to pick him." If you stack the deck, you'll always win! I've told countless classes of elementary school boys about how the point of recess is for everyone to have fun and have a chance to develop their skills. This includes a rotating list for team captains and quarterbacks.

Whether you parent a boy, a girl, or both, remind yourself that these gender differences reflect statistical averages. There are plenty of boys who are highly sensitive and empathetic to others as well as girls who struggle with the verbal interplay of other females. Michael Gurian and his associates refer to bridge brains when describing boys who use more verbal skills and girls who are more analytical in their thinking.[27]

EMPATHY AND THEORY OF MIND

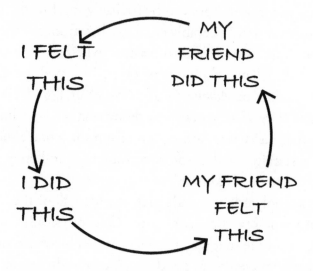

It's important to remember that most kids experience the same basic phases of social processing development. While most preschool children just play next to someone (as opposed to truly engaging in reciprocal play), the main idea is for them to try and use words for their feelings and modify any aggressive behavior. On a recent hike, I watched a preschool child and her older sister have a tiff over a pretty rock. The younger sibling felt rebuffed in her interests and blurted out: "I want to throw this rock at you!" Her mother looked at me and said, "That's a big improvement in using her words. Before, she would have just thrown it!"

While learning to use their words, preschool children still struggle with cause and effect in relationships and often feel victimized in social conflicts. A big reason for the lack of reciprocal play and this feeling of victimization has to do with their limited ability to see things from another's perspective.

As children enter kindergarten, they gain abilities related to theory of mind and start to perceive how they are impacting others' behaviors and how these behaviors are impacting them. As the young elementary student's thinking-feeling brain increases in functioning, you can start talking about the circle of behavior and how one's actions affect others and influence reciprocal behavior by their peers.[28] Kids in kindergarten are flexible in choosing playmates and will often engage in mixed-gender play during recess. Given their expanded ability to realize that others have different thoughts and desires in their heads, they are working on taking turns and demonstrating reciprocity with each other. They also have greater capacity to think about how the other person feels as well as express this empathy due to their increased Mirror abilities.

OLDER ELEMENTARY MIRROR DEVELOPMENT

In addition to basic cause and effect, early elementary children are also learning how to influence others to get what they want in upcoming play opportunities. While you are hoping they are taking turns and playing fairly (remember the old selection games like Bubble Gum and Rock, Paper, Scissors), the playground is rife with manipulative behaviors that dominate the rules of play.[29] In this regard, it's the expanded mirror neuron system that allows children to understand the emotional makeup of their peers and find ways to use it against them—just as the perpetrators of a Ponzi scheme dupe unwitting investors by exploiting their trust.

While mom and dad are still important to their identity, children in third and fourth grade increasingly begin to perceive

themselves through the eyes of their peers. As any parent knows, this peer-influenced self-image can be positive when your child is invited to play with a particular group of kids. It can also be damaging when your child comes home and says, "I don't have any friends." *Reputations begin to form based on the growing expectations for appropriate peer behavior as children hit the mid-elementary years.* If someone is behaving in a manner that the other kids think is babyish or just downright mean, the whole class of children may refuse to play with them.

As a child's Mirror continues to evolve early in puberty, sarcasm, pointing out the differences in others, and sexually inappropriate jokes might become commonplace. My son heard his first sex joke at the start of fourth grade, courtesy of a boy who had older brothers. I can recall the day I pulled out my new deep fat fryer and made catfish nuggets and fries for him and his friend. While I reached for the ketchup, I heard the boys giggling and saw them pointing at the plate. Looking down, I saw two nuggets placed at the end of a long fry. "Don't you get it, Dad?!" they said hysterically. "It's your dinner, just eat it!" I declared.

Mirror development in fourth grade females is characterized by smaller groups of girls just hanging out and talking. Despite the potential for gossip and power-brokering, these increased verbal interactions are fun opportunities to integrate the social perspectives of others. One fourth grade girl put it this way: "When we were little, we would just go out and play. Now, we spend half our time talking about what we are going to play. I just want to play and not do all that talking!"

In fifth and sixth grade, this expansion of sub-grouping and early adolescent efforts to fit in with one's friends continues. The expanded hormone system mentioned in section III triggers an upsurge in emotional processing during the day. Social mistakes are now obvious to the entire class. Girls notice everything around them and are more than happy to tell a friend. I was so pleased before school one morning when my daughter's sixth grade English teacher approached me and said, "Your daughter knows the difference between caring for a friend versus stirring the pot."

Fifth and sixth grade boys and girls are also more than willing to let you know how much you are embarrassing them. Many moms are heartbroken when their fifth grade sons don't want to be seen hugging them. Many fathers have also walked away stunned and confused when their daughters no longer think their fathers' sense of humor is all that funny in front of their friends. As my daughter, with great expressiveness in her body language, pronounced early in fifth grade, "Dad, you are an embarrassment!" While this might seem very foreign to you at first, these verbal and nonverbal advances are setting the stage for the emancipation of your teen and young adult.

Pre-teens become increasingly aware of what's going on in modern culture and what issues they hear other teenagers talking about. If your pre-teen has older siblings, you can be assured that they are listening to everything you and their older siblings are talking and arguing about. Growing up with a brother who was five years older and two older sisters, I heard about everything that was happening with the hippies: from boys with long hair to drugs and war protests; and from sex before marriage to the secret meanings behind Beatles songs when the album was played backward. Today, older elementary students are aware of depression, sexual harassment, bisexuality, gender neutrality, school shootings, and cutting.

These movements toward emancipation also mean the expansion of nonverbal processing related to romance and sexuality. While younger children will often imitate seductive looks and sexy posturing that they have observed in contemporary culture, the art of flirting really picks up for tweens. In fifth and sixth grade, most of the girls are paying closer attention to their style and makeup choices, and some of the boys are starting to groom more often and use cologne. If you decide to allow your child to use these products, the trick at this age is to talk to your daughter about how makeup should be applied so that others barely recognize that she is wearing any, and remind your son that only a spritz of Axe need be applied. It's also important to talk about not staring at those they are romantically interested in or staring at specific body parts. In my annual spring talk with sixth grade boys, we also talk about appropriate modesty when having an erection. It's a good idea for boys at this age to avoid wearing tight-fighting swimsuits at the pool and use good old briefs and blue jeans for holding things in place.

Take advantage of natural opportunities to discuss sexuality at an early age. While most fifth or sixth grade students have the annual "birds and bees" science talk or museum visit, it's important to supplement formal education talks by discussing sexuality with your own kids. This shows that you are approachable and open to these discussions as your children enter their teens. While discussing sexuality with their parents might seem taboo or awkward, kids can surprise you with an out-of-the-blue question at an odd time.

BRAIN ACTIVITY: VISUALIZING PERFORMANCE

In addition to helping us understand ourselves and others, a child's mirror neuron system can help them relax and feel better through visualization. Let's say your third grader has a class presentation coming up. After finishing the script and diorama, have them rehearse it with you a couple of times. Give them a few pointer tips such as looking up at the audience, smiling, or pointing to the diorama. Before rehearsing again, stop and help them visualize what they are about to do using the following technique.

1. *Sit comfortably and take some deep yoga breaths together as described previously in chapter 8.*
2. *Close your eyes and in a soft voice help them visualize the presentation by talking them through it.*
3. *For example, you might say, "See yourself walking calmly to the front of the room. Notice how you look relaxed and are smiling at your teacher and classmates. Now start your talk. Notice how your voice is clear and loud. See yourself smiling and looking up at the class. Picture all the kids smiling back at you as you move smoothly through your speech. Now, imagine yourself pointing out the details of your diorama. You are standing up straight and are confident. Now you are getting ready to end, so take a nice breath, smile, and say thank you."*

As you go through the visualization, your child's mirror neurons will fire the pathways for these practiced behaviors.[30] *In order to burn the pathways in further, practice the exercise together again and then have your child practice it on their own. The morning of the presentation, have them take a couple of minutes to practice their visualization again. Amazingly, with enough repetitions, mirror neurons will help enact visualized behaviors while your child is actually performing.*

Once you've taught your child how to visualize, you can use this technique for all sorts of upcoming activities. For years, athletes have used visualization in the locker room prior to going on the field. If your kids play baseball, encourage them to visualize what they want to do, how they want to look, and how they want to feel when walking up to the plate for their turn at bat. I use visualizations myself for about a minute or two out in my car before a lecture.

I picture myself speaking clearly, smiling, and having a lot of fun interacting with my audience. Pitching coach Bob Tewksbury creates audio recordings for his clients to listen to before game time. In a quiet space, the player closes his eyes, breathes deeply and listens to Tewksbury lead him through various game situations.[31]

You can also use visualizing for children who have a hard time falling asleep.[32] *At the end of your bedtime ritual, ask them what they would like to think about and visualize while falling asleep. Most children will pick a joy from that day or a future joy for tomorrow. This helps them focus on something positive instead of the day's worries that might be crowding their mind.*[33] *Then give them a kiss as they close their eyes. While using visualizations is not foolproof, it gives your children another tool for feeling in control as they fall asleep and go about mastering their worlds when they are awake.*

Parents of younger children might utilize Guatemalan worry dolls. The legend is to take a doll out of the box, tell it your worry, and then place it under your pillow. The dolls are said to make your worries go away so that you can get a good night's sleep. For other children, a dream catcher hanging close to their beds works in the same way. It catches their bad dreams and only lets the good ones through so that they can sleep through the night.

Finally, tune in to the mindfulness and visualization strategies that your child's teacher might already be using in the classroom. Recently, when I visited a first grade classroom, I found all the children lying flat on the floor and breathing deeply as they watched a mindfulness video on the smart board.[34]

Why the big push toward mindfulness in the classroom? Michele Borba explains that brain research "shows that practicing mindfulness—even minutes a day for a few weeks—can reap such positive benefits as boosting immune systems, reducing stress, increasing resilience, enhancing focus, stretching attention, and improving memory. But mindfulness can also nurture empathy and compassion as well as increase children's willingness to help others."[35] A 2015 study found that mindfulness programs in the schools helped to regulate stress in fourth and fifth graders; they were kinder, more helpful, and improved their performance in math.[36] In 2013, one study on mindfulness in the schools found that at-risk third graders' behavior and focus improved significantly, another 2013 study found that elementary students improved their self-control, classroom participation, were able to pay more attention, and displayed more respect for others.[37]

When it comes to mindfulness, I believe that if you visualize it, you have a better chance of making it happen.

CHAPTER 12

MOVING UP THE SPECTRUM

The midday sun beat down on the roof of our '68 Dodge station wagon as the giant thermometer on the gas station roof pushed past one hundred degrees. "Where is Dad?" we cried and complained to our mother. The gas tank was already full, but we continued to swelter in the heat. "You know your father," she replied.

After what seemed like an eternity, our dad returned. My four siblings and I demanded to know what took him so long. "I was just talking to the attendant about real estate prices in this area," my father replied. While we all knew this line of discussion had no basis in reality, we also knew that there was a deeper motive behind his topic of conversation. What mattered was his ingrained ability to strike up a conversation with nearly anyone on the planet. "People love to talk about themselves," he said with pride, "you just need to ask them a question to get them started." While we didn't appreciate it at the time, our father gave us the ability to strike up a conversation with just about anyone.

Just like Presidential functioning and a child's emotional temperament have genetic underpinnings, a child's placement on the nonverbal spectrum is at first determined by the genetic instructions inherited his or her parents. Then the mirror neurons grow and develop as children interact with others around them.[1] Think about your own childhood. Who taught you how to be cool? Did you have siblings who would give you feedback about your social behavior? I was fortunate to have four siblings who didn't hesitate to put me in my place if I engaged in anti-social behavior. While parents are concerned about their child's feelings being hurt, it's amazing how some negative feedback can prompt one's social development.

Children will also mirror their parents as they learn how to socialize.[2] As a parent, are you graceful and intuitive with your social interactions? Do you manage your frustration well and negotiate through problems with others? If you start to posture and act aggressively in your home, your child will mimic that behavior on the playground. According to a study of elementary and middle school students, kids of either gender who were exposed to domestic violence are the most likely to bully their peers.[3] In addition, the only common trait queen bees—the term used for the manipulative leaders of adolescent female social cliques—shared was having mothers who were quick-tempered and demonstrative, behavior that their seventh graders mirrored with gossip-laden, aggressive social interactions.[4]

One of my earliest memories is of my mother watching JFK's funeral procession. She stood before the TV in her powder blue dress and cried for the longest time. While I didn't really understand who President Kennedy was or what an assassination was, I knew that this was really important as I saw the throngs of people dressed in black crying as the horse-drawn carriage passed by. I also hated that my mom felt so sad. *At age five, my little brain mirrored my mother's emotions and the sadness of the whole nation.*

In addition to paying attention to your social modeling, you need to spend time teaching your child social sophistication skills. This process starts with understanding where they are on the Mirror spectrum and then identifying specific skills to increase their social abilities. Children on the lower end of the spectrum will need direct instruction on what's taking place, what others are thinking and feeling, and what would be a list of acceptable responses.[5] In addition, they often require encouragement to try new things and to ask questions when they are feeling confused. For example, with younger elementary children who struggle with joining free play at the school playground, try brainstorming what they like to play and what other children in the class like to play. Then have them practice looking for children who are smiling and making eye contact with others while they are playing. Have your child practice reciprocating the smile and eye contact while joining into the play. If they become confused by the rules of the game, coach them on how to observe what others are saying and doing. If need be, help them practice how to ask about the rules with one of the kids they feel most comfortable.

Also reinforce the basic courtesy of saying hi and saying goodbye. Our ancestral brains were wired to be startled when someone suddenly appeared or suddenly went missing. A friendly greeting lets others know they are safe, and a warm goodbye lets them know you are leaving and that something tragic didn't happen to you. In *UnSelfie*, Borba mentions some excellent strategies for handling inevitable conflicts, such as eye contact, a firm voice, and a strong body posture.[6] These simple techniques convey confidence and when you can notice the color of your friends eyes when you talk to them, your friend will know you are listening.

Parents who are natural social butterflies find it difficult to identify with a child who doesn't share their placement on the nonverbal spectrum. If this applies to you, try to appreciate how unnatural this process of reading others is for your child. It's analogous to attending a conference at an unfamiliar hotel in a strange city. Anyone—even those with a good sense of direction— can relate to getting lost in a maze of hallways with no familiar outside geographical reference points to guide you. To solve the confusion, you literally need to memorize the turns from your room to your destination. Now imagine that you were heading back to your room and found one of the hallways closed for cleaning and there were no directions for your needed detour. That's how children on the lower end of the spectrum feel when they walk into new or unstructured social situations. They panic.

Another way to empathize with a child who struggles with social cues is to analyze what characteristics you have that are on the high end of the social spectrum. Which traits enable you to accurately decode social cues and respond appropriately? What steps does your brain take to assess a social dynamic?[7] Try to dissect what your brain processed from the cues around you and relate that information to your child. I recently explained to a boy how to play the card game Uno. As we played a practice game, I used a monotone voice and even cadence to explain the rules. I also gave him some strategic advice. During the second game, I was down to one last card. As I set it on the table, I used a playful sarcastic voice and asked, "What color is it?" The boy responded by saying, "Do I have to guess that now?" as if this was a new rule. Then he said: "Wait, you have a trick face!"

Children on the high end of the spectrum require a much different approach. They are already socially aware and more naturally extend empathy to their classmates and others in the world. For these children, help them turn their empathy into action by developing harmony in the classroom, noticing and befriending the child who is left out, confronting cruel social behavior, and joining organizations and clubs for social change. Our school has a change-makers club, which is filled with empathetic students who want to spend a lunch hour each week implementing causes for social good. As one of my daughter's friends appropriately expressed one day: "I have a superpower—I can read what other people feel." At home, this young man is a great role model for helping his siblings and friends through life's ups and downs.

Some children with high Mirror abilities can use these skills for their own selfish needs. These children need guidelines to keep them from using their nonverbal abilities to take advantage of others. Exceptional mirroring can be a double-edged sword as these children quickly come up with plausible excuses for breaking parental rules: "I bought the soda pop because my friend was coming and I wanted her to feel special." (See chapter 13 for more Mirror strategies).

THE IMPORTANCE OF FREE PLAY

In addition to the Mirror growth at home are the hundreds of Mirror experiences children have when they are playing and laughing with their peers. Human children—as well as children of all mammal species—have an inherent urge to play.[8] Have you ever noticed how kids just seem to be looking for opportunities to play? Like puppies romping around together, looking for a playing companion fills children with excitement. For years scientists thought that these urges were nature's way of prompting the young ones to practice survival skills such as fighting and hunting. If you watch canine puppies at play, they will bite each other's necks as if fending off an enemy or when attacking prey. If you watch closely, however, you see that they are just mouthing the other dog's neck and are quick to release their grip if the other puppy yelps. So, it appears that puppies are learning those survival skills but are also mirroring the feelings of the other puppy.

So, what does play do for the rest of us?

The latest research on play shows that free, unstructured play helps children of all mammalian species learn how to relate to each other so they can succeed in a group as they get older.[9] Just like the puppies, human children mirror each other and engage others in play, negotiating through the conflicts that emerge. Boys will often engage in physical activities that require subtle signs not to push their playing partner any further. When the other child makes a pained face or says, "Stop," your child is learning restraint in addition to respect for his or her playing companions. One of the critical social skills for boys is navigating the fine line between good-natured roughhousing and physical violence—reading the social cues that indicate when a peer is no longer having fun. Playing like puppies is how boys develop these skills.

The physical contact that comes with unstructured play deepens the emotional bond between kids. Physical touch increases our oxytocin levels. Oxytocin is known as the "bonding" hormone and increases our feelings of connection with each other. All that movement and physical activity reduces our cortisol levels.[10] Lower cortisol levels will allow your child to return to the classroom refreshed, where they can face their academic demands without the overwhelming stress they felt before the unstructured play.

Even if physical contact isn't involved, the simple act of mirroring each other's emotions (from happy and excited to frustrated and sad) in free play helps move your child up the Mirror spectrum. It also helps children with learning how to negotiate, collaborate, and resolve conflicts. When my group of friends picked pro teams for baseball, we all wanted to be our hometown heroes—the St. Louis Cardinals. Utilizing skills in assertiveness and self-advocacy came in handy if you didn't want to be the hated rival team. Recently, I observed a group of second grade girls who were playing hospital. Using negotiation and collaboration, they decided who would be the patients, who would be the intake nurse, and who would be the doctors based on their own interests. They even determined who would be the hospital administrator.

In addition to increasing logical thinking, new research also found that children who spent more time engaged in free play showed greater abilities to set goals. These six- and seven-year-old children were more effective at breaking a goal down into manageable groups and then accomplishing the tasks related to each of these groups.[11] So, in addition to social bonding, play itself helps children grow new connections in their President, as well as the rest of their neocortex.[12] Another recent study found that those children who played well in third grade showed higher overall academic performance in eighth grade.[13] *The logical and Mirror skills that kids at play learn serve the most basic survival skills for our species—the ability to live and work with others in community.*

Most social play opportunities used to take place at daily recess. However, 40 percent of American schools, in order to focus on test preparation, have considered getting rid of it, or eliminated recess all together.[14] Contrast this with findings from the Centers for Disease Control and Prevention, which tell us that consistent, high-quality recess helps students feel more positive, engaged, and safe throughout the school day.[15] An additional study by the American Academy of Pediatrics reports that intelligence and cognitive growth directly result from play, and that play can strengthen the parent-child relationship and boost a child's social skills.[16]

Whether it is school recess or after school play, children who regularly spend time outside "show more empathy, as well as increased confidence, social skills, and collaboration."[17] *Time* magazine also reports that getting out into the sunlight might help your child's mood by boosting levels of serotonin.[18] For children and adults, spending time outdoors is linked to lower rates of heart disease and other chronic illnesses, and can reduce stress and anxiety, improve concentration, and even decrease nearsightedness.[19] In terms of academic performance, one article in *Experience Life* magazine points out: "The average student in the Finnish education system, which routinely ranks among the best in the world, spends fifteen minutes of every hour outdoors."[20] While we as parents are obsessed with foot protection during summer months, we might be protecting our children from a bee sting or a cut, but we are also taking away the relaxation that comes from walking barefoot in the grass and helping their "foot microbes flourish."[21]

The laughter that often accompanies play has many benefits, as well. Have you ever noticed how contagious laughter is with kids? Once they start mirroring each other, they can hardly control it. There even seems to be one or two kids in a class who are particularly vulnerable to this mirror frenzy of laughter and end up peeing in their pants! In addition to great mirroring opportunities, laughter increases oxygen intake and dopamine levels, which in turn increases Presidential alertness. It also sharpens a child's memory because the brain constructs deeper memories when emotions are involved.[22] Perhaps you can recall an elementary school teacher who was fun to be around and who helped to reduce the stress of school with humor and laughter.

A teacher with an engaging sense of humor who understands the benefits of unstructured play is your child's best ally. Sadly, children who are trapped in today's data-driven educational hysteria are expected to spend more time than ever sitting in a classroom for hours on end and must complete more homework than ever. In addition, the proliferation of team sports, many of which are year-round—along with other structured activities for kids—leaves virtually no time for improvised, unstructured play. According to one recent study, there has been a 50 percent drop in "free play" from 1981-1997 among children.[23] Students also saw a 200 percent increase in homework over the same period.[24] Michele Borba advises that if you want to carve out a little more free play for your child, try cutting out one activity a week.[25]

RELAX AND LET THEM PLAY

When you become a parent, you have to resist joining the fear parade. Freakonomics host Stephen Dubner states that, "Parenting is an exercise in risk assessment."[26] We must constantly weigh the potential benefits from an activity with the potential risks. Unfortunately, as parenting author Bryan Caplan points out, parents are poor at risk assessment when it comes to their kids.[27] The Magic Hat Brain Activity in chapter 9 illustrated how, like children, parents often focus on the probability of something random happening as a way to control anxiety.

Unstructured play can be a major source of anxiety as the world around us seems more dangerous than ever. Fear of kidnapping (a one in a million annual event) and injuries has limited many free-play options for kids.[28] Instead of spending afternoons on spontaneous treks through the neighborhood, our children now are busy with homework, group practices, and parent-organized play dates. Unfortunately, by overprotecting our children from the big things that can happen to them, we rob them of thousands of smaller and extremely valuable learning experiences that free play provides. Recently, the state of Utah—concerned about the lack of freedom for children and the fear parents face of getting in trouble with child protective services for negligence—passed a free-range parenting law. This law allows parents the freedom to let their kids participate in unsupervised activities in order to promote a child's independence. Other states are considering similar legislation. This perspective was reinforced in a 2018 *New York Times* article by a cognitive scientist at the University of California, Irvine, who states, "They [children] have *some* rights, and not just to safety. They have the right to some freedom, to some independence . . . to a little bit of danger."[29]

> Overprotecting our children robs them of valuable learning experiences.

At the center of it all is parent and child advocate Lenore Skenazy. Based on her own family experiences, she coined the term "free-range kids." In addition to lectures and media appearances, Skenazy recently started the Let Grow Project.[30] Her nonprofit is designed to encourage parents to let their child do something independently that they as parents were allowed to do when they were young. Activities include walking the dog, making a family dinner, walking to school alone or with friends, or running an errand.

TECHNOLOGY ISN'T FREE PLAY

Today's children are also held hostage by their smartphones, tablets, and game systems. Beyond the obvious physical health implications from too much screen time, *too much time in the virtual world impedes the development of your child's mirror neuron system.* Studies have found that infants, for instance, need authentic three-dimensional faces to develop their mirroring skills.[31] Without a functional mirror neuron system that is mirroring actual people to guide them, children struggle to develop empathy. In a review of research between 1979 and 2009, Stanford University found a sharp decline in empathy traits among college students over the last ten years. The culprit, researchers concluded, was the students' increased dependence on technology.[32] On a neurological level, neuroscientist Maryanne Wolf explains in her book *Proust and the Squid,* that the speed and superficiality of the tech experience thins the neural experiences that develop empathy.[33] Think about it: can you really understand how someone feels without gazing into their eyes? Do emojis really trigger our deeper emotional and Mirror abilities? Amazingly, one study found that children who spent time reading fiction books, however, were more empathic.[34] The act of placing yourself in the characters' lives and feeling their emotions develops your mirroring abilities.

Many of the benefits of free play are missed when children spend too much time with multiple electronic devices and not enough time socializing with other children. Presidential functioning is compromised by "continuous partial attention,"[35] during which children try to complete a task while bouncing from one electronic activity to another as they are interrupted by the sound of an arriving text or email. Modern problem-solving seems to have suffered as well as children impulsively reach out to parents on the cell phone with immediate requests and demands instead of relying on their President to resolve a problem.

Electronic devices disrupt family intimacy in addition to hindering Mirror development and empathy.[36] Last year, I asked fourth graders what they liked about living in our current culture. One of their top answers was technology and Internet access. When asked what they didn't like, they identified their parents' overuse of technology at home and in the car. When referencing *Highlights* magazine's "2014 State of the Kid" survey of 1,521 six- to twelve-year-old children, Borba writes, "sixty-two percent of school-age kids said that *their parents* [original emphasis] are too distracted when they try to talk to them. The top distraction: cell phones."[37] After all, they're kids. And kids need and deserve their parents' undivided emotional attention.

I had a chance to hear clinical and organizational psychologist Rob Evans comment on this disconnect at a conference for Independent School Educators: "There are many reasons to have a TV in a child's bedroom or in the family dining room—none of them are good."[38] Today, we'd have to add that there are also many reasons—all of which are bad—to have a cell phone in a child's room or at the dinner table. That applies to parents as well, so try going without cellular use in the car or while having family time. Your Mirror interactions and emotional contact with each other will have a much better chance of flourishing.

I fully support the guidelines for smartphone use as outlined by Michael Rich, founder of the Center on Media and Child Health at Harvard Medical School. First, he recommends you don't give your child a smartphone (or other electronic tools) until they really need it. Second, start out with a flip phone as an electronics learner's permit. If your child has a smartphone, don't allow the use of the alarm clock. Doing so creates the temptation for kids to check their messages long into the night. Finally, he recommends that the whole family take an electronic Sabbath day once a week. That means no electronics for everyone. Just old-fashioned connection time.[39]

More information about managing electronics is discussed in chapter 13.

BRAIN ACTIVITY: I'VE ALWAYS WANTED THAT!

Have you ever had the experience going into a store or watching a commercial where your child sees something for the first time and exclaims, "I've always wanted that!" While this response reveals a President that has not yet mastered impulse control, it also speaks to how advertisers and media producers understand the importance of mirroring with kids. The stereotypically played out male and female actors in the commercials are all having so much fun playing with that new toy. In an instant, your child's Mirror lights up as they imagine themselves being right there with the other children. For even greater mirroring action, throw in a child celebrity or sports star with whom children identify. "If that star likes it, then I will like it as well," goes this Mirror response.

Another great example of mirroring in action is at the toy store or the local department store. In order to boost profits, advertisers extensively research which products will appeal to this important demographic through the use of focus groups. You know you've hit the girls' aisle when you see the color pink everywhere. Almost every toy has bright colors and speckles on the packaging to make it even more attractive to that young girl walking down the aisle. She can literally see herself in every doll dress and hair style. If there is a picture of a famous Disney actress on the box, that's even better for mirroring purposes. Round the corner into the boys' aisle and see balls and action figures. What boy couldn't imagine throwing a football like the boys on the box or not feel a rush of power and fantasized domination with that super cool race car with the flame thrower headlights?

Young children are particularly susceptible to these identification and affiliation advertising techniques as they are not able to "critically comprehend TV advertising messages and are prone to accepting these ads as truthful, accurate and unbiased."[40] In 2004, advertisers spent 12 billion dollars a year directed toward the youth market. Given that the average child was exposed to forty thousand TV adds a year at that time, it makes great sense to start advertising conversations early on.[41]

Child advocates and consumer groups are also concerned about online targeted advertising to children under thirteen (the age YouTube's terms of service warns against use). Targeting occurs when companies such as Google sell advertising space to the kid-directed programs it packages. These companies then track information such as IP addresses, search history, and other personal data so that ads can be specifically tailored to the viewer. In 2018, the Center for Digital Democracy filed a complaint with the Federal Trade Commission regarding these practices.[42]

In order to help your children be aware of targeted advertising, take some time to explore together how mirroring is used in the world around you. The Got Milk campaign that started in 1993, featured milk mustaches on a variety of celebrities. Ask your child if they think this is a positive use of Mirror functioning and could improve the health of those encouraged by the ads to drink it? What about some of the beer commercials on TV that often use cute animals or funny party scenes to advertise their products? Identify the possible target audiences for these ads. What is your child's impression of these products? You can also discuss the subtle, almost subconscious art of product placement employed by advertisers in film and television. Did your child notice the brand of soft drink the star had? What does your child think of that product?

In terms of body image, help your kids explore the "ideal" body types being portrayed to both boys and girls. How would a child feel if they didn't have that body type? Are there ways advertising could promote healthier eating and lifestyle choices without using photo shop and pandering to the stereotypes? The body image of teens often starts much earlier in childhood so it's not too early to start these types of conversations with your kids when they are in second or third grade.

Another way to frame this discussion is to use the dichotomy I set up every year with my fifth grade students. I start by separating the board into two areas and place a heading above each. One says "What Advertisers Tell You," the other, "What Advertisers Don't Tell You." We then start the series off by talking about products and toys. I often start by reminiscing about my own Mirror-driven foolishness when watching the product demonstrations at Denver's annual stock show. It's like I'm holding that miracle mop myself and am watching the dirt fly off the floor. Like so many products the year before, I'm left disappointed and feel tricked when I think about how the demonstrations are rigged for maximum performance. (When my son and I go now, we enjoy having a laugh while figuring out how they are making the products work so great.)

We then move on to the products the kids bought with their own money only to find themselves as disappointed as I am. We list what features were promised in an advertisement compared to what the company actually delivered. The bottom line is that companies pay advertising firms to maximize their products' appeal.

CHILD SUPPORT SYSTEM
Mirror Reference Guide

High Mirror Used for Positive
- Positive reinforcement for empathy and building community
- Integrate deeper thinking and prosocial values
- Reinforce being a role model for others

High Mirror Used for Negative
- Slight increase in structure if periodic
- Strict guidelines and increased structure if frequent
- Immediate consequences
- Monitor manipulations
- Consistent adult monitoring and communication
- Emphasize responsibility taking
- Emphasize empathy for others

Low Mirror
- Increased structure
- Teach social norms and coach through struggles
- Positive reinforcement for nonverbal awareness and observations
- Advance planning and assist with visualizing new activities
- Positive reinforcement for flexibility when plans change
- Assistance with problem-solving

SECTION V

MAKING JELL-O

"You know what ELSE everybody likes? Parfaits!
Have you ever met a person, you say, "Let's get some parfait,"
they say, "Hell no, I don't like no parfait?"
~Donkey-Shrek (2001)

In section V, you will learn how all three systems work in harmony to help a child plan ahead, respond to changes with emotional restraint, and empathetically combine his or her own wants and needs with those of others. Understanding how developing brain centers function in concert with one another will help you provide the right amount of structure for a child. Once structured, parents can then focus on the three key areas of positive messages, emotional connections, and problem-solving. The fruit of these labors will be realized in amazing family adventures and community service in chapter 15.

CHAPTER 13

SELECTING THE RIGHT BOWL

Before the grocery store started selling premade Jell-O cups, my mother used to make the best orange Jell-O filled with mandarin oranges. She would open up a couple of boxes of the orange powder and pour them into her big sturdy mixing bowl. Then she'd pour boiling water into the bowl and mix it all together. After adding the oranges, she'd place this treat into the fridge where it would harden over the next several hours. It was pure joy as my siblings and I dug into our dessert bowls.

Now, what would happen if my mother's Jell-O bowl had developed a crack? If it was just a small fissure up near the top, she might have seen a small drop of hardened Jell-O when she pulled it out of the fridge. Even worse, what if the bowl had cracked open at the bottom as she placed it on the fridge's shelf? The orange treat would have spilled out all over the shelf and flowed down onto the items below. What a mess. It would then be time for a new sturdier bowl.

In this analogy, the Jell-O represents your child and the genetic mix of their President, Factory, and Mirror with which you as parents endowed them. After figuring out what comprises their mix, you must then select the right bowl for your child's needs. Some kids are born with a diluted Jell-O mix that takes a long time to harden. These kids need a thick bowl made up of extra structure and rules. Other kids seem to inherently possess the consistency of those premade Jell-O cups at the grocery store. They are already firm and require less structure.

So how do you pick the right bowl for your child? *Start with the basic philosophy that you want to use the least restrictive environment possible to get the job done.* You are parenting for independence, so you don't want the size of the bowl to overmatch your child's abilities. At the same time you need to keep them safe, so you don't want to overestimate your child's abilities either. Start with the least restrictive bowl your child needs and then work your way down to less structured support as your child matures—like my mother did when she checked the Jell-O in the fridge to see if it was hard enough to transfer to the smaller dessert bowls.

CONSIDER THE MIX OF YOUR CHILD

Consider the mix of a child who has good Mirror processing. The child uses this to build harmonious friendships, an even emotional temperament (including high verbal abilities for expressing feelings), and high-level Presidential functioning. This child doesn't need a large, sturdy bowl. He or she will be ready to try new activities, can be trusted with more freedoms, and is ready for those endless hours of summer fun running around the neighborhood. The old parent-structured play dates can quickly transform into kid-driven fun and independence. While these children still need to check in with you now and then, keep it to a minimum. When they make a mistake, you can simply talk to them about the emotional impact the mistake had on them and others and ask them what they could have done differently.

> Mirror skills can be used positively or negatively.

Unfortunately, some children use their innate, God-given Mirror skills to dominate their playmates.[1] These children will need a thicker bowl. Before sending them out to play, reinforce the rules of play time and remind them that you will be checking in now and then to see how it's going. Make sure to empower the other kids and their parents to contact you should something go wrong. A good consequence for manipulative behavior is to end the play time and have your child write a sincere apology note to the play partner and his parents before going back to play. Don't budge if your child tries to deny the behavior or blame others. Be careful about talking too much or you will find yourself being manipulated. *Be consistent about the consequences for manipulative behavior and hold your child accountable for his or her actions.* Make sure to give them lots of positive reinforcement for using their Mirror abilities for social harmony.

As you select the right bowl for your child's unique makeup, follow some of these basic considerations:

Higher levels of Presidential functioning and even temperaments

Children with higher levels of Presidential functioning and even temperaments, for instance, need less structure as they go through school and play. *Praise and positive reinforcement will keep them on track.* When they do make a mistake, don't overreact; instead, let them figure out how they should respond when a similar situation arises in the future. When it comes to parents having different parenting styles, this child can adapt and respond to these variations.

Lower levels of Presidential functioning

Children with lower levels of Presidential functioning, however, *need more structure and specific feedback.* Boys, in particular, need clear rules for physical play, especially if they are Excitable Eds. The basics include: no contact with the eyes and no contact to the private areas. Children with less Presidential control also need guidance about appropriate humor at school and at home. This includes humor that is overly sexualized or discriminatory based on race, ethnicity, gender, or sexual orientation. As the brain becomes less concrete, children also need guidance and limits on sarcasm. While some people like sarcasm as a form of playful humor, many don't, so help your children think about their audience. Give them specific guidance in when to tell a joke, when not to, and let them know that they should not repeat the same joke over and over.

Anxious, frustrated, or melancholic temperaments

Children with anxious, frustrated, or melancholic temperaments will need more assistance with working through these emotions. One important strategy for helping these children through their moods is to focus on the **process** of their emotions rather than on the **content** of what they are distressed about. If you start offering solutions to the content they are stressed about, you will find yourself heading down a rabbit hole where even your best solutions will be met with a "but" response. Offer one solution for your child to try. If met with a "but," it's time to focus on the emotional process. Try a statement and question such as, "You seem to be feeling [anxious/frustrated/sad] about this. What do you think you can do to decrease your emotions?"

Intense emotional reactions

If your child is more emotionally reactive, then he or she will need coordinated observation and support. You will need to reinforce the stop response to regulate the intensity and duration of your child's emotional reactions. Help your child with some strategies (chapter 14, Problem-Solving) for thinking through his or her emotions and applying that thought process to the behavior. If your child decides to try the strategy, give plenty of positive reinforcement. Failure to implement the strategies, or at least try them, should result in consequences. Parental communication and coordination is vital to this process.

Overly anxious

If your child is a Paralysis-by-Analysis Pete, he or she will need some extra guidance and structure at first, but try to loosen the reins once the process gets going. For those initial days of drop-off at preschool or kindergarten, make a plan for a special hug and kiss after you walk your child to the door or drop him or her off at the bus stop. When your child transitions to the teacher or bus driver, make a hasty exit. Use lots of positives for tiny steps forward *and be careful about being overly anxious yourself.* Too much structure and discipline can make the Pete's of the world even more anxious and risk avoidant.

It's also important to help an anxious child learn to find their voice in academic and social situations. Often times, it's helpful if you give them a set script for how to respond to various situations. The current classic response to taunting is a simple, "Whatever." When it comes to picking the recess game, the statement "Let's both give our ideas" sets the stage for your child to have their turn. In addition to positively reinforcing risk-taking behavior at home, let your child's teacher know that you are working on "finding a voice" and ask that the school supports this as well.

Fear of joining new groups

For a child who is afraid to join in new group activities, start with something they like to do. One year, I was visiting with a boy who didn't feel comfortable with playground activities and only felt comfortable playing with Legos. I asked his second grade teacher if the children could have a Lego Tuesday inside the classroom. She was happy to set it up and within a couple of weeks this boy had ten other children piling in to join in the fun. With this success as a base, we then brainstormed how he could go outside on the other days and find a few of those children who had shown an interest in Legos and talk with them.

Lower levels of Mirror skills

Going out into the larger world can be particularly frightening for children with lower Mirror skills. For example, it's good to help your child paint a mental picture of what is going to happen or even process beforehand like finding one's locker or how to place an order at a restaurant. I once had a sixth grader who froze in fear over the prospect of making a fast food order on a field trip. When I asked him about it, he explained that his mother always ordered for him. His mom later told me that, for years, she had tried to get him to talk to wait staff, but when the waiter would ask him what he wanted, he would just sit silently. Because she was concerned about taking up too much of the wait person's time, she would jump in and order for her son. While that approach helped relieve his fear, it wasn't helping him with long-term problem-solving. We then broke down the scenario into manageable strategies, which started with her son simply pointing to the menu item and then moved to more verbally successful responses.

Children who are lower on the Mirror spectrum and also have an anxious or frustrated temperament will need more structure and guidance. When they try new things, you will need to coach them and paint a picture of what the new environment will be like. They will also need direction around observing social norms such as displaying appropriate manners. Don't overdo negative consequences for poor Mirror abilities because these children truly don't understand what is appropriate or how their behaviors impact others around them. As they grow, your guidance will be geared toward helping them develop age-appropriate behaviors and responses. In the book *Seven Steps to Improve Your Child's Social Skills*, the three authors identify several key nonverbal skills that include: eye contact, body language, personal space, listening, reciprocity, timing, and vocal quality.[2]

Because children on the lower end of the Mirror spectrum struggle with anticipating how others will emotionally react to their words and actions, you will have to be more specific about what is OK to say and not say or do. For instance, we can look at one third grade boy who heard a comedian using the N-word on a YouTube video. He didn't have any insight into the history and oppression dynamics surrounding that word, but when he started using it at school, you can imagine the teachers' shock and dismay. Finally, when it comes to managing social conflicts, children with lower Mirror skills are going to need more tools than simply saying, "Please stop, you are hurting my feelings," as they get further in elementary school. Simple phrases like "whatever" or "no excluding" are easy-to-remember tools. These children show growth by practicing appropriate responses and being rewarded for stepping outside of their comfort zone and implementing these skills.

THE COMPLETE CHILD SUPPORT SYSTEM

For a quick reference on how to respond to your child's unique brain makeup, utilize the Child Support System outlined below. First, look at the strategies for your child's President. Second, look at the strategies for your child's Factory. Last, add in the strategies that correspond to your child's Mirror. For children whose Presidential functioning might demand more structure, but whose Factory or Mirror might require less, simply do an average of the strategy.

CHILD SUPPORT SYSTEM Presidential Reference Guide	
HIGH PRESIDENTIAL	• Decreased structure • Positive reinforcement for good choices • Promote self-problem-solving
LOW PRESIDENTIAL	• Increased structure • Clear guidelines and rules • Reinforce "Stop" • Increased adult consistency and communication at home and school • Emphasize Presidential awareness and responsibility taking • Positive behavioral reinforcement for impulse control, self-regulation and use of President • Model strong Presidential functioning

CHILD SUPPORT SYSTEM Factory Reference Guide	
OPTIMISTIC TEMPERAMENT	• Positive reinforcement for flexibility and emotional recovery • Increased unsupervised play
ANXIOUS TEMPERAMENT	• Plan ahead for potential anxieties • Limit "content" discussion, focus on anxiety "process" • Promote self-problem-solving • Positive reinforcement for small steps and "letting it go" • Limit expressed parental anxiety
ANGRY TEMPERAMENT	• Reinforce "stop" and increased structure for negative behavior • Limit content discussion and focus on anger process • Increase adult consistency and communication • Promote self-problem-solving • Positive reinforcement for small steps and "letting it go" • Consequences for aggressive behavior or refusal to try positive solutions

CHILD SUPPORT SYSTEM Factory Reference Guide	
SAD TEMPERAMENT	• Promote positive thoughts to combat negative thoughts • Limit negative self-talk and "victim" thinking • Limit content discussion and focus on sad process • Promote self-problem-solving • Positive reinforcement for small steps and "letting it go" • Extra TLC when needed and encourage gratitude
EXCITABLE TEMPERAMENT	• Embrace spontaneity but also self-regulation of behavior • Increase structure if getting carried away or for constant demands • Provide coaching for disappointment surrounding unfulfilled expectations
ANALYTICAL TEMPERAMENT	• Encourage attachment of emotions to thoughts • Encourage reflection on other's emotions • Help with shortening long, detailed explanations

CHILD SUPPORT SYSTEM Mirror Reference Guide	
POSITIVE HIGH MIRROR	• Positive reinforcement for empathy and building community • Integrate deeper thinking and prosocial values • Reinforce being a role model for others
NEGATIVE HIGH MIRROR	• Slight increase in structure if periodic • Strict guidelines and increased structure if frequent • Immediate consequences • Monitor manipulations • Consistent adult monitoring and communication • Emphasize responsibility taking • Emphasize empathy for others
LOW MIRROR	• Increased structure • Teach social norms and coach through struggles • Positive reinforcement for nonverbal awareness and observations • Advance planning and assist with visualizing new activities • Positive reinforcement for flexibility when plans change • Assistance with problem-solving

PARENT-CHILD MISMATCHES

As you select the right bowl for your child, start with looking at your own placement in the three brain areas we discussed. If you and your child struggle with Presidential functioning, it might be unnatural and difficult to provide your child with the structure they need. At the same time, if you are high on the Presidential scale and your child isn't, you may become more easily frustrated with your child's inability to learn and follow basic organizational demands in the morning or evening. You'll have to guard against the temptation to see all of your child's behavior as purposeful. Likewise, impulsive words in an argument can cut deep into a parent's heart, so you'll have to remind yourself that your child simply doesn't have the stop mechanism that you possess.

Perhaps the most difficult parent-child relationship issue is when you and your child don't match in temperament. Recently, Michael Thompson gave a talk about the sadness of parents who have easygoing, positive temperaments, but their child has more anxiety, sadness, or anger. His advice, "You have to respect and accept a child's individuality."[3]

When you start getting into combinations of mismatches, things can get pretty difficult. For example, let's take a closer look at parents who are both even keeled and structured in their approach to problems in family life and value deep, insightful discussions to help their child flower into a well-mannered, empathetic, and morally driven adult. When problems arise with their moody child who has a low-functioning President, their impulse is to have a calm discussion and reason the child out of his or her moods or into more respectful behavior in the family. While that might be possible later on, the chaos of the moment is going to demand a thick bowl and structure around the child's outbursts.

A mismatch of parent-child Mirror-emotional processing can also have its challenges. Take, for example, a mom who was reticent as a child and couldn't stand the girlie-girl gossiping and drama. Unfortunately, her fifth grade daughter thrives on it and is well-established as the class queen bee. This parent has to learn how to bite her tongue and think things through from her daughter's brain perspective before she responds. *Your job as a parent is to get the job done using the approach your individual child needs.*

ENVIRONMENTAL DEMANDS

These bowl sizes are based on your general environment and day-to-day functioning. If you live on a busy street, letting your younger kids ride their bikes freely around the neighborhood might not be the best choice. Once you have tailored your bowl size to your typical environment, you need to be ready with variable bowl sets when environmental demands necessitate a change. *A general rule of thumb is that increased structure is needed when you increase the number of kids.* Imagine if my poor mother let us five kids argue over who got the front seat every time my siblings and I raced to the car. Her solution was to have one day of the week for each child. Being the fourth in birth order, I was the Thursday kid.

This increased structure is also helpful when you have a larger group of kids over for play time or a special activity. When taking my group kids on field trips, we always started by reviewing the rules from start to finish and left little up to chance. In addition to our normal positive reinforcement system for behavioral cooperation, we pulled out the big bowl called the three-strike rule. I tell the kids what behaviors will earn them a strike and if they get three during the trip, it's just like baseball, "You'll be out for an hour sitting with me."

An enhanced bowl is also helpful when you are taking the kids to Target, a sporting event, or some new amusement venue. Pre-plan your trip and make sure to consider every possible difficulty before you go. In addition to safety concerns, think about the potential for impulsive demands that could derail your family fun. Many trips have been ruined when a strategy hasn't been thought through for the gift shop or the plethora of high-priced, sugar-laden snacks for sale. Before you go, let your children know exactly how many snacks they may have or how much money will be available if they want to buy a souvenir. Anything extra is up to them.

Extra support is also needed when you or your kids aren't at your best. Since a lack of sleep dramatically impacts your child's Presidential emotional control abilities, make sure you have a plan for the day after your kids have had a late night. Quiet reading time an hour before normal bedtime can prevent conflict.

If your family has suffered a loss or a trauma, it's helpful to get your kids back to their normal routine as soon as possible. I have helped many different communities through a variety of losses and have found that getting back to school and work is necessary for Presidential functioning and a sense of emotional normalcy.

Summertime is great for getting out of the school year bowl and letting children have more free play and fun family activities. However, they still need structured routines for completing summer reading and math. Children need to know their camp schedules, daily chores, when electronics time can take place, and those blocks of time when you need a break and expect them to entertain themselves. Ask any parent around the end of July, and you'll find a consensus that it's time for the kids to get back into their school year bowls. Even the firmest Jell-O can melt in the summer sun.

Finally, just as my mother took care when she poured Jell-O into the bowl, care needs to be taken when children transition between activities. Research into behavioral problems in schools demonstrates that discipline issues are more likely to occur when students are in transition.[4] You may have experienced a delightful ride to the grocery store with your child safely buckled in only to have them quickly unbuckle and dart out into the parking lot the moment the car stops. Walking down the hall, waiting for a class to start, or standing in the lunch line are less structured moments and offer a host of opportunities for acting out. Ask any teacher and they will tell you that when kids are working on a structured activity, their behavior quickly improves.

NINE TOOLS FOR THE PARENTAL TOOL BOX

Just as your child grows and matures emotionally and socially, your parenting abilities grow and change in relation to your kids. Each phase of their Presidential, Factory, and Mirror development brings new challenges to the structure and guidance you previously provided. Also, parenting approaches change with each additional child in the family. For most parents, the first child is your starter project. You take endless photos of them, read lots of books, and experience a great deal of anxiety as they experience joys, successes, worries, and sorrows. For subsequent kids, you have some parental experience under your belt and the new phases of development don't seem to be quite as shocking. While siblings will bring their own unique challenges, parents are generally a little more relaxed with their approaches and have less anxiety. However, we are continually expanding the parental tool box as we raise our kids and learn new strategies from other parents.

Establish boundaries with your kids

Almost all kids have a hard time imagining that their parents had lives prior to their birth. In their minds, you exist in order to take care of them. This mind-set can lead to lots of problems with over-enmeshment, a sense of entitlement, and demanding behavior. While these demands might result in immediate gratification for your child, giving in to these behaviors will actually hinder the development of their President and Factory control and increase the likelihood that Mirror abilities are used for negative power and control.

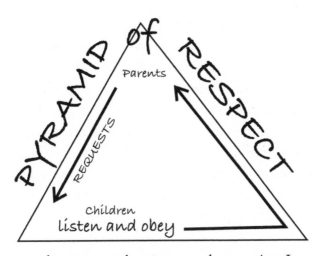

Look at the pyramid picture above. As I explain to kindergartners every year, the children are at the bottom and the adults are at the top. Teachers and parents set the rules and tasks and communicate these downward. The child's job is to show respect to those above them by listening and obeying. After a couple of fun role plays with real firefighting equipment, we learn about how a team of firefighters, a classroom, or a family can only function effectively when everyone shows respect for the pyramid. We also look at how cooperation means moving up the pyramid as you grow older and earn greater freedoms and greater responsibilities.

While shared power and lateral decision-making, or freedom-based management theory, is a popular management style, these participative systems are based on equal power and equal intellectual capacities.[5] This shared authority should be the case for parents but is not the case with your kids. In order to set the pyramid, start early by separating your bedroom from the kids' world. **No child should be allowed free access into their parents' room without first asking for permission.** This simple rule will establish your family pyramid and benefit your marriage.

It will also slow down your kid's impulsive requests. Rather than talk about demands in front of your children, simply say, "I/we will think about it later and get back to you." Then retreat to the privacy of your room where you alone, or you with your spouse, can process the request in peace and quiet. If you do this in front of the kids, you open yourselves to manipulation as the watching child looks for the slightest crack in the bowl between the two of you that they can leverage. This act alone will slow your kids down and validate your resolve and consistency while cementing your place at the top of the pyramid.

Watch for manipulations

Don't underestimate how sneaky children can be when it comes to getting things they want when they are with their friends. Older elementary children know that if they ask you something with a friend standing there, it increases the likelihood of a yes. This also applies when you are talking to another parent and your child insists, "My friend's mom said it would be OK." Be prepared for calls or texts from your child asking for playtime to be extended (usually these calls come within thirty minutes of the end of playtime). These negotiations often begin with, "My friend's mom said she thought the pick-up time was 5:00 so I don't think I should leave my friend here alone at the mall." As the saying goes, *You kids are trying to pull a fast one on us!*

Avoiding manipulation starts with a brainstorm about all the possible holes in your child's bowl that could occur in an upcoming situation. Then, be very clear about what the rules and boundaries will be. Parenting experience helps with this, and it does get a little easier with each additional child. Even so, it's not always possible to predict every possible hole.

After brainstorming and setting your rules, slow down when a spontaneous request is made from your child, especially if you are getting a gut feeling that the request sounds sneaky. Take a few seconds, then respond with, "Let me talk with your dad/mom/the other child's parents." As for parents, children are great at determining who the easy target is. With my daughter, I know that numerous questions will be coming my way after mom has left the house or when I'm picking her up from school. After numerous attempts, I use a broken record and tell her, "You'll have to ask your mom."

Finally, if you do get taken advantage of by a "fast one," make sure you follow up with a consequence. "I'm coming to pick you up right now" is a zero-tolerance message for your child. If you only complain about it and then don't follow through with a consequence, you are reinforcing your child's sneaky efforts in the future.

Talk like you mean it

I've met some amazing teachers over the years, who, in the sweetest manner, let the children know exactly what the behavioral expectations are. While not all of us can maintain that composure, the words *short* and *direct* come to mind when I think about addressing behavior problems. If you say too many words, you'll open yourself up to a variety of child logic manipulations. You also need to look and sound like you mean business. Model good body posture and make your body language support what you're saying—in other words, look and sound like you mean it. You don't need to yell or intimidate, but simply convey through your tone and body language that you sit firmly at the top of the pyramid. As a parent, you are the reference point for reality. *Nonnegotiable* is a great word for cutting down opportunities for arguing.

If you are going to consider negotiating rules with your child, don't bargain by indulging their impulsive demands. In our home, Sunday is the set day for my daughter to make requests about purchases or privileges during the upcoming week. While some decisions have to be made more immediately, a great many of them can be slowed down with, "We will discuss that on Sunday." If she doesn't negotiate in good faith, then negotiations are over. Remember, if you say no, it means no. Your decision is final. After you practice this consistently, soon your kids will know that if they accept your no and walk away, sometimes you might consider their wishes later. After you have time to yourself to reconsider their requests, you can always let them know later that you have decided to adjust the rules in a measured, appropriate fashion. As you carefully deliberate their impetuous demands, you have the added benefit of modeling impulse control and proper decision-making.

Establish routines

In addition to being essential for effective organization, every parent knows that a consistent bedtime routine is essential for getting your child to sleep. If you get out of that routine too often, you pay the price with a tired President. In fact, "tucking in the kids at inconsistent times can hurt their cognitive development."[6] A British study found that there is a correlation between irregular bedtimes at age three and lower scores in reading, math, and spatial development at age seven.[7] More kids necessitate more routines for all aspects of family life. Meal planning, shopping, and preparation get a lot easier when the routine is laid out. As a single parent for many years, I quickly realized the importance of routines in nearly every area of our lives to maximize efficiency as I carried out the tasks of two parents.

Establish age-/grade-based responsibilities and freedoms

How would most people feel if their employment contract had no stipulations for when and how their income and benefits would be adjusted? No doubt, there would be a fair amount of disgruntlement among the employees. The same is true at home. At an early age, create a list for your child that specifies what needs to be accomplished in order to earn free time and other age-appropriate freedoms. A dry erase board in the room or a chart in the kitchen works great for writing down the basics of getting dressed, brushing teeth, and throwing clothes in the hamper. On the first day of the new school year, or shortly after your child's birthday, let them know what additional expectations are being added. These could be chores like unloading the dishwasher, taking out the trash, mowing the lawn, and cleaning the bathroom. In exchange, let your child know their freedoms have increased in proportion to their added responsibilities. Provided they complete their tasks, they will now enjoy a later bedtime, increased electronic time, or the ability to run around with their friends in the neighborhood. Some schools start out the year with special tasks that are grade specific, such as the fifth graders having the privilege of raising the flag and tending to the recycling. A simple reminder for your child can be, "Ten-year-old freedoms means ten-year-old responsibilities."

This age-based approach also plays into a child's natural desire to have more freedom and decision-making in their lives.[8] They want to be able to do things and manage themselves without constant parental reminders. To this day I'm thankful that when I asked my fifth grade son to complete his chore, I controlled my response as he retorted from his bedroom, "Stop telling me what to do!" While the authoritarian part of me wanted to jump out of my chair, instead I replied, "Excuse me?" in a questioning voice. To my relief he said, "I don't want you to keep reminding me of my chores. I want to do them on my own." That's a developmental milestone that every parent is hoping for, which I would have destroyed if I had overreacted. That very evening, we made a plan where he was in control of completing his chores up until 8:00 p.m. At 8:01, I was allowed to remind him.

While playing up the freedoms they will earn, you'll also need to discuss the consequences for noncompliance. As a fifth grader, I knew that I had to mow the lawn by noon on Saturday in order to earn my allowance. If the lawn wasn't mowed, it wouldn't matter what I was doing at 12:01 when my dad came marching in to send me outside to complete my job. If he had to find me, I also didn't get paid. Like a contractual obligation, I agreed to finish the lawn by noon or forfeit my allowance. My dad was simply holding me accountable.

When you lay out child responsibilities and freedoms, it also decreases demanding behavior for many years to come. Let your kids know things like when they can start hosting and going on sleepovers, have a cell phone, get their ears pierced, get an iPad, use the internet without parental supervision, start using Nerf guns, walk or ride to school on their own, move up to airsoft guns, and when they can start going to the mall with just their friends. *These new realities will hit you before you can blink your eyes, so confront them before they come knocking at your door.* Starting now will also give you a template for the upcoming teen years.

This planning process is harder with the first born and will hinge in large part on your child's brain chemistry and developmental maturity. While you will get feedback from your friends about their standards, the beauty is that you get to set the standards for your own family and it doesn't matter what anyone else is doing. If something seems too restrictive for your day-to-day or your longer-term standards, you can always plan a family meeting and change them. In addition to adjusting responsibilities and freedoms, these family meetings can be used to lay down the law for compliance. I'll never forget one Sunday afternoon when my father sat my brothers and me down to discuss our disrespect of our mother. His exact words were: "Gentleman, you need to understand that your mother is my girlfriend and that when you mess with a guy's girlfriend, that guy is going to mess with you." Given my own dreams for a girlfriend someday, I completely understood what he meant.

Support the school

When asking your teacher to help reinforce the structure in your village, it's also imperative that you as parents support the school. If you asked me what has changed in the last thirty years of my work, the answer I most often give is the lack of support from parents when a behavioral issue has occurred at school. Rather than holding the child accountable, parents are quick to challenge the teachers by blaming others and accusing the teacher of missing out on some hidden bullying that they believe is taking place. While I often find large class sizes to be a major problem with cracked bowls, I was amazed by a Filipino teacher who told me she had forty-five students in her sixth grade class. "How do you keep them all focused?" I asked her. "It's not a problem at all," she replied. "You see, in the Philippines, I am treated with great respect. Everyone knows me and is polite to me in the market. If I have to call a student's parent about a problem, the kids all know that they will be in big trouble when they get home." When parents and teachers work more effectively together, it not only keeps kids accountable at school, in their communities, and at home, but it also promotes healthy early adolescent development.[9]

Teachers generally dislike making phone calls about a student's behavior. It only makes it harder when they receive a defensive response on the other end of the line. If you want your child's teacher to be part of your village, then back up your child's teacher the majority of the time. *No parent should ever utter the words, "Not my child, he or she could never do that."* You are in denial if you think this way. Every child is capable of making mistakes and being the cause of some unkind behavior. While some mixes are more prone to unkind behavior than others, they all need a bowl.

Implement the half/double rule

As mentioned earlier, discipline has two functions when raising children. The first is to either stop or start a behavior. *The second and most important purpose is to build your child's insight into their behavior.* A simple way to do this is by using the half/double rule. It starts by having a set consequence for misbehavior. For instance, my son would lose one episode of Disney's *Lizzie McGuire* as a standard consequence. If he accepted his consequence without complaint, and then admitted what motivated his behavior and verbalized his strategy for responding to similar situations in the future, then he could earn half the show back. If he complained about the consequence or refused to talk about it, then he would lose two shows.

This simple technique promotes the value of taking responsibility for one's behavior as well as expanding your child's insight. You can

Discipline should build insight.

also weave in empathy development by focusing on the feelings of others as well as thinking about what the perspectives were for others involved in the situation. By having these discussions, you are helping your children expand their stained glass window for how they perceive social relationships and understand cause and effect.

Sometimes, you won't need a consequence at all. Recently, two sixth grade girls confessed how they snuck a couple of iced teas from my school office. They then told me how bad they felt and promised never to do it again. I thanked them for their honesty and reminded them to always let their feelings be their guide.

Empathy as a verb

My parents taught all of us to notice those who were in need and then take care of them. At age ninety-three, my mother is still involved in all sorts of social ministry activities. Every Christmas, she collects one hundred art calendars and hand writes one hundred

Christmas cards (with a crisp five-dollar bill tucked inside) for our church program that serves adults and families who are suffering from severe mental illness (see chapter 15). In her words: "I want them to have art and beauty in their lives and let them know that they are loved."

However, a 2014 Harvard study points out that four out of five teens said their parents cared more about achievement or happiness than caring for others.[10] I wholeheartedly agree with Borba's concept that parents should expect social responsibility and her phrases, such as "sticking your neck out" and "moral courage," that describe children who stand up for others.[11] In country folklore, there is the concept of three types of people in the world: the wolves, the sheep, and the sheep dog. We need children who are willing to be sheep dogs in their own unique way when trying times are at hand.

For elementary aged children, I like to teach them how to identify an unkind behavior that's excluding or gossiping. For my sixth grade students, we talk about how cliques behave and what strategies they use to dominate others. We then brainstorm a whole list of strategies for taking a stand in the classroom (for example, ignoring the behavior, turning to others who feel the same way, using humor, or seeking adult guidance). We end the year role-playing a dramatic scene based on the example of Anne Frank. I ask them, "Who was responsible for the holocaust?" We talk about how Nazis were responsible, but that the many people who denied or hid from the truth were also responsible. There is always a look of shock when I read a cuss word from one of my favorite lines from Dante's *Inferno*, "The darkest places in *hell* are *reserved for those* who maintain *their* neutrality in times of moral crisis."

Manage electronics

There are many positives to the electronic world that can help families connect with each other and help your child connect socially with others. Unlike my father, who could never get away during the nine-to-five workday, parents today have a lot more flexibility to attend their children's events because of the freedom that online work allows. Parents who travel also love to be able to connect with their families by using interactive technology such as Skype or FaceTime. While I'm still a much bigger fan of IRL (in real life), person-to-person contact, I have been known to enjoy a video game or two at the local arcade. Video parties and online gaming also allow kids to have fun with each other as they compare scores or team up to defeat the newest enemy. In fact, the American Academy of Pediatrics (AAP) has recently acknowledged that some exposure to online media can be constructive.[12]

The key to managing your family's use of electronics is to avoid going too far with it (the average eight- to eighteen-year-old is plugged in to a digital media device about seven and a half hours a day) and thus limit your family time. Borba reports that the percentage of parents who say they now spend less time socializing as a family tripled in just two years.[13] The AAP has recently recommended new guidelines according to age:

> 0-18 months – video chatting only
> 18-24 months – snippets of educational programming with emphasis on unplugged playtime
> 2-5 years – one hour of high quality educational programming
> 6+ years – consistent limits set with parenting rules

They also warn that "problems can arise when media use displaces hands-on exploration and face-to-face interaction."[14] As mentioned in the introduction, there is clear evidence that an inadequate environment can have substantial consequences on a child's developing brain. According to Dr. Michael Rich, "Technology is a poor environment for brain development compared to the stimulation of our natural environment."[15]

If you do allow electronics during the week, I recommend that you start with limiting the time to thirty to forty-five minutes a day and no screen time an hour before bed. For weekends and summer days, consider two forty-five-minute blocks a day. An Oxford study found that restricting gaming to an hour or less a day made kids more sociable.[16] To avoid unnecessary arguments around interrupting a TV episode, I recommend that, when you can, plan dinner on the hour or half hour. Then you don't interfere with the allowed viewing. Some exceptions might include a favorite family movie or sporting event, where you make a special night of watching the movie or game while you eat dinner in front of the TV. Otherwise, family dinnertime should be electronics-free. I also suggest the same thing when you are driving in the car together.

According to former President Jimmy Carter, you have two loves in your life: God and the person who happens to be in front of you at any time.[17] Is it really possible to show that level of love and respect if your time together is spent answering the cell phone, checking email, texting under the table, or running to check if your tribe was attacked in the virtual world?

In addition to preserving your family intimacy time, make sure you have been very clear and consistent about your rules for all aspects of electronic activity. This includes an extra focus on cyber-safety, bullying behavior, and sexting activity. Your kids will need to know ahead of time exactly what will happen to their devices and privileges if these standards are violated. At the same time, let your child know that they can earn more electronic privileges by showing responsible use of what they have now (for instance: Use the flip phone well and you can have a smartphone later on).

For help with monitoring these standards, there are many programs for parents on how to protect your kids in the cyberworld as well as classes for children on being safe online. A great resource for all parents is Common Sense Media.[18] Some of the best electronic structuring techniques I've learned from parents include keeping the chargers in a basket in their bedroom and requiring that all phones, laptops, and game controllers be turned in at bedtime. Another rule is to keep the modem and router in your bedroom and turn it off at night. Especially for younger children, allow electronic usage only in family spaces. If you let your children use electronics in the bedroom, have an open-door policy. However, remember that kids are pretty good at switching what's up on their screen when an adult comes by. You could also implement a "no deleting" rule on text messages and have your kids show you their electronic devices immediately upon request. *Finally, never underestimate what's online that your child might be viewing and playing.* It's going to be hard to promote the concept of internal beauty if your kids are playing games like Beauty Clinic Plastic Surgery, by Woki Toki Kids Games.

Another way to help keep tabs on electronic device use is to hold off getting your children smartphones until they are in eighth or ninth grade. While our daughter has a flip phone, my wife and I recently signed the pledge for wait until eight (www.waituntil8th.org). As emphasized by Dr. Rich, "Kids don't have the executive functioning to self-regulate and control impulses."[19] This is especially the case with the many temptations a smartphone brings into your child's life. Kids are spontaneous and impulsive enough without the many temptations—with legal and lifelong impact—that smartphones bring into their chaotic world. When it comes to the school environment, France passed a nationwide law prior to the 2018-2019 school year, which bans phones for children in the French equivalent of preschool through ninth grade.[20] I also support other child advocates who recommend not allowing your child to use Facebook's Messenger Kids.[21]

In addition, don't forget to think about your children's relationship with the virtual assistant Alexa. Have you noticed how they boss her around? A Carnegie Mellon study confirms that some children order smart speakers—like Alexa or Amazon's Echo—around like servants.[22] Many wonder if that rudeness could transfer over to real life with others. Even more frightening, a 2015 unpublished study found that 93 percent of eight- and nine-year-olds would rather talk about a personal problem with a virtual voice assistant because they think it is too embarrassing to bring up to their friends or parents.[23] Needless to say, educating ourselves as parents, teachers, and counselors about security concerns and checking the device's privacy settings is essential.

The World Health Organization recently added gaming disorder as a new classification to addiction.[24] The American Psychiatric Association noted that "gaming prompts a neurological response that influences feelings of pleasure and reward, and the result, in the extreme, is manifested as addictive behavior."[25] The Center for Humane Technology also says that "many apps are engineered specifically to capture our attention, often to our detriment," making them "part of a system designed to addict us."[26] While your child is most likely not addicted, it doesn't mean that his or her gaming is not out of control. If you are concerned that your child's electronic use is getting to be too much, National Public Radio's Anya Kamenetz recommends that you ask yourself if the following five statements are true:

1. It is hard for my child to stop using screen media.
2. When my child has had a bad day, screen media seems to be the only thing that helps him or her feel better.
3. My child's screen media use causes problems for the family.

4. The amount of time my child wants to use screen media keeps increasing.

5. My child sneaks using screen media.[27]

If you find yourself answering yes, then it's time to add limits to your child's usage. Consider taking a total break from the game if your son or daughter is caught sneaking it, continually fights about turning it off, is becoming overly frustrated or emotional while playing, or is irritable afterward.

BRAIN ACTIVITY: ALLOWANCE HYBRID

In my generation, most kids were expected to do basic tasks like personal grooming and picking up after themselves. Then, each year you got older, you were given a chore such as doing the dishes, taking out the trash, mowing the lawn, or feeding the animals. At the end of the week, you were paid a set amount if you did your chores. Even better, my mom had a jar with slips of paper that listed an extra chore that could be done and the amount of money we could earn for doing it. If we wanted extra money to buy something, we could pick out a slip at any time. I always loved washing our colonial style window panes across the front of the house. This "make them earn it" approach was recently supported in Money Magazine *by contributing editor Farnoosh Torabi who notes, "Requiring kids to earn some wants through chores or a job can help curb entitlement.[28]*

However, in the '70s, there was a big shift in how allowance for kids was conceptualized. Psychologists started talking about how work around the house is part of family life and that you shouldn't pay your child for performing basic family responsibilities.[29] According to this theory, these tasks should be more intrinsically motivated and therefore, by paying for chores, you would hinder this internal motivation in your child. Instead of tying work to the allowance, you should just give them a set amount of money each week for the purpose of learning how to save and manage money. The amount received was also inflated to a suggested rate of one dollar for each year of the child's age per week. Additional incentives were added such as a matching program for money placed into a savings account.

When my son reached first grade, I was leaning toward the old-fashioned system. While I value intrinsic motivation and basic cooperation around the house, I also like reinforcing the idea that if you do your work, you earn your living. My son's mother, on the other hand, liked the newer version of allowance. Our solution was to combine the two together. If he was still breathing at the end of the week, he would receive half his age-based allowance. If he also completed his additional chores (we started with feeding the fish when he was in first grade and then added a new chore at the start of each school year), then he would receive the other half of his money.

During Friday pay day at our house, our daughter pulls out her three wallets that she has labeled Giving, Savings, and Spending. Twenty percent goes to each of the first two wallets. The remaining 60 percent is hers to spend. In addition, be very cautious about allowance advances when your child sees something he or she wants to buy and doesn't have enough spending money saved up. Remember, no child's life is going to be ruined by waiting a couple of extra weeks. If you decide to give an advance, make sure to help your child calculate just how many weeks of allowance that loan amounts to. Some parents also add on interest to a loan to help their children understand how the real world works.

CHAPTER 14

THE FRUIT OF POSITIVE MESSAGES, EMOTIONAL CONNECTION, AND PROBLEM-SOLVING

POSITIVE MESSAGES FOR "BEING" AND "DOING"

The best part of my mother's orange Jell-O was the mandarin orange slices she added in. For your children, nothing is more fundamental to their future sense of self, resiliency, and social success than what I call the *three solid blocks of child development*. Once you understand the makeup of your child's President, Factory, and Mirror and find a metaphoric bowl that fits, you can mix in the fruits of positive messages, emotional sharing time, and enhanced problem-solving abilities.

Put another way, in my first interview for the Attention Deficit Disorder Association's national newsletter in 1993, I was discussing a card shop poster that read: "There are two things we as parents give our children: one is roots, and the other is wings." The roots are the fruits of positive messages and emotional sharing time. The wings are the fruits of ongoing problem-solving.[1]

To highlight the importance of the fruit of positive messages, let's begin with a simple exercise I use with my speaking audiences. Close your eyes and think back to your own childhood, somewhere between kindergarten and sixth grade. See if you can recall a time when someone made you feel included, special, or cared for with positive words. Now, spend a couple of seconds thinking about a negative message someone said to you during your childhood, a comment that made you feel different, excluded, or inferior to other children.

When I process this exercise with audiences, I ask those who could remember a positive message from childhood to raise their hands. I then ask for a show of hands from those who could remember a negative message. In the hundreds of times I've done this activity, nearly 80 to 90 percent of the audience recalls a negative message. On average, about 50 to 60 percent of participants remember a positive message. Obviously, on an emotional level, turning off negative messages can be very difficult.

Related to the content of positive memories, most audiences share times when they felt unique, included with their peers, or were enjoying a special occasion. I can still remember my third grade teacher's lesson on similes. When she commented, "For instance children, I could say that Craig's eyes are as blue as the ocean," my heart filled with joy and I immediately had fantasies of running off to a deserted island with the fair Miss Hunter.

For negative memories, the feelings that stick with most of us include feeling different from the other children and excluded by them. Early in elementary school, my pleasure connection with reading was negatively impacted for years to come when the majority of my classmates were in the giraffe and monkey reading groups while I was placed in the turtle reading group with a couple of other students. Recently, I published my experiences with this reading group in the book *Easy to Love but Hard to Live With: Real People, Invisible Disabilities, True Stories*. My chapter, "Happy Reading," details my negative reading experiences and how my parents and certain teachers turned it around for me.[2]

While children receive feedback from others, a child's positive emotional foundation comes from you. As they get older and expand into the community, children will receive a formative mix of positive and negative messages from peers, teachers, religious mentors, pop culture, and the media, among other influences. However, your persistent positive messages, both for *being* and *doing*, can offset some of the destructive feedback your child receives from the world.

Being messages or statements, such as, "I love you," "You're just the sweetest thing," "God put a little extra sugar in your sweet tea," and "Our world wouldn't be the same without you," lift a child's spirits. Children also love nicknames. There is an old proverb that states, **A child with many names is well loved.** When I played with my son as a preschooler and kindergartner, we would often use nicknames: Mac for him and Bob for me. Mac and Bob's many adventures represent some of our most cherished father-son moments. The use of our nicknames had the added benefit of helping me during difficult parenting moments. If my son was stubborn, I would say, "I'm not sure Mac would treat Bob that way." Very often, the act of referring to our emotionally connected nicknames would de-escalate the situation. For our youngest daughter, just the utterance of Little Lils, Shrimpy, or Baby brings a huge smile to her face.

Children also benefit from *doing* compliments. These statements acknowledge academic and athletic achievements, or any other aspect of your child's demonstrated success. Praise in public is the most effective way to recognize your child's successes, and conversely reprimand in private minimizes embarrassment when your child needs honest, even harsh criticism for their actions. When it comes to positives for doing, it's most important to emphasize your child's effort and hard work. In psychology, this is considered *earned self-esteem*. While participation ribbons and trophies for everyone have become a trend over the past couple of decades, by the age of six or seven, children know when they have truly earned accolades for their efforts. Offering praise for a small accomplishment may even be taken as a slight.[3]

In particular, take notice when your child demonstrates empathy and takes action to act upon it. An act of kindness or standing up for a friend shows character. I love to talk to children about Martin Luther King Jr. and his message about judging people on the content of their character, not the color of their skin or any other superficial quality that our modern world or culture deems popular. In *UnSelfie*, Borba mentions how aligning praise with character creates more empathetic children and helps to build their moral identities.[4]

As children get older, they also begin to realize that while they have specific strengths, they also have weaknesses. While our brains learn and grow, the reality is that the vast majority of students will not be capable of getting straight A's all the way through college. In fact, praising students for their grades alone may even be counterproductive. Research has found that praising fifth graders for how smart they are resulted in less risk taking with harder problems due to the fear of making mistakes. Praising for effort, however, resulted in confident students who wanted to take on the task they could learn from.[5]

While some parents might emphasize performance perfection, the ability to get up after a fall and continue to strive toward goals will help your child survive throughout life. No program better epitomizes this philosophy than the ELM acronym from Stanford University's Positive Coaching Alliance program for youth sports.[6] The "E" stands for effort: Did your child give their best effort today? The "L" stands for learning: Did your child learn something today? The "M" stands for mistakes: Was your child willing to take risks and make mistakes today? For social and emotional success, it is imperative that parents, teachers, and coaches not only impart these values to young athletes today but apply these three questions to every aspect of a child's learning. Additionally, strong effort and hard work always beats natural ability with inconsistent effort.

Understanding hard work will serve your child well and build tolerance for trying times.

As your children mature, they will need to learn positive self-talk if they are to keep marching forward through difficult times. *One's sense of self as an adult needs to come primarily from within and not from others.* You can help foster this self-reliance by providing a solid base of both *being* and *doing* positives. Give your children the gift of positive messages and find those times when they need a special pick-me-up. At the age of forty-five, I received an amazing gift shortly before my father's stroke. He knew I had struggled emotionally in the aftermath of Columbine and through a divorce, and one day he said, "You are a hell of a man." At that moment I couldn't have asked for anything more than his positive blessing.

EMOTIONAL SHARING TIME AND FLY FISHING FOR FEELINGS

If you've ever seen an episode of the children's sitcom *Leave it to Beaver*, which ran from 1957 to 1963, you might recall the standard closing scenes. After the Beaver (the young main character) had messed up, he'd sit obediently across from his father's desk while Ward dished out the consequences for those offenses. After the last commercial break, the final scene would show Ward and Beaver sitting on the bed in Beaver's bedroom. As they played sock basketball, Ward would talk to Beaver about his emotions and the deeper issues that drove Beaver's behavior.

This one-two combination is the perfect example of discipline discussions and emotional sharing time. In the scenes described above, appropriate consequences and follow-up sharing were aimed at increasing Beaver's insight into his emotions. While I like to think that children have a "window to their soul" that opens and closes at seemingly random times, such as when we are hurriedly cooking dinner or dashing out the door, the one thing that will promote greater emotional control is having a regular sharing time with your child. As Michael Thompson says, "You can't make quality moments; they jump out at you when the child is ready."[7] With my son, and now with my daughter, I have found that the driving time to school the next morning gives us a great opportunity to process any behavior issues from the night before or discuss how to handle social situations in the day ahead. This special time allowed us to emotionally repair our discord as well as frame the experience into a life lesson, which hopefully will prevent future difficulties.

These sharing opportunities can take place after a conflict or occur organically as they develop. While the bedroom or car can be a good place to talk, many kids will open up while you are sitting at the playground or working around the house together. Building models or doing crafts together are great bonding moments and might also be opportunities for your child to discuss emotional and social struggles while you wait for the glue to dry.

In order to make the most out of the experience, I like to use what I call "fly fishing for feelings." If you have ever fished with a hook and worm before, it's a pretty simple process. You cast the baited hook into a lake and wait. It's a pretty straightforward process. In emotional sharing terms, this would be like saying to your kid, "So how was your day?" Unless you get really lucky, you'll get the F-word response: "Fine." If the next statement out of your mouth is, "So how much homework do you have?" then you might as well put your fishing rod away for a while. That fish is gone.

Fly fishing, on the other hand, is much more subtle in nature since you are trying to trick a fish into thinking that your artificial fly is actual food. You have to study the river, see what they are biting on, and pick the perfect time to cast. Before greeting your child from the school day, spend some time thinking about what has been going on that day: maybe there was a test; maybe you heard that the class was changing seating positions; or maybe you heard about an ill classmate from another parent. Also think about something you did or heard about that relates to them: perhaps their favorite sports team just signed a new player. You might say, "Hey [nickname], I just heard on the radio that we signed Bob Johnson for the upcoming season. What do you think of that?!" Listen while your child responds and then wait a couple of seconds before you mention a potentially stressful situation at school, such as "I heard that Mrs. Smith was going to have you switch seats around today," or "What were the best parts of your day?" See what you might reel in and then throw out a few more tidbits if needed. After some meaningful conversation transpires, you can say something like, "I'm hoping we can [play ping-pong/play a board game/watch that show] tonight. Do you think your homework will take you very long?" If they bite this "fly," then you can help them plan out their evening schedule and how their homework will get done. While students with low Presidential abilities may need you to ask if they have all of their assignments fairly quickly before leaving carpool or after arriving home, the first words out of any parent's mouth should not be about homework.

Once emotional conversations get going, you can help your child value the importance of talking about their feelings. Like a pot on a hot stove with a lid on it, most kids know what's going to happen to that pot if some of the steam isn't let out. These conversations also offer a host of other opportunities. For instance, you can weave your family values into the discussion. While my mom was clear about us not watching any James Bond movies, she would let us know the value behind it: "I don't want my boys to grow up thinking that girls are nothing more than bikinis." While I was resentful, I also knew my mother was teaching us an important lesson: the sexual objectification of women is wrong. I appreciate the values she instilled in me back then and the continuing lessons she imparts today.

It's vital that you as a parent communicate your value system to your child. Ideally, you should explain and reinforce these values of good citizenship on an ongoing basis, not just when your child is in trouble for breaking them. Your children need to learn the basic tenets of good citizenship early on—essentials like looking out for their own safety and the safety of others, for example. From the moment they begin to grasp these concepts (thanks to their expanded President, Factory, and Mirror abilities), they should be able to understand, verbalize, and demonstrate values such as honesty, personal responsibility, integrity, social conscience, and their wants versus needs. Other invaluable lessons include respect for all of their classmates (and their personal space), identifying exclusionary behaviors and avoiding them, and appropriate restraint.

While you feel your child is special, you need to remind them that all children are special, and therefore their peers have equal rights and must be treated with dignity. One study at Ohio State University found that if parents "overvalue" their children by telling them they are more special than other children or deserve something extra

All children are special.

in life, then their children showed higher signs of narcissism when tested later. One of the researchers explained that "Children believe it when their parents tell them that they are more special than others. That may not be a good thing for them or for society."[8]

Your older elementary child's dignity for others includes clear boundaries around bullying and sexual harassment. As kids get into fifth and sixth grade, when social awareness skyrockets, they can be incredibly cruel (many times this is unintentional, but it can also be quite intentional). Regrettably, taunts about race, sexuality, body image, gender orientation, and sexual orientation of others are not off limits for fifth and sixth graders. This is where you have a wonderful opportunity as a parent and teacher to enforce and reinforce cultural competence that emphasize respect for others, regardless of their differences. In my annual fifth grade puberty talk with boys, I advise them to think of one simple thing before making a sexually oriented comment to a female or male classmate: "How would your mother feel if you said that?"

If you see your child participating in bullying or harassing behaviors, or witness them not executing basic human decency by defending themselves or their peers, you can say, "What kind of person do you want to grow up to be?" While many books point out how damaging shaming can be for children, there are times when you want a child to be ashamed of his or her behavior. It's the human ability to feel shame that will change antisocial behavior in the future. Another great parenting line in these moments is: "I love you always, but I don't always like your behavior."

In addition to addressing morality, allocate time to address high-risk behavior. While kids don't often think about risk when they are excited and hyper-focused on their friends, intervening with a discussion at the right moment could turn on a light bulb in your child's head before he races out into the street on his bike.

SOCIAL AND EMOTIONAL LESSONS

Conversations that transcend small talk and carry emotional weight allow your child to gain perspective on the many ups and downs they experience every day. Whether you realize it or not, your children listen to what you say and internalize your belief system, and those messages tend to stick. Below, I've included a list of character-building stories and allegories that I employ at home, when I'm teaching classes or when I work individually with a child. You can use these as a way to support your child's behavioral, emotional, and social development.

How's your President, Factory, or Mirror?

You can use the many stories and activities from this book to explain these three areas that make up your child's social brain. Remind your child ahead of time to prevent a problem or to talk about a problem after it has happened. Give enthusiastic praise when you see development in each of these areas.

Be the best friend you can be

This is something I've been saying to students for years. Dr. Borba calls this "Developing your best possible self."[9] A study cited in *Research in Human Development* had participants write a brief description of their "best possible self" each day. They found that doing so provided a dramatic boost in optimism, bolstered a sense of self-efficacy, and encouraged the ability to change the perceived realities of their world.[10]

Just wear a smile

I can't tell you how many times I heard my mother respond with this phrase when we worried about what we would wear. My father had a similar expression: "It's not what you have to say, it's how you look when you say it." Next time your children have a speech to give or need to resolve a conflict, remind them that if they are smiling and look confident, others will listen.

"*He* always spoke highly of *you*"

This was my father's favorite line whenever we were worked up about someone else's behavior. This line will slow down your child's emotions, help them see the situation from the other person's perspective and hopefully come to the conclusion that, "Maybe I'm being too judgmental."

People are like Swiss cheese

Another way to increase your child's perspective on themselves and others is to use the old psychoanalytic concept of the Swiss cheese ego. Simply put, none of us are cheddar. We all have holes in our moral and behavioral functioning. The key is to help your child realize that someone else's hole doesn't mean they don't have plenty of other solid qualities. Then, help your child build awareness and motivation into filling their own holes.

Well, some kids . . .

When I am responding to a child's complaints about another child, I try to keep things general. This might include saying something like, "Some kids like to have a little more control in their relationships." This kind of statement helps children not take it so personally. When it comes to teasing and horsing around, I might say, "Some kids like to play hardball and some kids like to play softball, and you get to decide which group to play with."

I remember the time . . .

Children learn a great deal through story telling. In particular, elementary children love to hear stories about the "olden days" and often get a kick out of your social and emotional mistakes. For years after I've told a particular story, students will plead with me to tell it again and laugh with great joy as if this was the first time they were hearing it. Telling these stories will help your child feel like you can understand what they are going through.

Sometimes you are the hammer and sometimes you are the nail

This is one of a series of metaphors that are designed to help keep life's frustrations in perspective. "The Serenity Prayer" by Reinhold Niebuhr, was crossed-stitched above the living room TV in my childhood home. It read: "God, Grant me the courage to change what I can change, the patience to accept what I can't change and the wisdom to know the difference."[11] As for the hammer and nail, a student suddenly shouted: "And sometimes you are the thumb!" I think he understood it.

Watch a few others first

All children struggle with trying something for the first time at some point in their development. Often, they may wish to avoid it and stall for as long as possible, but this approach only makes them more nervous and probably more likely to struggle given their decreased Presidential functioning. In these situations, recommend that they position themselves third or fourth in line. They can watch a couple of kids do it first and then get their attempt over with.

Like flowers in the garden

Walk into any fifth or sixth grade classroom and you'll notice a wide range of body shapes and sizes. Sometimes, the early blossoming children might feel like they are cooler than the other kids and the ones who haven't yet developed may feel inadequate in comparison. When talking about puberty, I remind kids that just like flowers in the garden, everyone has their time to blossom. Some children are like the tulips, which come out early, some are like the daisies of midsummer, and some are like the late blooming chrysanthemums. There isn't one time for everyone, and no one is better than anyone else.

You can make more of your own friendship choices at home

Kids will naturally play with whomever they want at recess but must also be reminded that inclusion is the rule at school. That means, if another child wants to join in, he or she will be included and treated with respect. At home, your child can have more of a voice about who comes over for a play date. Make sure your child knows that you will not tolerate negative comments about the visiting friend or discussions about kids who were not invited to a birthday party. While children will learn the lesson that *You don't always get to play with who you want*, it should be a lesson that is learned slowly over time.[12]

You don't have to play sports to fit in

Over the last thirty years, our country has been obsessed with children playing team sports. Help your child discover his or her area of joy and giftedness such as rock climbing, art, creative play, nature discovery, or reading.

Remember the lone zebra

The largest study ever on bullying was conducted in Norway in the 1970s.[13] One of the questions that Norwegian research psychologist Dan Olweus looked at was, who is more likely to be targeted by a bully: thin kids, obese kids, kids with glasses, or kids with braces, etc.? The study found only one common variable: kids who were loners were victimized by bullies.[14] It makes sense that those who are alone have no one to protect them or stand up for them. One doesn't need to have a ton of friends, but having one or two is essential for social development and in forming an alliance of mutual protection.

Teasing is like fishing

If a fisherman goes to a particular cove and gets a couple of bites, where will he go the next day? The same spot. If there are no bites for several days in a row, what will he do? Move on. When the fisherman gets even the slightest bite, he will reel it in. He will remember that fishing hole and return every day, as long as he continues to get bites. And what does a fisherman want the fish to do when he hooks it? He wants it to fight like crazy, because that's where all the fun is. And the harder the fish fights, the more ensnared it becomes on the hook. I tell kids that if they react to teasing, the teaser will probably come their way again. If they really react, the teaser is guaranteed to return and take pleasure in his ability to provoke their reactions.

The friendship pyramid

If you want a great understanding of friendship dynamics among children, check out the many books written by Michael Thompson. In his classic *Best Friends, Worst Enemies*, Thompson and his co-author Catherine O'Neill Grace describe the naturally occurring social classifications among kids. Imagine a horizontally divided pyramid with the top 15 percent being very popular, the next 45 percent being accepted, the next 20 percent being average or unclassifiable, and the bottom 20 percent being overlooked, controversial (think bully), or rejected. That means that 80 percent of all kids are doing pretty well with friends.[15] These kids may sometimes need a small nudge or some goal setting to enhance the development of their social brain while the kids in the bottom 20 percent will need more aggressive support and counseling. As far as popularity goes, there are no guarantees about what will make a child popular or not. For boys, being athletic or of larger stature can help. Being more verbal or attractive can help for girls.[16] I like to remind kids that what is more achievable and more desirable than popularity is shooting to be among the 65 percent of kids who are having fun with friends and to be comfortable in their own skin. On the other hand, a child who is trying to become popular may be at greater risk for self-destructive tendencies as they move through middle and high school. Author Rosalind Wiseman labels females in this group as the wannabes.[17]

YOUR CHILD'S MOST DIFFICULT TIMES

When it comes to moments of loss, children become easily distraught when they are separated from a primary attachment figure. *Even small changes can be hard.* Most parents have experienced a child's homesickness when they are spending the night at a friend's house or attending a sleepaway camp. These same feelings can arise if you travel for business or pleasure. The best strategy in these situations is to stay in contact with your child using technology. Crossing off the days till you reunite on the family calendar helps your child feel excited. This calendar can be helpful for children of divorced parents. I also like to remind them: "You are a two house family now, but you still have one heart around you."

The price for empathy is suffering

The ultimate blessing of the brain's drive to empathize with others is that we feel attached to other people and to all aspects of life. When others extend empathy to us and we extend it to them, we feel like we are connected. However, this also means that we will feel the pain and suffering when those we are attached to suffer, and we will feel our own shame when our actions cause pain to others. Ultimately, we will feel great pain and suffering when our attachments come to an end. When your child's empathy is causing them to suffer, remind them that acceptance of suffering is a small, temporary price to pay for living in a world where we feel love and attachment. A good statement to use is, "You are sad because you are attached." You can also talk about resiliency (discussed in section III).

Grief and loss is like falling on a hike

Having helped hundreds of children through a variety of loss and grief experiences, I've developed a few analogies to process it all. One comes from a set of stick-drawing images in my office of a child going on a hike in the mountains with his family on a beautiful, "normal" day. I then say, "Without noticing, you could trip over a rock and fall down an embankment." We then process the various feelings that come next: shock, hurt, anxiety, and anger. Then I ask, "If you did fall down, what would you do?" Almost every time, the response is, "I'd try to get out." I then draw a line and explain how sometimes they might start to move up and then they might drop down (in other words, your child might start to feel a little better and then remember something upsetting again). We talk about how this process will continue for awhile until eventually they get back to a new place on the trail. I also mention how one of the strategies to getting back up is to look for the "ropes" of support that surround us and find hope and inspiration in various activities and events as we search for a way out. During follow up visits with children, I will often pull this picture out again and have them tell me about their ups and downs and where they are on their path out.

The stained glass heart

When a child experiences a death in their life, I like to use a picture of a heart made out of glass and say, "One day the heart falls from its shelf and breaks. The first thing you should do now is stop and look for all the big pieces that you can find." I then ask the child to tell me memories of their departed loved one. As the child talks, I write each memory on a broken piece of heart glass that I had previously cut out of paper. (One child used the word *bacon* to describe the memory of his grandmother because when he visited her it was the scent he smelled upon waking.) Finally, I show how the pieces get rearranged into a stained glass shape of a heart again and tell them that even though they are feeling the pain of loss now, their feelings of love will come back. I point to the lines of pewter holding the stained glass heart together and explain that they are the scars of life that we all have. They do fade with time.

A loving object

Don't forget the importance of a loving object for younger children as they experience grief. Several years ago, a first grade student experienced the death of his mother. I had breakfast with him and his younger brother and brought along the Sad and Fear plush toys from the movie *Inside Out*. I talked to the boys about how they could hold on to them when they were feeling sad and afraid. When they hugged them, they could imagine that they were hugging their mom. I also told their dad to give each boy one of their mother's soft scarves to use as a blankie. The smell of her, I explained, will be comforting to them. That first grader is now a rising fourth grader and he and his brother are taking the plush toys with them as they move overseas with their dad and their new mom.

Just listen and hug

Sometimes listening is the best thing you can do. You might not always be able to explain the experiences your child is having or give them a nice and tidy framework. You can, however, listen with empathy and compassion. Your child will know they aren't alone in their suffering. According to a University of Colorado at Boulder study cited in *Men's Journal*, holding hands, hugging, and a back rub can be incredibly soothing and can even help reduce a loved one's sense of physical pain.[18]

Just listening in a non-judgmental way with a group of children who have experienced the same trauma can be incredibly powerful and helpful. Of the many traumas I've helped with, the aftermath of the Columbine massacre was the most difficult. As devastating as some of the high school students' stories were, perhaps the ones I remember most came from the elementary students I met with to discuss their experiences. Accounts of being locked-down in their classrooms for hours without knowing if their brother or sister was still alive reverberated among the children. One child in particular said: "I just had a fight with my brother that morning before school and then I was worried that he was dead and that I didn't get to tell him I loved him."

EFFECTIVE PROBLEM-SOLVING

The third fruit you are adding into your child's bowl is the ability to problem solve. Once you've had sharing time, the important part is that you have them transition from talking about feelings into taking action where you can. The Paralysis-by-Analysis Petes will often want to keep talking about problems, miring themselves in a repetitive soundtrack of negative emotions. Parenting brings out our anxieties and anxious parents have a tendency to "interview for pain."[19] The questioning can go on and on, and in my own experience, parents have a harder time letting go of emotional burdens than their kids. If you get overinvolved in your kids' problems, Thompson tells us that you will also strip them of their chance to become autonomous beings.[20] Children have a fundamental drive to master their worlds and *the handling of tough social situations will give them the mettle to conquer future problems.* When my daughter said to me, "Stop trying to comfort me, Dad." I knew it was time for me to stop talking. Once I stopped, she walked confidently into her classroom ready to tackle her problem.

It is essential to load up your child's thinking-feeling brain with successful strategies and the positive emotional memories of conflicts resolved. As described in some of the previous brain activities, start with shared insights about their unique Presidential and Factory functioning and then help them with a basic self-talk technique for handling difficulties. For those after-school chats, I use a strategy that includes the following five questions: 1) "What am I feeling?" 2) "What is the problem?" 3) "What did I do to contribute to the problem?" 4) "What are others thinking and feeling?" and 5) "What are three things I could do about it?"

During a recess pickup soccer game, a nine-year-old captain asked his classmates, "Who wants to be goalie?" After he selected one of the kids, a boy stormed off into the corner of the gym, sat down with his arms crossed, and told me, "I didn't get picked to be goalie because the captain thinks I stink." I replied, "Can you think of other reasons he didn't pick you?" He said, "Well, maybe I was waving my hand in his face too much when he asked who wanted to be goalie." We discussed this possibility, and I suggested that he could jump in the game with a positive attitude and that he would get his rotation later.

After the game, we processed what had happened earlier. We started by brainstorming the possible reasons the boy wasn't selected at first. Then, I had the boy ask the captain why he wasn't picked. To all of our surprise and joy the captain said, "Well, one of the girls was raising her hand and my mom told me to always let girls go first." What a sweetheart.

We ended the discussion by talking about the tendency of the boy who wasn't picked for goalie to negatively interpret a situation he perceives as unfair. This is a tendency all of us have to varying degrees. This discussion combined with a follow-up reinforcement system for thinking positively increased his ability to internalize the day's lesson, as well as expand his self-talk abilities.

For those children who like cute posters and acronyms, you might consider using a picture of a large star with the word STAR inside. Each letter forms a list of four things to do when having a problem: stop, think, act, review. You can practice this strategy by having the children use their President to stop, and then kick in the thinking-feeling brain to process the problem and think of some strategies to try.

RULER is another acronym developed by Yale University's Center for Emotional Intelligence (the center's evidence-based approach to integrating emotional intelligence in schools and curriculum) that stands for *recognizing* emotions in self and others; *understanding* the causes and consequences of emotions; *labeling* emotions accurately; *expressing* emotions appropriately; and *regulating* emotions effectively.[21]

If you are strapped for time, stick to the two most important questions for building insight into your child's behavior and having empathy for the other child. First: "What was I thinking or feeling that caused my behavior?" Second: "How would I feel if that happened to me?" If you want deeper reflection, write these two questions down and have your child write out a thoughtful response before they are free of their consequences.

PROMOTING COGNITIVE FLEXIBILITY

A big part of successful emotional and social problem-solving is having the ability to think flexibly as you search for solutions to problems. However, children sometimes need your support in brainstorming different solutions. I like to start with the one they are stuck on and help them see how that solution might circle back to the same result they are experiencing (you can write it down and draw an arrow leading to the result). Then offer a slight change to their solution and brainstorm where that might end up. Continue this process until they can see the wisdom of the new solution. A child might even come up with a novel solution on his or her own. I was working with a third grade girl who was struggling (often unconsciously) with picking her nails and the skin on her forehead until it bled. The other children at school would often have negative comments about her scabs. Her parents and I were so pleased when one night they came into her room to say good night, and found her with a sock over each hand. Noticing their surprise, the girl explained that this would help her from picking at herself during the night and while she was falling asleep.

If your child is having more frequent social struggles, spend some time talking with the teacher and the two of you can analyze any problematic behavior your child might be having. *Approach your child from a needs-base of wanting to have more social success.* This means talking about how a behavior is impacting your child's friendships rather than how it is impacting you. If you start yelling out, "Stop that, you are driving me nuts!" you'll probably get more of the same behavior. First, help them identify the strengths and positives they possess for making and keeping friends and help them figure out how they could emphasize those strengths. Next, explore their growth areas and then develop social and emotional goals for them to work on. Ask the question, "How could you be a better friend?" This question alone sends the message that we are moving past being victims and exerting control over what happens to us and how we are treated.

When a goal is established, you can positively reinforce change and offer tips and specific suggestions for accomplishing the goal. When that goal is accomplished, try adding on to it. For instance, a sensitive fourth grader might start crying when a relatively small conflict occurs. Start with limiting crying to bigger things as the first goal. Next, you can add not running to the teacher every time a small problem happens in the classroom and then learning how to ignore these so-called problems. Finally, help them learn a few creative comebacks so they can stand up for themselves. For instance, when being teased by a boy at her Catholic school that "Boys are better than girls because God created Adam before Eve," a fifth grade girl retorted, "Adam was God's rough draft!"

When helping your children reach their goals and become more effective at solving their social, emotional, and behavioral struggles, you will have to accept some very basic realities in the lives of your kids. *First, you have to accept that your kids are not always going to be happy.* Ever since Happy Meals and half-birthday celebrations, our culture has been obsessed with childhood happiness. If life were perfect for our kids, we would rob them of those problem-solving opportunities. While joys and successes are part of our human story, so are struggles and sorrows. Award winning actor Will Smith put it this way when talking about his family: "We call it leaning into the sharp parts. Something hurts, lean in. You just lean into that point until it loses its power over you. There's a certain amount of suffering that you have to be willing to sustain if you want to have a good life. And the trick is to be able to sustain it with your heart open and still be loving. That is the real trick."[22]

Leaning in can happen when your child makes a mistake (chapter 9). When you allow your child to feel the pain of that mistake, it means that you don't rush in to solve it for them or make some last-second attempt to rescue them from the impending consequences. No child's life is going to be ruined because a book report was left behind on the kitchen table. Ninety percent of the mistakes your child will make in elementary school have low stakes attached to them. Children need to feel the pain of a mistake in order to make needed changes and it is better that they learn when the stakes are low versus carrying old patterns into the high stakes world of adolescence. As mentioned in chapter 1, one of your main jobs is to parent for independence.

Leaning in can also apply when your child has harsh realities come into their lives or when they are trying their hardest to excel. For my daughter, I was so proud of her when she pushed herself to the limit during a cross-country meet. I found her bent over at the finish line crying out that she was about to throw up. I responded, "Way to go baby! I'm so proud of you!" While this concept takes a great deal of personal strength that emerges more fully in adolescence, it's never too early to talk to your child about how we all must suffer at points during our lives if we are truly going to be great. In other words, life isn't always going to be rainbows and butterflies.

Social and emotional development is no different than any other concept a child learns in school. It takes practice, mistakes, and a lot of repetition before kids get it right. However, throughout the learning process, some mistakes will hurt others. For 95 percent of these situations, a parent should respond by staying calm and avoid overreacting or getting involved. Sometimes it's hard to fight those impulses. I couldn't believe how mean the little girls at the pool could be when I first started taking my daughter to swimming lessons. I wanted to scold the girls and then talk to their parents. Fortunately, I had my wife's "wash and wear" philosophy tucked in my feeling-thinking brain and reminded myself that everyone is just learning.

It's also important to embrace a very broad definition of what is considered normal behavior throughout your child's social development. A good parenting skill to acquire is learning how to accept *all* child behaviors instead of getting uptight or overreacting to them. I often get calls from teachers or school administrators asking me if I thought a particular situation or behavior was abnormal for a child. In thirty-five years, I can only remember two times when I thought a child's conduct was more troubling than "normal."

This acceptance of normal social conflict is especially significant given our country's recent obsession with the topic of bullying. Mistakes are part of the learning process for kids, and they are still capable of outgrowing troubling behavior. As such, your child should never hear you identify another child as a bully. That word inflames the situation and only increases the chance that, in a misguided attempt to protect them, you will deny your child the opportunity to problem solve and gain independence.

When you hear about another child or parent who has had some difficulties, it's helpful to remember the phrase: *There but for the grace of God go I.* As parents, we all try to follow our internal script of how to raise children and what will lead to their success. When others vary from this script, we tend to judge them and pull away from their missteps. However, as you parent through high school, college, and beyond, you begin to realize that no parent or child is immune to problems, despite all our best efforts. Don't rush to judge others in your community, as you and your child could become the next ones being talked about. *As parents, we are all in this together and it's a forgiving heart that helps us all survive.*

By accepting these basic realities, you can be the parent with a lot of "teeth marks in your tongue." In other words, biting your tongue can help diffuse a situation and provide a learning opportunity. When your child brings up a problem, take a pause, and then start thinking about how you could empower your child to handle it. You aren't trying to figure out parent or adult solutions, but rather, you are helping to figure out what the *child* solutions to the problem might be.

In slowing yourself down, it's helpful to keep in mind that some negative peer feedback and a little embarrassment can actually benefit your child's social functioning. I learned pretty quickly in sixth grade to stop picking my nose in public when two of the popular girls turned around and said, "Gross!" Your kids are being socialized through both positive and negative messages from their peers. If you feel the negative messages are tipping the scale, then seek help from your child's teacher or a mental health professional.

While I have enumerated many ways to help shape your child's social and emotional development, you must also accept the reality that you can't pick your child's friends or choose all of the ways in which they will socialize. According to Thompson, you can only do four things: 1) Embrace and support their friends (rather than expressing dislike for a friend, a show of support might actually increase the chances that your child will come to you with friendship issues, or these friends might actually tell you more about your child than your child would ever tell you); 2) Give them a place to play; 3) Let them play alone; and 4) Give them food.[23]

Unless your child is in that bottom 20 percent who really do need more specialized adult support and ongoing therapy, I suggest you remember that *it's probably not as bad as you think it is.* Thanks to the brain's hard wiring and genetic guidance system, your child probably knows more than you think they do. Perhaps the best gift you can give your child is to communicate that you have high expectations for their social behavior and that you believe they can solve their own problems. In *Cat's Eye*, Margaret Atwood follows the story of a young girl who didn't have much in the way of parental advice when a group of girls are teasing her. The moment when she achieves self-efficacy is all the more remarkable. She stands up to the girls and says, "I don't know and I don't care. . . . I'm amazed at myself. . . . .It's like stepping off a cliff believing that the air will hold you up. And it does."[24] That's the kind of confidence you want your child to feel as they head into the uncertainty of adolescence. Imagine what your child is capable of with just a touch of informed insight from you.

BRAIN ACTIVITY: ATTITUDE OF GRATITUDE AND AN ABUNDANCE MIND-SET

Helping your child have an attitude of gratitude might be the best gift you ever gave them. Berkeley scientist Robert Emmons has been studying the daily benefits of focusing on gratitude for years.[25] Emotionally, gratitude increases positive emotions such as joy, pleasure, optimism, and happiness. Social benefits of gratitude result in greater helpfulness, generosity, and compassion. People who focus on gratitude feel less isolated, are more outgoing, and more forgiving as well. Our family has a nightly bedtime ritual where we say what we are thankful for that day. This is a great way to help your child focus his or her mind on gratitude before falling asleep. You can also create a family journal or poster board of all the things you are grateful for.

That attitude of gratitude goes hand in hand with an abundance mind-set. Children can whine a great deal about what they don't like and how their lives aren't as good as other kids. If you want to change your child's deprivation mind-set, take a challenge from entrepreneur and marketing expert Noah Kagan and go a day without complaining.[26] *Once you are aware of your own negative attitude, you can start a complaint jar for your whole family. Make a complaint and put money in the jar.*

BRAIN ACTIVITY: HOLDING A BABY BIRD

I use the analogy of a baby bird to remind younger students about the importance of freedom in friendships. I first have them imagine that they have found an abandoned baby bird, and then I ask, "If you were going to pick it up, how would you do it?" The kids show me by carefully reaching down and gently picking up the imaginary bird in the palm of their hands.

Next, I ask them to imagine that the bird tried to struggle or maybe pecked them a little and say, "What would you do? You wouldn't close your hands and smother the bird would you?" We talk about how they would keep their hands open and whisper to the bird, telling it to stay calm and not to worry. Later, when the bird was strong enough to fly away, I ask them, "What would you do?" Instinctively, the kids raise their hands up and let the bird fly away.

One of the cutest things in the world is seeing all the kids raise their hands up to free the imaginary bird. Afterward, we talk about how the bird relates to freedom in their friendships and how our ancient brain gets very anxious when we worry about being left out. This worry might make us want to take control of our friends by saying something like: "If you are friends with her, you can't be friends with me." I tell the kids, "That would be like closing your hands around the bird and smothering it."

We also discuss how they need to stay calm and, rather than controlling their friend, they can tell their friend to feel free to fly away and play with others. Or they can let their friend know that they are happy to join in, or are happy to keep playing and will be there if their friend wants to come back. "If you try and control them," I say, "they are very likely to fly away and never come back."

CHAPTER 15

FAMILY PARFAIT

FAMILY RITUALS

For as many years as I can remember, every Sunday held the same pattern when I was growing up: church, a roast beef dinner, playtime while my parents napped, football in the yard with my dad, and then a supper of grilled cheese and tomato soup followed by an episode of *Bonanza* in the family TV room. This familial ritual provided fun, joy, family unity, and a cocoon of security from the world around us. It didn't matter what was going on during the turbulent '60s; our Sunday routine was a constant stabilizing force that reconnected us after a chaotic week. As we grew older, card games like Uno and Hearts supplanted *Bonanza*. Today, during our family reunions, each night ends with a rousing game of poker. You'd have to see it to believe it, but my ninety-three-year-old mother with her white hair and dark sunglasses can still bluff us all—an amazing feat for a woman who is practically incapable of telling a lie.

Established family rituals, like game night, ground you and your children and have long-term emotional benefits. Research on children who grew up in alcoholic homes showed one subgroup that seemed more resilient despite experiencing the same disruptive childhood environment as the other subjects.[1] Subsequent research found that family rituals mitigated the emotional trauma.[2] Those chaotic families who still had traditions, such as holiday activities and birthday celebrations, produced children who were scarred by alcoholism but were also able to emotionally rebound as adults.[3] The other group, whose members were trapped in chaotic environments with no family traditions, fared poorly as adults. The rituals observed in the first group provided the kids with an anchor in stormy seas and proved constant amid the turmoil.[4]

If you haven't already, start some daily, weekly, monthly, or yearly family rituals. They don't have to be elaborate or expensive. Nightly bedtime rituals for children ground them emotionally after a long day and fill them with great love. My wife and daughter share a variety of kisses (Eskimo, butterfly, hand-on-heart) each night.

Some rituals might be seasonal, while others might happen just once a year. As a kid, I could always count on going hunting with my dad on Saturdays in the fall. While we never hit many birds, walking in the woods together gave my dad a break from work and family stress, and gave me a respite from school and social stress. On our drive back, we'd stop at some small diner for pie and then listen to football games on the radio. To this day, any time I hear the voice of iconic sportscaster Keith Jackson, I'm transported back in time to the front seat of my father's station wagon.

Likewise, families who participate in faith, school, or other social communities have many opportunities to observe rituals. Activities such as potlucks, carnivals, and holiday celebrations, bring families and communities together to socialize, celebrate, and become active in social change. An Orthodox Jewish Rabbi friend of mine explained his observance of the Sabbath from sundown Friday until sundown on Saturday in this way: "Think about it, you get to spend one day every week just connecting with your friends and your family. There is no work stress and nothing that has to be done. Just pure connection time."

Families going through a divorce face an important decision: Which traditions will you maintain? What new rituals will you establish? For my son and I, going to Colorado University's football games and continuing the tradition of chopping down our Christmas tree in the mountains were important customs to maintain. These and other, newer rituals reminded both of us that not everything had to change; we could adapt to our new reality by shaping our futures together.

These family rituals are the sweet whipped cream that fortifies your family parfait. If you have ever made homemade whipped cream, you know it takes time to set but that it is well worth it. Rituals take time to solidify, but they get you into the flow of your kids' lives and offer a break from the whirlwind of demands that disrupt family life.

For all the faults in our culture, the increased involvement of parents—especially dads—in their children's lives is a notable positive. This increased engagement can be the perfect tonic for nature-deficit disorder (NDD), a hypothesis advanced by Richard Louv in his 2005 book *Last Child in the Woods*. Louv's theory for NDD, a condition that is not recognized in medical diagnostic manuals, asserts that a lack of time spent outdoors is the cause of modern-day behavior problems in children.[5] Regardless of nature-deficit disorder's debated status as an actual disorder, there is a clear link between staying indoors plugged into electronics and social ineptitude. Planning outdoor adventures with your kids and their friends gives all of you opportunities to problem solve, manage frustrations and anxieties, develop real-life, person-to-person social skills, and put your family values into practice. My favorite car in the school parking lot is one that is plastered with thirty or so stickers from our country's national parks. Talk about a statement of that parent's outdoor, adventurous values.

While we all enjoy vacations in various resorts, make sure that you take some time to get out of the resort. You don't want your child to develop the impression that the entire world is nothing but lavish resorts and all-you-can-eat buffets. Help your child see and experience the reality of the people who live outside the resort areas. It is human nature to empathize with those who are like us and getting outside the tourist zone helps children to expand their "familiarity circles to those 'not like them' [and] opens the path to empathy."[6] Unfortunately, research has also shown that when we have more money, we often become more focused on ourselves and are less likely to care about other's feelings.[7] Even if it's just a cab ride on the way to a resort, help your children see how others, who are not like them, live.

Whether it's spending time outdoors or at resorts, regular, planned adventures are another important ingredient in the whipped-cream topping on your family parfait.

ADVENTURE TIPS

Your adventures don't need to be far-flung, expensive excursions to remote locations. You can have a great time on free, unplanned adventures together. Here are a few suggestions:

- Go crawdad fishing at a nearby creek.
- Watch the giant equipment at a construction site.
- Poke around your local junk yard.
- Start adventures early with your kids and scale your activities to their maturity levels. A short hike with your six- and seven-year-olds might pave the way for climbing a fourteen thousand foot mountain when they are older.
- Include friends in these family adventures as a fun way to boost your child's social development.
- It doesn't matter what your adventure is or where you are going, it's about sharing unique experiences with your kids. I call it having an "adventure mind-set."

Although you are physically active and most likely outside, it's not so different from the Orthodox Rabbi's description of observing the Sabbath: You are creating a bubble around yourselves and not letting the stresses of day-to-day life intrude on your time together. Even mistakes and misadventures are cherished experiences and result in time well spent with your kids. My son and I had a great time after we broke down on the side of the highway far away from any gas station (I was trying to see how far a Prius could go on battery power after the gas ran out—not far, it turns out!) While we waited for help, we pulled out his bag of army men and made little bunkers and forts in the dirt off to the side of the road. While the delay could have consumed us with frustration, we turned it into an adventure that I wouldn't have traded. You can even have a great time stuck in traffic for hours if you can appreciate that any time spent with your kids is sacred.

Some of the most formative adventures a child can experience occur away from family members. Like author Michael Thompson, I believe that sending your children to sleepaway camps is one way to combat nature deficits.[8] In addition to being outdoors and mastering the many challenges that arise when kids are out of their element, camp gives kids the opportunity to make new friends and play in a less structured environment than typical adult-run sports and activities. They also learn to manage their anxieties and function independently. As a parent, you might appreciate the break from the sometimes whiney, demanding behavior that accompanies any parent-child relationship. Take note, though, that your strong, independent camp kid often regresses into a needy malcontent when mom and dad show up. Fortunately, that camp confidence and friendship success is somewhere in there and will take root over time as your children mature. Maybe, just maybe, they will be a little less whiney and a little bit more appreciative when they come home.

COMMUNITY SERVICE: TOPPING YOUR FAMILY PARFAIT

Several years ago, I heard an interview on NPR with Dr. Nathaniel Branden, the psychologist who, in 1969, coined the term "self-esteem."[9] In discussing how his original concept had been muddled over the ensuing decades, he expressed dismay over two important aspects. When he coined the term, Dr. Branden's intention was that children would feel good about themselves because they knew they had worked hard to achieve something. "Nowadays," he said, "kids get ribbons for just about everything without really having to work for it."[10]

He also expressed disappointment that people had seen the goal of helping children attain high levels of self-esteem as an end unto itself. Dr. Branden wanted children to feel good about themselves (self-confidence and self-efficacy), but not for their own enrichment; rather, his intent was that self-esteem would result in selfless community service. *Instead of simply serving the child, self-esteem is supposed to help the child serve the community.*

I agree with Dr. Branden's original self-esteem concept and share his exasperation at the distorted, feel-good version of the term so ubiquitous today. If you value independence and acts of kindness for your children, you will find that the perfect cherry to top your family's life is volunteerism. Instead of just talking about your values, your kids will see these values in action as you intentionally seek out regular volunteer activities. In the words of the Dalai Lama: "I have always had this view about the modern education system: we pay attention to brain development, but the development of warm-heartedness we take for granted."[11] More simply stated, the development of empathy doesn't happen in a vacuum. **In your family, make empathy a verb.**

In addition to serving your community, these activities will reap huge benefits for the growth of your child's President as he or she takes on the challenges and problem-solving situations that often occur in volunteer work. You'll also see your children's confidence grow as they tackle these challenges and work past frustration and anxiety. On an emotional level, community service gives children a break from the stress of homework and extracurricular activities. Kids can also form deep attachments with those they help and learn how to keep their struggles in perspective when they see what life for others is really like. Imagine all the extra thoughts and memories they will have in their thinking-feeling brain the next time they start to feel entitled or sorry for themselves.

Thanks to our Mirrors and the power of empathy, we, as human beings, instinctually come together following a community crisis or tragedy. Recently, the *Today Show* featured a high school football team's commitment to volunteerism. Longmont, Colorado, a rural community that is forty miles north of Denver, is best known for the six state football championships that reside in the trophy case at Longmont High School. However, since 2007, the Trojans have spent one day of training camp every summer performing community service. In July 2014, the team spent a day helping the area rebuild from the 2013 flood that had ravaged much of the state. The players fixed homes damaged by the flood, helped rebuild an at-risk youth center, and assisted local farmers who suffered property damage in the disaster. "I believe football is the best game in the word," head coach Doug Johnson told the *Today Show*, "but giving to other people is way beyond that. It's helped us be unselfish. If we finish all those projects we said we were going to do, we start the season 1-0."[12]

In September 2017, Hurricane Irma wreaked destruction on the island of St. Thomas. In a follow up interview on NPR, the director of a mental health treatment center for troubled adolescents choked up as she talked about the heroic actions of her young men. As the nursing home next door was flooding, her clients left their locked residential facility and transported bedridden seniors to higher levels of the building as the water rose and the structure fell apart around them. They sat with the elderly patients in the dark and protected them from spraying glass.[13] Their actions saved countless lives that day. In helping others in need, they may have experienced something that will change their lives forever.

Like the players at Longmont High School and the young men in St. Thomas, your children will also reap social and health benefits of volunteer work for years to come. At the most basic level, our brains are wired to receive a boost from altruistic behaviors. In one study, toddlers who gave their snacks to others were found to be happier than those who ate the snacks themselves.[14] Another study revealed that nine- to eleven-year-olds who committed three kind acts per week, such as picking up litter or helping a peer, experienced increased happiness and more popularity among their peers.[15] Some researchers refer to this feeling as a helper's high.[16] Later in life, studies suggest that acts of kindness lower cortisol levels and relieve feelings of stress, depression, and social isolation.[17]

The pay-it-forward movement exploded in the 2000s. At local Starbucks across the nation, people happily paid the bill for the customer behind them. While this practice not only made the adult driver of the car happy, imagine how the children sitting in the back seat of the car at the drive-up window felt. They were probably giddy with excitement and felt even greater happiness than their parents. Altruism, generosity, selflessness, and acts of kindness are powerful words to use and even more powerful actions you can model on a daily basis.

In psychology terms, superordinate goals focus on a common mission and help work toward the greater good. A 1954 study performed by Turkish-American social psychologist Muzafer Sherif demonstrated how superordinate goals helps us bond.[18] In the study, two groups of boys that often displayed their innate competitive tendencies were paired in a camp setting. The two groups teamed up with their cabin mates and started a rivalry with the other cabin. Predictably, the boys quickly began to posture and engage in a variety of competitions and antagonistic behaviors directed at the other group in a plotline straight out of *Lord of the Flies*. One day, the camp counselors reported that a staff member had been lost in the woods and needed the boys' help. Instantly, the boys dropped their competitive stance toward each other and worked together to save their lost camp counselor. That primal hostility melted away when given a chance to serve their community.[19]

One of the greatest joys in my life was starting a program at my small, local church in 1985 for people with schizophrenia and other chronic mental health disorders who live extremely difficult and isolated lives within our cities. Our small program, called the Prince of Peace Social Club, started with a handful of volunteers ranging from young adults to parents with kids to senior citizens. Once a month, we gather together and host a home-cooked dinner with a social activity like Bingo (with all sorts of basic necessity prizes) for our fifty or so guests.

Over the past thirty-three years, we have been blessed with generations of volunteers and guests and have grown in size, adding a clothes bank and a food bank. As I've lived out my own joys and sorrows, running this program has served as a constant in my emotional life. I believe that getting out of our heads and helping others is the best therapy. In my estimation, community service truly is what life is all about.

The Prince of Peace Social Club also kick-started my son's passion for volunteerism. He started coming when he was three-months-old, sitting in his car seat as I carved turkeys and hams. As he grew older, he learned how to help out with a variety of chores and take on some leadership responsibilities, which made his confidence grow. His respect for people who suffer from mental illness is genuine, and I never heard him ask about why these people were odd, different, or weird. They were just his friends. Once these enacted values began to flourish in his life, they took on a life of their own. He earned the eighth grade volunteer award at his school in recognition of his service, and now that he's out of college, my son continues to volunteer. As a medical school student, he intends to spend his career serving others.

Our daughter, Lily, has also volunteered in the same program and is absolutely thrilled when the last Monday of the month rolls around. She likes to help out by babysitting some of our guest's children and by calling out numbers during the bingo game. You've never heard a squeal of delight until you've heard Lily yell, "We have another bingo!" into the microphone.

Thankfully, community spirit and volunteer mind-set appears to be alive and well in America's youth. St. Anne's Episcopal School in Denver recently became a Changemaker School (a program developed by Ashoka to cultivate empathy, teamwork, leadership, and problem-solving).[20] Each week, students gather before school to brainstorm social problems and how they might make a difference. Thanks to the sixth graders, my office now has a bucketful of pop tops from cans that will be donated to help fund Denver's Ronald McDonald House. Traditional programs like Peace Corps are still running strong as well as mission trips and medical relief trips. Perhaps the best example of this enthusiasm is the environmental movement. From conservation to resource management to environmental technology, kids, teens, and young adults demonstrate more concern for the fate of the planet than preceding generations. Hardly a day goes by that my daughter doesn't remind me about a dribbling faucet or how to recycle something.

If you are looking for ways to build your child's awareness of social concerns or find service opportunities, spend time with your older elementary student and look at the newspaper or online news sites. My daughter watches every morning as I spread out my two newspapers on the counter top. We've had many discussions about local, national, and international societal problems, which include conversations about Black Lives Matter, the Me Too movement and, most recently, the March for Our Lives movement generated by students at Stoneman Douglas High School. I felt tears well up in my eyes as I watched my daughter place flowers and a handmade poster on her school's alter during a memorial service for the students who lost their lives at Stoneman.

PARENT WITH OPTIMISM

I still hold a great deal of pain from my experiences with the Columbine High School students.[21] I wouldn't have thought that we would still be suffering from school shootings two decades later. The pain and anguish was so horrendous that, certainly, I believed we would find a way to end this scourge on our children. I personally became involved in confronting media outlets about their coverage of the tragedy and the glorification of violence through their focus on the shooters.[22] Part of my own psychological and emotional survival following Columbine and several other tragedies with which I've had to deal has to do with believing in the hope which children bring into the world. My faith in this amazing social wiring that we are blessed with at birth was reinforced on a recent Easter morning as I watched the interactions between my preschool-aged granddaughter and my preschool-aged great nephew. He was shy when he first arrived at our house. Instinctually, she reached out to him and offered him her new stuffed bunny. Later, as she struggled to get into the plastic play car due to her Easter dress, he came over and steadied the car for her. Both expressed empathy and kindness without even saying a word to each other.

Fortunately, my career has allowed me to witness other miraculous transformations through the power of human relationships. I've been collecting memories, most related to children, in a file labeled Things of Beauty That Make Me Cry. One of those memories was of Bobby, a former group member, now deceased, who was losing his sight in late elementary school due to a degenerative neurological disorder. While our groups are very active with games and sports, it was becoming increasingly difficult for Bobby to participate. The group came up with a solution for him; we cut a ball open and placed a small bell on the inside. While Bobby couldn't see the ball, he could hear it as he played goalie during soccer. The other children rallied around him and were more excited about Bobby's participation than they were about their own fun and games.

In addition to holding on to memories that give you hope and optimism, you can parent with optimism when children begin to understand how their brains work and have increased insight into their emotions and social relationships. When you match that with purpose-driven self-confidence, these are the kids who will reshape the world. My fifth grade students have a surprisingly keen perception of the world around them, both good and bad, and how they'd like to change it.

You as a parent will more than likely feel helpless as your children go through various stages of development. *The key is to relax, let them play, and remember that your parenting has to be "just good" enough.* Your kids are who they are, and while you are there for guidance, their joys and struggles are their own. Some of the best parenting advice I've heard came from Rose Kelly, a former admissions director for St. Anne's Episcopal School in Denver, who was sadly taken by cancer. An amazing mentor for many young parents, Kelly had a relaxed attitude about parenting and liked to say, "Parent just this side of benign neglect. If you go past that, you're in for a world of drama."

Her philosophy also carried over into doing what works even if it's not something the professionals would recommend. One mother recently shared with me how she gave a chocolate mint to her dyslexic son every time he practiced a spelling word correctly. He got an A on his next test. Former Colorado pro football player and Olympic freestyle skier, Jeremy Bloom, tells a great tale of how he learned to speed ski as a child. His grandfather would take a bag of small candy bars on the ski lift and drop them off as they went up the mountain. He then challenged his young grandson to ski down fast so he could get them before anyone else did.[23]

The philosophy of not being an overinvolved parent was reinforced by a parenting episode on the world-renowned podcast Freakonomics. A variety of economists talked with the hosts about this generation's struggle with obsessive parenting. In the 1980s, college educated moms spent an average of thirteen hours a week on childrearing. Today, moms are spending an average of twenty-two hours. The reason? Economists correlated it to an increased competition in college admissions in the 1990s. It seems like all the extra child-based extracurricular activities could result in greater developmental gains as well as pad the college application.[24]

Like Dr. Barkley's concept of parents as shepherds (in the Introduction), these economists concluded that obsessive parenting has few long-term rewards for children, including long-term success. Of all the research into perceived child engineering, they could only find three parent behaviors that did have long-term impacts on kids who were raised in reasonable child environments. As you might guess, the first two—cigarette smoking and alcohol abuse—had negative impacts. The one behavior that had a positive impact? Kindness. Thanks to your child's mirror neuron system, the parental kindness that you demonstrate to those you interact with (restaurant workers, retail sales people) is highly contagious for your kids. Parent author and Freakonomics co-host

Steve Levitt tells us that "Parenting is about who they are, not what they do. All kids really need is to be loved." For nurturing your child, cohost Stephen Dubner adds, "The quality of your relationship with your child is what matters most."[25]

Backing off from all the activities and following this advice can be hard. There is always going to be the temptation to do more for your child. And you may hear a voice in the back of your head keep asking, "What if we *don't* do that?" It's also hard when your parent friends are signing up for the latest camps, classes, and activities and you aren't.

However, if you are going to be a dedicated parent, start by trimming down the number of activities each year as your child gets older. It's not possible for your child to be proficient at everything. Next, focus on one or two activities that both you and your child are passionate about. My wife took this approach with her son's obsession with little league baseball. Even though she sat countless hours in the stands on cold spring days and blazing hot summer afternoons, it wasn't hard for her because her son was deeply engaged in the sport. She never had to argue with him about being on time or demand that he practice at home. He lived baseball.

The experts on the podcast Freakonomics also recommend that you shouldn't invest in an activity if you are getting a negative return. At that point, either you or your child will feel resentment. All that extra time and energy spent on activities that aren't bringing positive returns can equal a lot of unhappiness in the household. For instance, if you are fighting over those music lessons, then drop them. Stephen Dubner says, "The happiest parents are the least stressed," and least anxious about what they are doing or not doing.[26] While this might not be true in every moment, happy parents equal happy kids.

While not a famous economist, author, or podcaster, my mother once told me what gave her the most satisfaction as a parent. She started to talk about her kids being happy but then stopped and said, "No, it's not that they are all happy; it's that they are all *responsible*." **Your primary job as a parent in the human community is to raise a responsible, morally driven, contributing member of society.** Great adventures and family rituals are important, but ultimately, they are a bonus. Focus on being responsible and reasonably happy for your kids and everything else will most likely work out in the wash. Former football and baseball superstar Bo Jackson put it this way, "If we don't teach kids structure and responsibility, they will be lost when they get older."[27]

BRAIN ACTIVITY: PLANNING ADVENTURES AND VOLUNTEER EXPERIENCES

- *Make a dream list of adventures that your children would like to go on.*
- *You can split the list into short, nearby adventures and long, far-off adventures.*
- *Start the list with things your kids are interested in. In cases where your child's natural interests don't necessarily match yours, I find that expanding your repertoire of adventure activities will help motivate your child's interests.*
- *Combine some of your short-term adventures into longer-term adventure dreams over the course of years. It took five summer trips for my son and me to retrace the Lewis and Clark route. This summer, I took my daughter on her first alpine slide ride just outside Denver. She loved it. Now we are planning on visiting other alpine slides in the state next summer.*
- *Take a weekend to organize your shed or garage so that you can easily go on your adventures. Nothing*

will spoil your adventure like realizing you left some vital piece of equipment back at home. If you have what you need all ready to go, you can load up the car and then put it all back when you return so that you are set for your next adventure. Use this same brainstorming technique for planning your family's volunteer opportunities. Most kids have experiences at school with fund-raisers and collection drives that support various populations. Just like any adventure, start with your child's interests.

AFTERWORD

NEVER WISH
A MOMENT AWAY

"You may not know it now, but you're gonna miss this."
~Trace Adkins

Throughout human history, the development and evolution of the human species has favored those who can live, work, and play in community. Fortunately, the evolution of the human brain has provided children with sophisticated biological neural networks that allow them to become mature, socially connected members of society. Now that you have read this book and used some of the activities, I hope you have a much better understanding of the interplay of the President, the Factory, and the Mirror, and that your children have become empowered and conscious, mindful users of their social brains. While we know that, genetically, some children will struggle in these three brain areas, you can provide the structure and guidance they need. If you are ever concerned that your child is having chronic stress in these areas, you can always seek out professional consultation from your school or your community's mental health providers. There are plenty of psychological testing instruments that can pinpoint your child's emotional processing and Presidential and Mirror spectrum placement. It's also useful to seek out guidance when your child's environment isn't good enough, or you have a temporary disturbance or change in your child's environment.

My final wish for you and your kids is that you embrace the challenges and energy unique to every phase of your child's life. Some of these phases will bring you great joy and pride in your child's development. Other phases may also cause you great disappointment and shame. You'll suffer and feel sadness when your child is suffering. While you have to separate your emotions from your child's emotions, remember that *you can only be as happy as your saddest child.* Even so, you have to accept each phase as it comes. Get ideas from other parents and your child's teachers, be creative, and enjoy the process of watching them mature. **Even in the toughest of times, never wish a moment away.** It all goes so fast, and in the blink of an eye, your children will be moving into the teen years when child development and parental challenges really start to speed up.

My Best,
Craig A. Knippenberg

ACKNOWLEDGMENTS

I first want to thank the thousands of parents who have trusted me with their children and families for almost forty years. I've learned so much from them and continue to learn from them every day.

I owe so much to my wife for her inspiration, patience, support, and understanding. She is my complete partner in every way. She's also my in-house editor and has been working on this book since day one. I offer love and gratitude to my son, Alex, and the many adventures we have shared through the years. He taught me so much about being a father and I couldn't be prouder of the young man he has become. My daughter, Lily, is now teaching me how to parent a young woman. She too, has had to cope with the stress of Dad's project and continues to fill our house with love and joy. Daniel, my stepson, was my first editor and was patient in teaching me how to be a better writer. And I am grateful to my stepdaughter, Elizabeth, whose energy and enthusiasm is channeled everyday into caring for her nursing patients. She has also given us the gift of a granddaughter, Shayna, who reminds us every week of the speed at which a preschooler's brain develops.

I also want to honor and thank my family of origin. While my father is no longer with us, I learned so much about being a responsible, socially connected, and service-driven man from him and my mother. My parents were role models for empathy expressed in action. I also want to thank my siblings. When you are the fourth of five kids, you learn quickly about social skills and emotional management. My older brother, Mark, is a gifted therapist and has been helping others for the past forty years. I have gratitude for my sisters, Janet and Lynn, who taught me how to understand and relate to women, and helped me through many difficult losses. Finally, I offer thanks to my brother John, who's been my best friend since he was born. We spent countless hours honing our athletic, social, emotional, and negotiation skills through playing and running around the neighborhood together. I simply can't imagine a world without him.

Many thanks to the students, parents, and faculty of St. Anne's Episcopal School in Denver—a school that all children should have. I especially want to thank my two heads of school: Ramsay Stabler and Alan Smiley. When he first hired me as the school's mental health consultant, Ramsay told me, "You can talk about anything you want as long as it is based in science." Thankfully, Alan allowed me that same freedom for the past thirteen years. I'll also be forever grateful to Alan for his steadfast leadership through our community's tragedies. He truly supported each of us and understood that we needed to grieve in our own way. And I offer thanks to our dear departed admissions director, Rose Kelly, who reassured thousands of parents as they went through their own difficult family times.

Throughout my professional development I've had great mentoring, inspiration, and support. Flowing from my professors' tutelage at Valparaiso University, the Graduate School of Social Work, Denver University, and the Iliff School of Theology, I walked into working with children and running behavioral, emotional, and social development groups (our *Connect* model) at Boulder County Mental Health Center. As a twenty-two-year-old grad student, they gave me and my fellow student, Mark Brooks, PhD, the freedom to develop the group model and just "rock 'n' roll." Also, I am thankful to my old roommate and friend, Rod North, who when asked what we've been doing professionally all these years, replied, "Collecting wisdom." Thanks to the hundreds of students at the Havern Center who helped me learn how to creatively engage exceptional students as they expanded their social and emotional skills.

I've also been blessed in hearing and speaking with many of the professionals who are cited in this book. Especially Michael Thompson, PhD, an extraordinary writer and speaker who has inspired me over the past twenty years. I also owe so much to Randi Hagerman, MD, medical director of the MIND Institute, a gifted speaker who can take the most complex brain concepts and make them fun and understandable to everyone in the audience. It's that same gift that I've loved bringing to children and parents and it's the reason I turned to her ten years ago to discuss the curriculum I was developing at St. Anne's. Also thanks to Michael Gurian and the Denver Boys Summit and Dr. Russell Barkley for always being willing to offer guidance with research and publishing.

For this manuscript in particular, I want to first thank the thousands of parents who have said to me after sessions or lectures, "You should write a book." While it took longer than I'd hoped, I finally did. Individually, I want to thank my brain editor, Nicole Tartaglia, MD, of Children's Hospital, Colorado. She was so patient in checking and correcting my brain explanations and metaphors. The gifted Jennifer Phelps was a lifesaver, as my content and copy editor and helped me through many struggling moments. Thanks to my artist, Liz Cohen, PsyD, a former graduate student who could cleverly put mental health concepts into her drawings for kids. A huge thanks to Larry Yoder, former book buyer for the Bookies Bookstore, for providing guidance and inspiration throughout the entire process. I would like to acknowledge Mike Klassen and the professionals at Illumify Media for taking me on as a first-time author. In addition, thanks to my author neighbor Jim Syring for his advice; author Steve Antonoff, PhD, for always being an inspiration to me; Sonny Hutchison who produced my *Will You Be My Friend?* video series on YouTube and shared his wisdom on developing a platform; and our friends at Denver Academy for all their support throughout the process, especially Philippe and Jenni Ernewein, two of Colorado's top educational specialists. Finally, I offer gratitude to my friend Daniel Yohannes, former US Ambassador, and his family for all their friendship and spiritual support.

I also want to give a special thanks to my office associates over the past thirty years. Their hard work with children and families fills me with joy everyday as I watch happy children and parents literally dance out of our office. Their hard work has allowed me the privilege of taking time off the last four summers to write this book.

Thanks, as well, to our volunteers and guests at the Prince of Peace Social Club. Those who struggle with long-term mental illness deserve to feel joy, and to feel that, they too, need opportunities to share their social and emotional gifts.

In closing, I can't possibly count the many special memories over my career. To say that I have been blessed in my profession would be an understatement. When asked what I do, I like to respond, "I get paid to play with kids all day." Yet, there have been many difficult moments, as well. The losses of children and parents to illnesses, accidents, and suicides are some of the most difficult moments I've been through. The experience as a mental health first-responder at the Columbine High School massacre and working in that community for years afterward still weighs heavily on my heart and soul. I also carry the memories of children and parents we have lost at St. Anne's, especially Grace and Sam. While I never intended to do grief and trauma work, it had a way of finding me. Thankfully, when I see children, I hang on to the belief that hope always conquers despair. Finally, I hold in my heart, dear, sweet Jonathan, our nephew who was taken from us way too young.

NOTES

Preface

1   Donald W. Winnicott, *The Child, the Family, and the Outside World* (New York, NY: Penguin, 1973), 173.

2   Russell Barkley, "ADHD and the Nature of Self-Control" (presentation, CHADD Annual International Conference on ADHD, San Antonio, TX, 1997).

Introduction

1   John J. Ratey, *A User's Guide to the Brain: Perception, Attention, and the Four Theaters of the Brain* (New York, NY: Vintage Books, 2001), 302-305.

2   Michael Thompson, "How to Raise Responsible Children" (lecture, St. Anne's Episcopal School, Denver, CO, March 12, 2018).

3   Michele Borba, *UnSelfie: Why Empathetic Kids Succeed in Our All-About-Me World* (New York, NY: Touchstone, 2016), xiv.

4   Borba, *UnSelfie*, xv.

5   Ratey, *A User's Guide to the Brain*, 302-305.

6   Harry Reis, quoted in "Deploy Random Acts of Kindness," *Time*, October 2, 2017, 32.

7   Sandra Aamodt and Sam Wang, *Welcome to Your Child's Brain: How the Mind Grows from Conception to College* (New York, NY: Bloomsbury, 2011), 173.

8   Daniel Goleman, *Emotional Intelligence: Why It Can Matter More Than IQ, 10th edition* (New York, NY: Bantam Dell, 2006), 4.

9   Jenny Brundin, "Q&A: Will Too Much Testing Sap Students' Creativity?" *Colorado Matters*, Colorado Public Radio News, April 29, 2014, http://www.cpr.org/news/story/qa-will-too-much-testing-sap-students-creativity.

10   Edmond McDonald as cited in Marian Wright Edelman, *Guide My Feet: Prayers and Meditations on Loving and Working for Children* (Boston, MA: Beacon Press, 1995), 7.

Chapter 1

1   David Scott Yeager, "Implicit Theories of Personality and Adolescent
    Aggression: A Process Model and Intervention Strategy" (Dissertation,
    Stanford University, 2011), https://webcache.googleusercontent.
    com/search?q=cache:UJqJVX7EWHUJ:https://stacks.stanford.
    edu/file/druid:hv373wm7082/yeager%2520final-augmented.
    pdf+&cd=2&hl=en&ct=clnk&gl=us.

2   Jed Yalof, "Right Hemispheric Disorders and Emotional Disturbance,"
    in *Emotional Disorders: A Neuropsychological, Psychopharmacological,
    and Educational Perspective*, ed. Steven G. Feifer and Gurmal Rattan
    (Middletown, MD: School Neuropsych Press, 2009), 52.

3   Study cited in Rachael Rettner, "'Helicopter' Parents Have Neurotic
    Kids, Sutdy Suggests," *LiveScience*, June 3, 2010, http://www.livescience.
    com/10663-helicopter-parents-neurotic-kids-study-suggests.html.

4   Borba, *UnSelfie*, 198.

5   Adam Sternbergh, "With American Families Shrinking in Size, the
    Middle Child May 'Go Extinct,'" *All Things Considered*, National Public
    Radio, July 12, 2018, https://www.npr.org/2018/07/12/628546595/
    with-american-families-shrinking-in-size-the-middle-child-may-go-
    extinct.

6   Thompson, "How to Raise Responsible Children."

7   Russell A. Barkley, *Taking Charge of ADHD, Revised Edition: The
    Complete Authoritative Guide for Parents* (New York, NY: Guilford Press,
    2000), 48.

8   Eva Jablonka and Gal Raz, "Transgenerational Epigenetic Inheritance:
    Prevalence, Mechanisms, and Implications for the Study of Heredity and
    Evolution," *The Quarterly Review of Biology* 84, no. 2 (2009): 131-176,
    and Jack P. Shonkoff and Deborah A. Phillips, eds., *From Neurons to
    Neighborhoods: The Science of Early Childhood Development* (Washington,
    D.C.: National Academy Press, 2000).

9   "Boy Brains, Girl Brains," *Newsweek*, September 18, 2005, http://www.
    newsweek.com/boy-brains-girl-brains-118279 and R. K. Lenroot, N.
    Gogtay, D. K. Greenstein, E. M. Wells, G. L. Wallace, L. S. Clasen, J.
    D. Blumenthal, J. Lerch, A. P. Zijdenbos, A. C. Evans, P. M. Thompson,
    and J. N. Giedd, "Sexual Dimorphism of Brain Developmental

Trajectories During Childhood and Adolescence," *NeuroImage* 36, no. 4 (2007): 1065-1073.

10   Nicole M. Else-Quest, Janet Shibley Hyde, H. Hill Goldsmith, and Carol A. Van Hulle, "Gender Differences in Temperament: A Meta-Analysis," *Psychological Bulletin* 132, no. 1 (2006): 33-72. doi:10.1037/0033-2909.132.1.33 and Madhura Ingalhalikar, Alex Smith, Drew Parker, Theodore D. Satterthwaite, Mark A. Elliott, Kosha Ruparel, Hakon Hakonarson, Raquel E. Gur, Ruben C. Gur, and Ragini Verma, "Sex Differences in the Structural Connectome of the Human Brain," *PNAS* 111, no. 2 (2013): 823-828. doi:10.1073/pnas.1316909110.

11   Andrew Lawrence, "We Know Football Is Dangerous. So Why Are We Still Letting Our Sons Play It?" *Men's Health*, July 10, 2018, https://www.menshealth.com/health/a21346159/should-kids-play-football/.

12   Daniel H. Daneshvar, David O. Riley, Christopher J. Nowinski, Ann C. McKee, Robert A. Stern, and Robert C. Cantu, "Long Term Consequences: Effects on Normal Development Profile after Concussion," *Physical Medicine & Rehabilitation Clinics of North America* 4 (November 2011): 683-700, doi:10.1016/j.pmr.2011.08.009.

13   Seann Gregory, "New Study Links Playing Youth Football to Later Brain Damage," *Time*, September 19, 2017, http://time.com/4948320/football-brain-damage-consussions-study/.

Chapter 2

1   Kelly Lambert and Craig Kinsley, *Clinical Neuroscience* (New York, NY: Worth, 2005), 84.

2   William W. Blessing, *The Lower Brainstem and Bodily Homeostasis* (Oxford, England: Oxford University Press, 1997) and Ratey, *A User's Guide to the Brain*, 10.

3   Aamodt and Wang, *Welcome to Your Child's Brain* and Jukka M. Leppänen and Charles A. Nelson, "Tuning the Developing Brain to Social Signals of Emotions," *Nature Reviews Neuroscience* 10 (2009): 37-47. doi:10.1038/nrn2554.

4   Aamodt and Wang, *Welcome to Your Child's Brain*, 156.

5   Aamodt and Wang, *Welcome to Your Child's Brain*, 178.

6   Jon H. Kaas, "Evolution of the Neocortex," *Current Biology* 16, no. 21 (2006): R910-R914.

7   Aamodt and Wang, *Welcome to Your Child's Brain*, 173.

8   Aamodt and Wang, *Welcome to Your Child's Brain*.

9   Judith Graham and Leslie A. Forstadt, "Children and Brain Development: What we Know About How Children Learn," Cooperative Extension Publications, University of Maine, 2011, https://extension.umaine.edu/publications/4356e/.

10   Ratey, *A User's Guide to the Brain*, 19.

11   Ratey, *A User's Guide to the Brain*, 19.

12   Ratey, *A User's Guide to the Brain*, 25.

13   Graham and Forstadt, "Children and Brain Development."

14   Aamodt and Wang, *Welcome to Your Child's Brain*, 42.

15   Dale Purves, George J. Augustine, David Fitzpatrick, Lawrence C. Katz, Anthony-Samuel LaMantia, James O. McNamara, and S. Mark Williams, eds., *Neuroscience* (Sunderland, MA: Sinauer Associates, 2001).

16   Nicolas Chevalier, Salome Kurth, Margaret Rae Doucette, Melody Wiseheart, Sean C. L. Deoni, Douglas C. Dean III, Jonathan O'Muircheartaigh, Katharine A. Blackwell, Yuko Munakata, and Monique K. LeBourgeois, "Myelination is Associated with Processing Speed in Early Childhood: Preliminary Insights," *PLOS ONE* 10, no. 10 (2015). doi: https://doi.org/10.1371/journal.pone.0139897.

Chapter 3

1   Jablonka and Raz, "Transgenerational Epigenetic Inheritance," 131-176.

2   Thom Hartmann, *Attention Deficit Disorder: A Different Perception* (Grass Valley, CA: Underwood Books, 1997). I take a deeper look at ADHD in chapter 4 and define it in relation to a child's Presidential functioning.

3   K. Kersting, "Brain Research Advances Help Elucidate Teen Behavior," American Psychological Association 35, no. 7 (2004): 80. http://www.apa.org/monitor/julaug04/brain.aspx.

4   "Boy Brains, Girl Brains."

5   Ratey, *A User's Guide to the Brain*, 32.

6   Ratey, *A User's Guide to the Brain*, 21.

7   Ratey, *A User's Guide to the Brain*, 33.

8   Ting Tao, Ligang Wang, Chunlei Fan and Wenbin Gao, "Development
        of Self-Control in Children Aged 3 to 9 Years: Perspective from a Dual-
        Systems Model," *Scientific Reports* 4, no. 7272 (2014). doi:10.1038/
        srep07272.

9   Russell A. Barkley, ed., *Attention-deficit Hyperactivity Disorder, Fourth
        Edition: A Handbook for Diagnosis and Treatment* (New York, NY:
        Guilford Press, 2015), 378.

10   Jerneja Macek, David Gosar, and Martina Tomori, "Is There a
        Correlation Between ADHD Symptom Expression Between Parents
        and Children?" *Neuroendocrinology Letters,* 33, no. 2 (2012): 201-206.
        http://www.researchgate.net/publication/230625179_Is_there_a_
        correlation_between_ADHD_symptom_expression_between_parents_
        and_children.

11   Laurie Miller, Wilma Chan, Linda Tirella, and Ellen Perrin "Outcomes
        of Children Adopted from Eastern Europe," *International Journal of
        Behavioral Development* 33, no. 4 (2009): 289-298,
        doi:https://doi.org/10.1177/0165025408098026 and "The Disorder
        Named ADHD," *CHADD*, n.d., http://www.chadd.org/Understanding-
        ADHD/The-Disorder-Named-ADHD-WWK1.aspx.

12   John Medina, *Brain Rules: 12 Principles for Surviving and Thriving at
        Work, Home, and School* (Seattle, WA: Pear Press, 2008), 241.

13   Alexandra Sifferlin, "Why Girls' Brains Mature Faster Than
        Boys' Brains," *Time*, December 19, 2013, http://healthland.time.
        com/2013/12/19/why-girls-brains-mature-faster-than-boys-brains/.

14   "Boy Brains, Girl Brains."

15   Tom Chiarella, "The Problem with Boys…Is Actually a Problem with
        Men," *Esquire*, July 1, 2006, http://www.esquire.com/news-politics/
        news/a865/esq0706sotamboys-94/.

16   Randi J. Hagerman and Robert L. Hendren, eds., *Treatment of
        Neurodevelopmental Disorders: Targeting Neurobiological Mechanisms*
        (Oxford, England: Oxford University Press, 2014).

17   Nic Swaner, "10 Cases of Natural Gender Inequality," *Listverse*, August
        2, 2010, http://listverse.com/2010/08/02/10-cases-of-natural-gender-
        inequality/.

18   Swaner, "10 Cases of Natural Gender Inequality."

19   See http://www.gurianinstitute.com/ for more information.

20   Michael Gurian, "Boys and Girls Learn Differently," n.d., http://www.gurianinstitute.com/.

21   Gurian, "Boys and Girls Learn Differently."

22   Mark E. Mahone, "Neuropsychiatric Differences Between Boys and Girls With ADHD," Psychiatric Times, 29, no. 10, October 4, 2012, accessed May 6, 2019, https://www.psychiatrictimes.com/adhd/neuropsychiatric-differences-between-boys-and-girls-adhd.

23   Phyllis Brown, "Teens with ADHD More Likely to Drop Out," Futurity, August 31, 2010, http://www.futurity.org/teens-with-adhd-more-likely-to-drop-out/.

24   Walter Mischel, Ebbe B. Ebbesen, and Antonette R. Zeiss, "Cognitive and Attentional Mechanisms in Delay of Gratification," Journal of Personality and Social Psychology, 21, no. 2 (1972): 204-218.

25   Terrie E. Moffit, Richie Poulton, and Avshalom Caspi, "Lifelong Impact of Early Self-Control," American Scientist, September-October 2013, 353-59.

26   Terrie E. Moffit et al., "A Gradient of Childhood Self-Control Predicts Health, Wealth, and Public Safety," Proceedings of the National Academy of Sciences 208, no. 7 (2011): 2693-98.

27   Jonah Lehrer, "Don't! The Secret of Self-Control," The New Yorker, May 18, 2009, https://www.newyorker.com/magazine/2009/05/18/dont-2.

Chapter 4

1   Margarita Tartakovsky, "The Curious Case of Phineas Gage and Others Like Him," Psych Central (blog), August 28, 2011, http://psychcentral.com/blog/archives/2011/08/28/the-curious-case-of-phineas-gage-and-others-like-him/.

2   Tartakovsky, "The Curious Case of Phineas Gage and Others Like Him."

3   John Fleischman, Phineas Gage: A Gruesome but True Story about Brain Science (Boston, MA: Houghton Mifflin Harcourt, 2004).

4   Gregory A. Fabiano and William E. Pelham, "Impairment in Children," in Assessing Impairment: From Theory to Practice, ed. Sam Goldstein and Jack A. Naglieri (New York, NY: Springer, 2009), 105-120.

5   Thomas Phelan, *1-2-3 Magic: Effective Discipline for Children 2-12*, 3rd
     ed. (Glen Ellyn, IL: ParentMagic, 2003).

6   Noelle Phillips, "Northeast Denver Chess Club Won't Let One Bad
     Move Block Winning Strategy," *Denver Post*, August 3, 2018, https://
     www.denverpost.com/2018/08/03/northeast-denver-youth-chess-club-
     donations/.

7   David Shannon, *David Goes to School* (New York, NY: The Blue
     Sky Press, 1999) and Bruce Hale, *Clark the Shark* (New York, NY:
     HarperCollins, 2013).

Chapter 5

1   Ratey, *A User's Guide to the Brain,* 125.

2   Pat Wolfe, "The Adolescent Brain and Addiction" (lecture, Learning and
     the Brain Conference, San Francisco, CA, February 20, 2009).

3   Wolfe, "The Adolescent Brain and Addiction."

4   John J. Ratey and Catherine Johnson, *Shadow Syndromes* (New York,
     NY: Bantam Books, 1997), 322.

5   Aamodt and Wang, *Welcome to Your Child's Brain,* 77 and BJ Casey,
     Stephanie Duhoux, and Matthew Malter Cohen, "Adolescence: What
     Do Transmission, Transition, and Translation Have to Do With It?"
     Neuron 67, no. 5 (2010): 749-760. doi:10.1016/j.neuron.2010.08.033.

6   Bernice E. Cullinan, "Independent Reading and School Achievement,"
     School Library Media Research Journal, 3 (2000). https://www.
     researchgate.net/publication/291793658_Independent_reading_and_
     school_achievement.

7   Michael Rich, interview by Nathan Heffel, August 1, 2018, "Worried
     About Your Kid's Smartphone Use? Start Them On A Flip Phone, Plus
     More Advice," *Colorado Matters*, Colorado Public Radio, https://www.
     cpr.org/news/story/worried-about-your-kids-smartphone-usage-start-
     them-on-flip-phones-and-more-advice.

8   Wolfe, "The Adolescent Brain and Addiction."

9   Royce Flippin, "What Is ADHD Hyperfocus?" *ADDitude: Inside the
     ADHD Mind*, n.d., https://www.additudemag.com/understanding-
     adhd-hyperfocus/.

10   David L., "Dopamine, Games, and Motivation," *Learning Theories*,
     February 2, 2016, https://www.learning-theories.com/dopamine-games-
     motivation.html.

11   "Marijuana and Dopamine: The Science Behind It," *LeafScience*,
     May 10, 2014, https://www.leafscience.com/2014/05/10/marijuana-
     dopamine-science/.

12   Deborah Blum, "The Plunge of Pleasure," *Psychology Today*, September
     1, 1997, last reviewed on June 9, 2016, https://www.psychologytoday.
     com/articles/199709/the-plunge-pleasure.

13   Aamodt and Wang, *Welcome to Your Child's Brain*, 124.

14   Bob Tewksbury, "Head Games," *Sports Illustrated*, April 23, 2018,
     https://www.si.com/vault/2018/04/17/head-games.

Chapter 6

1   See www.interventioncentral.org for more information.

2   E. S. Shapiro, S. L. Durnan, E. E. Post, and T. S. Levinson, "Self-
     monitoring Interventions for Children and Adolescents," in *Interventions
     for Academic and Behavior Problems II: Preventive and Remedial
     Approaches*, ed. M. R. Shinn, H. M. Walker, and G. Stoner (Bethesda,
     MD: NASP, 2002), 913–938.

3   "Mindfulness Said to Boost Academics," Colorado Academy News, n.d.,
     http://news.coloradoacademy.org/mindfulness/.

4   Erich Kasten, "Ruled by the Body: How Physical Illness Affects the
     Brain," *Scientific American Mind* 22, no. 1 (2011), 57.

5   Fiona Macrae, "Water On the Brain: Grey Matter Literally Shrinks
     Without Hydration," *Daily Mail*, May 20, 2010, http://www.dailymail.
     co.uk/health/article-1279840/Water-brain-Grey-matter-literally-shrinks-
     hydration.html.

6   Philippa Norman, "Feeding the Brain for Academic Success: How
     Nutrition and Hydration Boost Learning," *Camino Island Mills*, August
     31, 2014, https://www.camanoislandmills.com/feeding-the-brain-for-
     academic-success/.

7   Ratey, *A User's Guide to the Brain*, 35.

8   "Feed Your Willpower," *Men's Health* (December 2012), 98.

9   Norman, "Feeding the Brain for Academic Success."

10   Ratey, *A User's Guide to the Brain*, 35.

11   Herman Pontzer, "The Exercise Paradox," *Scientific American Mind*,
     February 2017, https://www.scientificamerican.com/article/the-exercise-
     paradox/.

12   Medina, *Brain Rules.*

13   Aamodt and Wang, *Welcome to Your Child's Brain,* 127.

14   Ratey, *A User's Guide to the Brain,* 362.

15   John Ratey, *Spark: The Revolutionary New Science of Exercise and the Brain* (New York, NY: Little, Brown, and Company, 2008).

16   Centers for Disease Control and Prevention, *The Association Between School-Based Physical Activity, Including Physical Education, and Academic Performance* (Atlanta, GA: US Department of Health and Human Services, 2010), http://www.cdc.gov/HealthyYouth/health_and_academics/pdf/pape_executive_summary.pdf.

17   Yong, Ed, "A New Theory Linking Sleep and Creativity: The Two Main Phases of Sleep Might Work Together to Boost Creative Problem-Solving," *Atlantic,* May 15, 2018, https://www.theatlantic.com/science/archive/2018/05/sleep-creativity-theory/560399/.

18   Penny Corkum, Rosemary Tannock, and Harvey Moldofsky, "Sleep Disturbances in Children with Attention-Deficit/Hyperactivity Disorder," *Journal of the American Academy of Child & Adolescent Psychiatry* 37, no. 6 (1998): 637-646. doi:http://dx.doi.org/10.1097/00004583-199806000-00014 and Rosalina Silvestri, et al., "Sleep Disorders in Children With Attention-Deficit/Hyperactivity Disorder (ADHD) Recorded Overnight by Video-Polysomnography," *Sleep Medicine* 10, no. 10 (2009): 1132-1138.

19   Kristiaan Van der Heijden, Marcel G. Smits, Eus J.W. Van Someren, K Richard Ridderinkhof, and W. Boudewun Gunning, "Effect of Melatonin on Sleep, Behavior, and Cognition in ADHD and Chronic Sleep-Onset Insomnia," *Journal of the American Academy of Child & Adolescent Psychiatry* 46, no. 2 (2007): 233-241. doi:http://dx.doi.org/10.1097/01.chi.0000246055.76167.0d.

20   Joe Rubino, "Screens Have Big Effect on Kids' Sleep: CU Study Suggests Children's Eyes Absorb More Light," *The Denver Post,* November 2, 2017, https://www.denverpost.com/2017/11/02/americas-youth-looking-screens-like-never-before-studies-show-their-sleep-is-suffering/.

21   Rubino, "Screens Have Big Effect on Kids' Sleep."

22   Rich, interview by Nathan Heffel, "Worried About Your Kid's Smartphone Use?"

23   Van der Heijden et al., "Effect of Melatonin on Sleep" and Mark
      Hyman, "How a Light Bulb Can Help You Sleep Better," *HuffPost*,
      November 8, 2013, https://www.huffingtonpost.com/dr-mark-hyman/
      light-sleep_b_4239765.html.

24   Jiexiu Zhao et al., "Red Light and the Sleep Quality and Endurance
      Performance of Chinese Female Basketball Players," *Journal of Athletic
      Training* 47, no. 6 (2012): 673-678. doi:10.4085/1062-6050-47.6.08.

25   Mark Rapport et al., "Hyperactivity in Boys with Attention-deficit/
      Hyperactivity Disorder (ADHD): A Ubiquitous Core Symptom or
      Manifestation of Working Memory Deficits?" *Journal of Abnormal Child
      Psychology* 37, no. 4 (2009):521-34. doi:10.1007/s10802-008-9287-8.
      Also see John Cloud, "Kids with ADHD May Learn Better
      by Fidgeting," *Time*, March 25, 2009, http://psychrights.org/
      Articles/090325TimeMagFidgetingKidsMayLearnBetter.htm.

26   Sean Gregory, "The Shoddy Science Behind Fidget Spinners," *Time*,
      May 11, 2017, http://time.com/4775458/shoddy-science-behind-fidget-
      spinners/.

27   Valerie Strauss, "Schools are Banning Fidget Spinners, Calling Them
      Nuisances and Even Dangerous," *The Washington Post*, June 1, 2017,
      https://www.washingtonpost.com/news/answer-sheet/wp/2017/06/01/
      schools-are-banning-fidget-spinners-calling-them-nuisances-and-even-
      dangerous/?utm_term=.09c6889eb9f1.

28   Gregory Berns, "What Does Your Dog Really Want?" *Scientific
      American Mind*, August 9, 2017, https://blogs.scientificamerican.com/
      observations/what-does-your-dog-really-want/.

29   Mary Fowler, "Mindful Discipline for Distressed Learners," in *Emotional
      Disorders: A Neuropsychological, Psychopharmacological, and Educational
      Perspective*, ed. Steven G. Feifer and Gurmal Rattan (Middletown, MD:
      School Neuropsych Press, 2009), 279.

30   James M. Swanson, *School-Based Assessments and Interventions for ADD
      Students* (Madison, CT: K.C. Publishing, 1992), 122.

31   John Gottman, Jonni Gonso, and Brian Rasmussen, "Social Interaction,
      Social Competence, and Friendship in Children," *Child Development* 46,
      no. 3 (1975): 709-718.

32   Phelan, *1-2-3 Magic*.

Chapter 7

1   Kimberly Saudino, "Behavioral Genetics and Child Temperament,"
     Journal of Developmental & Behavioral Pediatrics 26, no. 3 (2005): 214-
     223.
2   Saudino, "Behavioral Genetics and Child Temperament."
3   Saudino, "Behavioral Genetics and Child Temperament."
4   Steven G. Feifer, "Social Brain Circuitry and Behavior: The
     Neural Building Blocks of Emotion," in *Emotional Disorders: A
     Neuropsychological, Psychopharmacological, and Educational Perspective*,
     ed. Steven G. Feifer and Gurmal Rattan (Middletown, MD: School
     Neuropsych Press, 2009), 39.
5   Aamodt and Wang, *Welcome to Your Child's Brain*, 224.
6   Feifer, "Social Brain Circuitry and Behavior," 40.
7   Shel Silverstein, "Three Stings," *Falling Up: Poems and Drawings by Shel
     Silverstein* (New York, NY: Harper Collins, 1996), 148.
8   Feifer, "Social Brain Circuitry and Behavior," 23.
9   Sharon Begley, "The Brain: How the Brain Rewires Itself," *Time*,
     January 19, 2007, http://content.time.com/time/magazine/
     article/0,9171,1580438-4,00.html.

Chapter 8

1   The amygdala has very strong connections to the hippocampus, the part
     of the brain that decides which information and experiences should be
     sent into longer term memory (Ratey, *A User's Guide to the Brain*, 188).
2   Steven G. Feifer, "Mood and Anxiety Disorders in Children," in
     *Emotional Disorders: A Neuropsychological, Psychopharmacological,
     and Educational Perspective*, ed. Steven G. Feifer and Gurmal Rattan
     (Middletown, MD: School Neuropsych Press, 2009), 136.
3   Feifer, "Social Brain Circuitry and Behavior," 53.
4   Ratey, *A User's Guide to the Brain*, 225.
5   Elizabeth Dougherty, "What Are Thoughts Made Of?, MIT, Ask an
     Engineer," April 26, 2011, https://engineering.mit.edu/engage/ask-an-
     engineer/what-are-thoughts-made-of/.
6   Paul Ekman, "Emotional Awareness" (lecture, Learning and the Brain
     Conference, San Francisco, CA, February 20, 2009).
7   Ratey, *A User's Guide to the Brain*, 238.

8   Gloria Willcox, "The Feeling Wheel: A Tool for Expanding Awareness of Emotions and Increasing Spontaneity and Intimacy," *Transactional Analysis Journal* 12, no. 4 (1982): 274-276. doi:https://doi.org/10.1177/036215378201200411.

9   Richard J. Haier, "What Does a Smart Brain Look Like?: Inner Views Show How We Think," *Scientific American Mind* 20, no. 6 (2009): 47.

10   Steve Ayan, "How to Control Your Feelings and Live Happily Ever After," *Scientific American Mind* 26 (2014): 52. doi:10.1038/scientificamericanmind0115-48.

11   Mandy Oaklander, "The Science of Crying," *Time Health*, March 16, 2016, http://time.com/4254089/science-crying/.

12   David Bianculli, "It's All in Your Head: Director Pete Docter Gets Emotional in 'Inside Out,'" *Fresh Air*, National Public Radio, June 10, 2015, http://www.npr.org/2015/07/03/419497086/its-all-in-your-head-director-pete-docter-gets-emotional-in-inside-out.

13   Ekman, "Emotional Awareness."

14   ESPN, "SC Featured: A 9/11 Hero's Lasting Impact on Rugby," August 28, 2016, video clip, http://www.espn.com/video/clip?id=17403649.

15   Ayan, "How to Control Your Feelings," 50.

16   Jeffrey Kluger, "Why We Worry About the Wrong Things: The Psychology of Risk," *Time* 168, no. 23 (2006): 66.

17   Claude Steiner, *The Original Warm Fuzzy Tale* (Los Angeles, CA: Jalmar Press, 1979).

18   Feifer, "Social Brain Circuitry and Behavior," 43.

19   Mike Klis, "Peyton Manning Adjusts Well to Playing With a Right-hand Glove," *The Denver Post*, January 8, 2013, http://www.denverpost.com/2013/01/08/peyton-manning-adjusts-well-to-playing-with-a-right-hand-glove/.

20   Jason Gay, "Mikaela Shiffrin Is Going to Be OK," *The Wall Street Journal*, February 16, 2018, https://www.wsj.com/articles/mikaela-shiffrin-is-going-to-be-ok-1518782939.

21   John Medina, "Rule #8, Brain Rules: Principles for Surviving and Thriving in School" (lecture, Learning and the Brain Conference, San Francisco, CA, February 20, 2009).

22   Aamodt and Wang, *Welcome to Your Child's Brain*, 223.

23   Alice Park, "How Playing Violent Video Games May Change the Brain,"
      Time, December 2, 2011, http://healthland.time.com/2011/12/02/how-
      playing-violent-video-games-may-change-the-brain/.

24   Borba, *UnSelfie*, 100.

25   Sean Coughlan, "Violent Video Games Leave Teens 'Morally
      Immature,'" *BBC News,* February 6, 2014, https://www.bbc.com/news/
      education-26049333.

26   Daniel Goleman, "The Experience of Touch: Research Points to a
      Critical Role," *The New York Times*, February 2, 1988, http://www.
      nytimes.com/1988/02/02/science/the-experience-of-touch-research-
      points-to-a-critical-role.html?pagewanted=all&mcubz=0.

27   Sue Gerhardt, *Why Love Matters: How Affection Shapes a Baby's Brain.*
      (Hove, East Sussex: Brunner-Routledge, 2004).

28   Fowler, "Mindful Discipline for Distressed Learners," 276.

29   Scott Carney, *What Doesn't Kill Us: How Freezing Water, Extreme
      Altitude, and Environmental Conditioning Will Renew Our Lost
      Evolutionary Strength* (New York, NY: Rodale, 2017).

30   Aamodt and Wang, *Welcome to Your Child's Brain*, 220.

31   Thomas G. Power, "Stress and Coping in Childhood: The Parents' Role,"
      Parenting: Science and Practice 4, no. 4 (2004): 271-317.

32   Ayan, "How to Control Your Feelings," 51.

33   Gay, "Mikaela Shiffrin Is Going to Be OK."

34   Timothy J. Schoenfeld, Pedro Rada, Pedro R. Pieruzzini, Brian Hsueh,
      and Elizabeth Gould, "Physical Exercise Prevents Stress-Induced
      Activation of Granule Neurons and Enhances Local Inhibitory
      Mechanisms in the Dentate Gyrus," *Journal of Neuroscience* 33, no. 18
      (2013): 7770-7777. doi:10.1523/JNEUROSCI.5352-12.2013.

35   Molly Fletcher, "The Key to Nick Saban's Success? Embracing Now,"
      (blog), January 9, 2017, https://mollyfletcher.com/key-nick-sabans-
      success-embracing-now/.

36   "Fight stress, positively: Dalai Lama," *Hindustantimes*, January 3, 2011,
      http://www.hindustantimes.com/india/fight-stress-positively-dalai-lama/
      story-eg49T0Yx1DIIZnpoWzYA6O.html.

Chapter 9

1   Yalof, "Right Hemispheric Disorders and Emotional Disturbance," 52.

2   Aamodt and Wang, *Welcome to Your Child's Brain*, 155 and Calvin A. Colarusso, *The Golden Age of Childhood: The Elementary School Years* (San Diego, CA: True Nature Productions, 2011).

3   Sigmund Freud, *Three Essays on the Theory of Sexuality*, trans. James Strachey (Eastford, CT: Martino Fine Books, 2011).

4   Aamodt and Wang, *Welcome to Your Child's Brain*, 162.

5   For more information about Stanford's Positive Coaching Program, see https://www.positivecoach.org/mission-history.

6   Louis Cozolino, "The Neuroscience of Human Relationships: Developing Social Brains" (lecture, Learning and the Brain Conference, San Francisco, CA, February 20, 2009).

7   Rene Montagne, "Experiment Tests If Teacher-Student Relationship Helps Performance," *Morning Edition*, National Public Radio News, October 13, 2015, http://www.npr.org/2015/10/13/448182553/experiment-tests-if-teacher-student-relationship-helps-performance.

8   I am also working on a third book for this series, *No One to Play With*, that addresses how effective coaching can help these children overcome the tremendous social struggles they face.

9   Cory Turner, "When Kids Start Playing to Win," *NPR Ed*, National Public Radio, August 5, 2014, http://www.npr.org/sections/ed/2014/08/05/331412567/when-kids-start-playing-to-win.

10   Paul Tough, "What if the Secret to Success Is Failure?" *New York Times Magazine*, September 14, 2011, http://www.nytimes.com/2011/09/18/magazine/what-if-the-secret-to-success-is-failure.html?mcubz=0.

11   Michael Kimmel, as cited in "The Above Average Guy: How Do You Rate?" *Men's Health* (June 2018), 140.

12   See Alyson Krueger, "15 Life-Changing Inventions That Were Created By Mistake," *Business Insider*, November 16, 2010, http://www.businessinsider.com/these-10-inventions-were-made-by-mistake-2010-11.

13   For more quotes from Albert Einstein, see https://www.brainyquote.com/quotes/quotes/a/alberteins148788.html.

14   For more quotes from Michael Jordan, see https://www.brainyquote.com/quotes/quotes/m/michaeljor127660.html.

15   The full teen experience will be explored in my second book in this series, *Dangerous Play*.

16   Aamodt and Wang, *Welcome to Your Child's Brain,* 77.

17   Lesley Gore, "It's My Party," *It's My Party* (Mercury Records, 1963).

18   IngBeth Larsson and Carl-Göran Svedin, "Sexual Experiences in Childhood: Young Adults' Recollections," *Archives of Sexual Behavior* 31, no. 3 (2002): 263-273 and Floyd M. Martinson, *The Sexual Life of Children* (Westport, CT: Bergin & Garvey, 1994).

19   For more quotes from Dr. Seuss, see https://www.goodreads.com/quotes/526257-cause-when-a-guy-does-something-stupid-once-well-that-s.

20   W. N. Friedrich, P. Grambsch, D. Broughton, J. Kuiper, and R. L. Beilke, "Normative Sexual Behavior in Children," *Pediatrics* 88, no. 3 (1991): 456-464.

21   Borba, *UnSelfie,* 181-82.

22   Ratey, *A User's Guide to the Brain,* 255.

23   Aamodt and Wang, *Welcome to Your Child's Brain,* 77.

24   Aamodt and Wang, *Welcome to Your Child's Brain,* 160.

25   For more quotes from Aristotle, see https://www.brainyquote.com/quotes/quotes/a/aristotle132211.html.

26   Tali Sharot as cited in "Fibbers Beware: Study Finds Small Lies Lead to Bigger Ones," Associated Press, October 24, 2016, https://mashable.com/2016/10/24/lying-study/#os30Jo0EUqqi.

27   Borba, *UnSelfie,* 54. Borba mentions that disappointment over anger is a better way to teach our kids.

Chapter 10

1   Ratey, *A User's User's Guide to the Brain,* 167.

2   *Diagnostic and Statistical Manual of Mental Disorders: DSM-5.* (Washington, DC: American Psychiatric Pub Inc., 2013). Asperger's syndrome is a diagnosis now considered on the higher functioning end of the autism spectrum disorder category and is characterized by impairments in social interactions, such as the use of nonverbal communication and a lack of social and emotional reciprocity. While these children have no significant delays in language and cognitive development, they might demonstrate repetitive patterns of behavior and interests that often involve preoccupations with parts of objects or a particular interest (such as military machines or the details of every

Pokémon card). An inflexible adherence to nonfunctional routines (such as having to only step on every third stair of a staircase) may also be present.

3   Simon Baron-Cohen and Sally Wheelwright, "The Empathy Quotient: An Investigation of Adults with Asperger Syndrome of High Functioning Autism, and Normal Sex Differences," *Journal of Autism and Developmental Disorders* 34, no. 2 (2004): 163-175.

4   Marco Iacoboni, *Mirroring People: The New Science of How We Connect with Others* (New York, NY: Farrar, Straus and Giroux, 2008), 42, 70, 162.

5   R. J. R. Blair, J. S. Morris, C. D. Frith, D. I. Perrett, and R. J. Dolan, "Dissociable Neural Responses to Facial Expressions of Sadness and Anger," *Brain* 122, no. 5 (1999): 883-893. doi: https://doi.org/10.1093/brain/122.5.883.

6   Penny Spikins, "Those Eyebrows Speak Volumes," *Science Friday*, April 13, 2018, https://www.sciencefriday.com/segments/these-eyebrows-speak-volumes/.

7   Iacoboni, *Mirroring People*, 42.

8   Temple Grandin and Catherine Johnson, *Animals Make Us Human: Creating the Best Life for Animals* (Boston, MA: Houghton Mifflin Harcourt, 2009).

9   Marc Bekoff and Jessica Pierce, "The Ethical Dog," *Scientific American Mind*, March 1, 2010, https://www.scientificamerican.com/article/the-ethical-dog/.

10   Grandin and Johnson, *Animals Make Us Human*.

11   Grandin and Johnson, *Animals Make Us Human*.

12   Nell Greenfield-Boyce, "The Tail's The Tell: Dog Wags Can Mean Friend or Foe," *Morning Edition*, National Public Radio November 1, 2013, http://www.npr.org/2013/11/01/242126859/the-tails-the-tell-dog-wags-can-mean-friend-or-foe.

Chapter 11

1   Iacoboni, Mirroring People, 11.

2   Iacoboni, Mirroring People, 112.

3   Helen Thomson, "Strange Stories of Extraordinary Brains—and What We Can Learn From Them," *Wall Street Journal*, June 29, 2018, https://

www.wsj.com/articles/strange-stories-of-extraordinary-brainsand-what-we-can-learn-from-them-1530286669.

4   Carl Zimmer, "Secrets of the Brain," *National Geographic*, February 2014, http://ngm.nationalgeographic.com/2014/02/brain/zimmer-text.

5   Martin Schulte-Rüther, Hans J. Markowitsch, N. Jon Shah, Gereon R. Fink, and Martina Piefke, "Gender Differences in Brain Networks Supporting Empathy," *NeuroImage* 42 (2008): 393-403.

6   Feifer, "Social Brain Circuitry and Behavior," 35.

7   Amanda MacMillan, "Resisting the Urge to Yawn Will Only Make It Worse," *Time Health*, September 1, 2017, http://time.com/4923855/resisting-urge-to-yawn/?iid=sr-link1.

8   Emily Anthes, "Youngsters Immune to the Contagious Yawn," *Scientific American Mind,* January 1, 2011, https://www.scientificamerican.com/article/immune-to-the-contagious-yawn/.

9   John M. Garruto and Gurmal Rattan, "School Achievement, Neuropsychological Constructs, and Emotional Disorders," in *Emotional Disorders: A Neuropsychological, Psychopharmacological, and Educational Perspective,* ed. Steven G. Feifer and Gurmal Rattan (Middletown, MD: School Neuropsych Press, 2009), 239.

10   Stephen M. Kosslyn and G. Wayne Miller, "A New Map of How We Think: Top Brain/Bottom Brain," *Wall Street Journal*, October 20, 2013, https://www.wsj.com/articles/a-new-map-of-how-we-think-top-brainbottom-brain-1382140494.

11   Lucina Q. Uddin, Jonas Kaplan, Istvan Molnar-Szakacs, and Marco Iacoboni, "Self-Face Recognition Activates a Frontoparietal 'Mirror' Network in the Right Hemisphere: An Event-Related FMRI Study," *Neuroimage* 25, no. 3 (2005): 926-935. doi:0.1016/j.neuroimage.2004.12.018.

12   Simon Baron-Cohen, Sally Wheelwright, Jacqueline J. Hill, Yogini Raste, and Ian Plumb, "The 'Reading the Mind in the Eyes' Test Revised Version: A Study with Normal Adults, and Adults with Asperger Syndrome or High-functioning Autism," *Journal of Child Psychology and Psychiatry* 42, no. 2 (2001):241-251.

13   Simon Baron-Cohen, *The Essential Difference: Male and Female Brains and the Truth About Autism* (New York, NY: Basic Books, 2003), 3.

14   Robert J. Sternberg, "The Theory of Successful Intelligence,"

Interamerican Journal of Psychology 30, no. 2 (2005): 189-202. See http://www.robertjsternberg.com/successful-intelligence/ for more information.

15   William Pollack, *Real Boys* (New York, NY: Henry Holt and Co., 1998), 346.

16   Louann Brizendine, *The Female Brain* (New York, NY: Broadway Books, 2006), 125.

17   Brizendine, *The Female Brain*, xix.

18   Takashi Ohnishi et al., "The Neural Network for the Mirror System and Mentalizing in Normally Developed Children: An FMRI Study," *Neuroreport* 15, no 9 (2004): 1483-1487. doi:10.1097/01. wnr.0000127464.17770.1f.

19   Madhura Ingalhalikar, Alex Smith, Drew Parker, Theodore D. Satterthwaite, Mark A. Elliott, Kosha Ruparel, Hakon Hakonarson, Raquel E. Gur, Ruben C. Gur, and Ragini Verma, "Sex Differences in the Structural Connectome of the Human Brain," *PNAS* 111, no. 2 (2013): 823-828. doi:10.1073/pnas.1316909110.

20   Kosslyn and Miller, "A New Map of How We Think."

21   Jeff Foxworthy, "Women Want to Talk," *Big Funny*, YouTube video, posted by Jeff Foxworthy, November 7, 2014, https://www.youtube. com/watch?v=2ecaNSiQN1g.

22   Brizendine, *The Female Brain*, 120.

23   Brizendine, *The Female Brain*, 31-38.

24   Louann Brizendine, *The Male Brain* (New York, NY: Broadway Books, 2010), 22 and Aamodt and Wang, *Welcome to Your Child's Brain*, 64, 67.

25   Michael Gurian, "Michael Gurian on Aggression Nurturance," posted by Devel Res, November 3, 2016, https://www.youtube.com/watch?v=9l_kaMEqG_U.

26   McKay, Brett, "Podcast #347: The Science of Social Awkwardness," *The Art of Manliness*, October 12, 2017, http://podcastrepublic.net/podcast/332516054.

27   Michael Gurian, *The Wonder of Boys: What Parents, Mentors and Educators Can Do to Shape Boys into Exceptional Men* (New York, NY: Tarcher/Putnam, 1997), 31-32.

28   Feifer, "Social Brain Circuitry and Behavior," 35.

29   Kang Lee, "Little Liars: Development of Verbal Deception in Children,"

Child Development Perspectives 7, no. 2 (2013): 91-96. doi:10.1111/
cdep.12023 and Shanna Williams, Kelsey Moore, Angela M. Crossman,
and Victoria Talwar, "The Role of Executive Functions and Theory
of Mind in Children's Prosocial Lie-Telling," *Journal of Experimental
Child Psychology* 141 (2016): 256-266. doi:https://doi.org/10.1016/j.
jecp.2015.08.001.

30   Edgar Blanco, "Seeing Is Believing: Harnessing the Power of
        Visualization," *Supply Chain Management Review* (September/October
        2013): 10-11.

31   Bob Tewksbury, "Head Games," *Sports Illustrated*, April 23, 2018,
        https://www.si.com/vault/2018/04/17/head-games.

32   Rich Presta, "Sleep, Your Child's Anxiety, and How to Make it Better by
        Tonight," The Anxiety-Free Child Program, n.d., http://anxietyfreechild.
        com/sleep-your-childs-anxiety-and-how-to-make-it-better-by-tonight/.

33   Amit Sood, *The Mayo Clinic Guide to Stress-Free Living* (Boston, MA: Da
        Capo Press, 2013).

34   For some great ideas on implementing yoga and mindfulness in the
        classroom, or at home, see www.radiantbeginningsyoga.com.

35   Borba, *UnSelfie*, 106-107.

36   Kimberly A. Schonert-Reichl et al., "Enhancing Cognitive and Social-
        Emotional Development Through a Simple-to-Administer Mindfulness-
        Based School Program for Elementary School Children: A Randomized
        Controlled Trial," *Developmental Psychology* 51, no. 1 (2015): 52-56.

37   Maryanna Klatt, Karen Harpster, Emma Browne, Susan White, and
        Jane Case-Smith, "Feasibility and Preliminary Outcomes for Move-Into-
        Learning: An Arts-Based Mindfulness Classroom Intervention," *Journal
        of Positive Psychology* 8, no. 3 (2013): 233-241 and D. S. Black and
        R. Fernando, "Mindfulness Training and Classroom Behavior Among
        Lower-Income and Ethnic Minority Elementary School Children,"
        Journal of Child and Family Studies 22, no. 7 (2013): 1242-1246,
        https://link.springer.com/article/10.1007/s10826-013-9784-4.

Chapter 12

1   Baron-Cohen, *The Essential Difference* and Iacoboni, *Mirroring People*,
        161-162.

2   Bethel Moges and Kristi Weber, "Parental Influence on the
    Emotional Development of Children," *Developmental Psychology
    at Vanderbilt* (blog), May 7, 2014, https://my.vanderbilt.edu/
    developmentalpsychologyblog/2014/05/
    parental-influence-on-the-emotional-development-of-children/.

3   A.C. Baldry, "Bullying in Schools and Exposure to Domestic Violence,"
    Child Abuse & Neglect, 27, no. 7 (2003): 713-732.

4   Rosalind Wiseman, "Girls' Cliques: What Role Does Your Daughter
    Play?" *Makeup Talk* (blog), November 6, 2006, http://www.makeuptalk.
    com/f/topic/33784-girls-cliques-what-role-does-your-daughter-play/.

5   Albert J. Cotugno, "Social Competence and Social Skills Training and
    Intervention for Children with Autism Spectrum Disorders." *Journal
    of Autism and Developmental Disorders,* 39, no. 9 (2009): 1268-1277,
    doi:0.1007/s10803-009-0741-4.

6   Borba, *UnSelfie,* pp 36-37.

7   Kristy Hagar, Sam Goldstein, and Robert Brooks, *Seven Steps to Improve
    Your Child's Social Skills: A Family Guide* (Plantation, FL: Specialty Press,
    2006).

8   Jon Hamilton, "Scientists Say Child's Play Helps Build a Better Brain,"
    NPR Ed, National Public Radio, August 6, 2014, http://www.npr.org/
    sections/ed/2014/08/06/336361277/scientists-say-childs-play-helps-
    build-a-better-brain.

9   Hamilton, "Scientists Say Child's Play Helps Build a Better Brain."

10 Aamodt and Wang, *Welcome to Your Child's Brain.*

11 Hamilton, "Scientists Say Child's Play Helps Build a Better Brain."

12 Dr. Sergio Pellis, Research & Innovation Services, University of
    Lethbridge, http://www.uleth.ca/research-services/research_profiles/dr-
    sergio-pellis.

13 Hamilton, "Scientists Say Child's Play Helps Build a Better Brain."

14 Judith Newman, "How to Let Kids Be Kids," *Redbook,* August 2008,
    188. Newman cites a study by the American Association for the Child's
    Right to Play, which surveyed 15,000 elementary school districts.

15 Centers for Disease Control and Prevention, "The Association
    Between School-Based Physical Activity, Including Physical Education,
    and Academic Performance," April 2010, https://www.cdc.gov/
    HealthyYouth/health_and_academics/pdf/pape_executive_summary.pdf.

16 Kenneth R. Ginsberg, "The Importance of Play in Promoting Healthy Child Development and Maintaining Strong Parent-Child Bonds," *Pediatrics* 119 (January 2007).

17 NAIS, "Using Nature to Boost Empathy, Imagination, and Well-Being," Winter 2018, https://www.nais.org/magazine/independent-school/winter-2018/using-nature-to-boost-empathy,-imagination,-and-well-being/.

18 Alice Park, "Why Sunlight Is So Good for You," *Time*, August 7, 2017, http://time.com/4888327/why-sunlight-is-so-good-for-you/.

19 NAIS, "Using Nature to Boost Empathy."

20 Stephanie Granada, "From the Outside In," *Experience Life*, 20, no. 5 (2018): 56.

21 Rob Dunn, "Play Dirty," *Men's Health*, March 2017, 111.

22 James L. McGaugh, "Panel: The Science of Memory and Emotion— How Emotions Strengthen Memory," *Project on the Decade of the Brain*, Library of Congress, January 3, 2000, http://www.loc.gov/loc/brain/emotion/Mcgaugh.html.

23 William J. Doherty, "Overscheduled Kids, Underconnected Families: The Research Evidence," Putting Family First, May 2006, http://web.archive.org/web/20060501041926.

24 Nancy Gibbs, "The Growing Backlash Against Overparenting," *Time*, November 30, 2009, http://content.time.com/time/magazine/article/0,9171,1940697,00.html.

25 Borba, *UnSelfie*, 161.

26 Stephen Dubner, "The Economist's Guide to Parenting (Rebroadcast)," *Freakonomics*, July 5, 2018, http://freakonomics.com/podcast/the-economists-guide-to-parenting-rebroadcast/.

27 Bryan Caplan, *Selfish Reasons to Have More Kids: Why Parenting is More Fun and Less Work Than You Think* (New York, NY: Basic Books, 2011).

28 Dubner, "The Economist's Guide to Parenting."

29 Kim Brooks, "Motherhood in the Age of Fear," *New York Times*, July 27, 2018, https://www.nytimes.com/2018/07/27/opinion/sunday/motherhood-in-the-age-of-fear.html.

30 See https://letgrow.org/ for more information. The website boldly states, "Treating today's kids as physically and emotionally fragile is bad for

their future—and ours. Let Grow counters the culture of overprotection. We aim to future-proof our kids, and our country."

31   Iacoboni, *Mirroring People*, 161-162.

32   Catherine Steiner-Adair, *The Big Disconnect: Protecting Childhood and Family Relationships in the Digital Age* (New York, NY: HarperCollins, 2014).

33   Maryanne Wolf, *Proust and the Squid: The Story and Science of the Reading Brain* (New York, NY: HarperCollins, 2007).

34   Keith Oatley, "In the Minds of Others," *Scientific American Mind,* 22, no. 5 (2011): 62-67, http://www.sscnet.ucla.edu/polisci/faculty/chwe/austen/oatley2011.pdf.

35   Ellen Rose, "Continuous Partial Attention: Reconsidering the Role of Online Learning in the Age of Interruption." *Educational Technology,* 50, no. 4 (2010): 41-46, http://unbtls.ca/teachingtips/pdfs/sew/Continuous_Partial_Attention.pdf.

36   Aamodt and Wang, *Welcome to Your Child's Brain.*

37   Borba, *UnSelfie*, 10.

38   Rob Evans, "Meeting the New Challenge of New School Governance" (lecture, Trustee/Head of School Workshop, Vail, CO, October 11, 2007).

39   Rich, interview by Nathan Heffel, "Worried About Your Kid's Smartphone Use?"

40   Dale Kunkel and Brian Wilcox, "Television Advertising Leads to Unhealthy Habits in Children; Says APA Task Force," *American Psychological Association,* February 23, 2004, http://www.apa.org/news/press/releases/2004/02/children-ads.aspx.

41   Kunkel and Wilcox, "Television Advertising Leads to Unhealthy Habits in Children."

42   Matt O'Brien, "Child Advocates Ask FTC to Investigate YouTube," *Denver Post,* April 9, 2018, https://www.denverpost.com/2018/04/09/youtube-ftc-investigaiton/.

Chapter 13

1   Victoria Talwar and Angela Crossman, "From Little White Lies to Filthy Liars: The Evolutions of Honesty and Deception in Young Children,"

Advances in Child Development and Behavior 40 (2011): 139-179. doi:10.1016/B978-0-12-386491-8.00004-9.

2   Kristy S. Hagar, Sam Goldstein, and Robert Brooks, *Seven Steps to Improve Your Child's Social Skills: A Family Guide* (Plantation, FL: Specialty Press, 2006), 40-45.

3   Thompson, "How to Raise Responsible Children."

4   Mary Louise Hemmeter, Michaelene M. Ostrosky, Kathleen M. Artman, and Kiersten A. Kinder, "Moving Right Along…Planning Transitions to Prevent Challenging Behavior," *Beyond the Journal*, National Association for the Education of Young Children, May 2008, http://journal.naeyc. org/btj/200805/pdf/BTJ_Hemmeter_Transitions.pdf.

5   Andrew Latham, "Four Types of Management Theory," *eHow*, November 9, 2016, http://www.ehow.com/info_8375509_four-types-management-theory.html.

6   Mike Darling, "14 Ways to Be a Good parent," *Australian Men's Health*, August 2016, https://www.menshealth.com.au/14-ways-to-be-a-good-dad.

7   Michelle Castillo, "Lack of Regular Bedtime May Affect Kids' Learning Skills," *CBS News*, July 9, 3013, https://www.cbsnews.com/news/lack-of-regular-bedtime-may-affect-kids-learning-skills/.

8   William Glasser, *Choice Theory: A New Psychology of Personal Freedom* (New York, NY: HarperCollins, 1999).

9   Jacquelynne S. Eccles and Rena D. Harold, "Parent-School Involvement during the Early Adolescent Years," *Teachers College Record* 94, no. 3 (1993): 568-587.

10   Richard Weissbourd and Stephanie Jones, "The Children We Mean to Raise: The Real Messages Adults are Sending About Values," Making Caring Common Project (Cambridge, MA: Harvard Graduate School of Education, 2014), https://mcc.gse.harvard.edu/files/gse-mcc/files/mcc-executive-summary.pdf.

11   Borba, *UnSelfie*, 179.

12   Ariana Eunjung Cha, "A Major Update Relaxes Screen Time Rules For Some Kids," *The Washington Post*, October 21, 2016, https://www.washingtonpost.com/news/to-your-health/wp/2016/10/21/big-updates-new-screen-time-rules-by-age-from-the-american-academy-for-pediatrics/?utm_term=.b45aaf124f5c.

13   Poll from the USC Annenberg Center for the Digital Future: "Family time Decreasing with Internet Use," http://www.digitalcenter.org/wp-content/uploads/2013/02/2009_digital_future_report-year8.pdf, and Borba, *UnSelfie*, 9.

14   Cha, "A Major Update Relaxes Screen Time Rules."

15   Rich, interview by Nathan Heffel, "Worried About Your Kid's Smartphone Use?"

16   Andrew K. Przybylski, "Electronic Gaming and Psychosocial Adjustment," *Pediatrics* 134, no. 3 (2014), www.pediatrics.org/cgi/doi/10.1542/peds.2013-4021.

17   Krista Tippet, "The Private Faith of Jimmy Carter," *On Being*, April 26, 2007, http://www.onbeing.org/program/private-faith-jimmy-carter/transcript/1321.

18   See https://www.commonsensemedia.org/ for more information.

19   Rich, interview by Nathan Heffel, "Worried About Your Kid's Smartphone Use?"

20   Sam Schechner, "France Takes On Cellphone Addiction With a Ban in Schools," *Wall Street Journal*, August 13, 2018, https://www.wsj.com/articles/france-takes-on-cellphone-addiction-with-a-ban-in-schools-1534152600.

21   Hamza Shaban, "Child Advocates Urge Facebook To End Messenger Kids," *The Denver Post*, January 31, 2018, Business, 11A. The advocates expressed concern to Facebook's CEO, Mark Zuckerberg, that "boosting the screen time of young children…would interfere with crucial developmental skills such as reading human emotion, delaying gratification and engaging with the physical world."

22   Alex Sciuto, Arnita Saini, Jodi Forlizzi, and Jason I. Hong, "'Hey Alexa, What's Up?': A Mixed-Methods Studies of In-Home Conversational Agent Usage," *Proceedings of the 2018 Designing Interactive Systems Conference* (2018): 857-868. doi:10.1145/3196709.3196772

23   Solace Shen, "Children's Conceptions of the Moral Standing of a Humanoid Robot of the Here and Now," Phd diss., University of Washington, 2015, ResearchWorks Archive https://digital.lib.washington.edu/researchworks/handle/1773/35303?mod=article_inline.

24   Associated Press, "Compulsive Video-Game Playing Could Be Mental Health Problem," *KDVR News*, June 18, 2018, https://www.apnews.com/309e0d17ea024b8b8a6bac92d8d3cd09.

25 Associated Press, "Compulsive Video-Game Playing."

26 Michael Liedtke, "How Apple's App Store Changed Our World," *Denver Post*, July 10, 2018, https://www.denverpost.com/2018/07/10/apple-technology-app-store/.

27 Anya Kamenetz, "5 Things To Know About Screen Time Right Now," *NPR Ed*, National Public Radio, January 3, 2018, https://www.npr.org/sections/ed/2018/01/03/572875689/five-things-to-know-about-screen-time-right-now.

28 Farnoosh Torabi, "Instill Gratitude, Not Attitude," *Money Magazine*, April 2015, https://archive.org/stream/Money_April_2015_USA#page/n33/mode/2up/search/instill+gratitude.

29 Susan Borowski, "Allowance for Kids—Types & How Much You Should Pay for Chores," Money Crashers, n.d., http://www.moneycrashers.com/allowance-kids-chores/.

Chapter 14

1 Craig Knippenberg, "Developing A Child's Self Esteem and Social Growth," *Challenge Newsletter* 7, no. 1 (January/February, 1993).

2 Craig Knippenberg, "Happy Reading," in *Easy to Love But Hard to Live With: Real People, Invisible Disabilities: True Stories,* ed. Tricia Bliven-Chasinoff and Lisa Davis (Pittsboro, NC: DRT Press, 2014).

3 Aamodt and Wang, *Welcome to Your Child's Brain*, 254.

4 Borba, *UnSelfie*, 34.

5 Carol S. Dweck, "Brainology: Transforming Students' Motivation to Learn," *Independent School Magazine*, National Association of Independent Schools (NAIS), winter 2008, https://www.nais.org/magazine/independent-school/winter-2008/brainology/.

6 For more information about the Positive Coaching Alliance Program, see https://www.positivecoach.org/mission-history.

7 Thompson, "How to Raise Responsible Children."

8 Jeff Grabmeir, "How Parents May Help Create Their Own Little Narcissists," The Ohio State University, March 9, 2015, https://news.osu.edu/news/2015/03/09/little-narcissists/.

9 Borba, *UnSelfie*, 42.

10 Laura K. King and Joshua A. Hicks, "Narrating the Self in the Past and the Future: Implications for Maturity," *Research in Human Development* 3, no. 2-3 (2006): 121-138.

11   Reinhold Niebuhr, "The Serenity Prayer," *Internet Resources*, http://skdesigns.com/internet/articles/prose/niebuhr/serenity_prayer/.

12   Michael Thompson and Catherine O'Neill Grace, *Best Friends, Worst Enemies: Understanding the Social Lives of Children* (New York, NY: Ballantine Books, 2001).

13   To learn more about Dr. Dan Olweus and the Olweus Bullying Prevention Program, see http://www.violencepreventionworks.org/public/olweus_history.page.

14   Dan Olweus, "Bullying at School: Basic Facts and Effects of a School Based Intervention Program," *Journal of Child Psychology and Psychiatry* 35, no. 7 (1994): 1171-1190. doi:10.1111/j.1469-7610.1994.tb01229.x.

15   Thompson and O'Neill Grace, *Best Friends, Worst Enemies.* Also see http://www.nesacenter.org/uploaded/conferences/sec/2013/handouts/thompson/bestfriendsworstenemies.pdf.

16   Thompson and O'Neill Grace, *Best Friends, Worst Enemies.*

17   Rosalind Wiseman, *Queen Bees Wannabes: Helping Your Daughter Survive Cliques, Gossip, Boyfriends, and the New Realities of Girl World*, 2nd ed. (New York, NY: Three Rivers Press, 2002), 94.

18   Gerald Imber, "Ask Dr. Imber," *Men's Journal* (June 2018): 111.

19   Thompson, Lecture presented at Graland Country Day School, Denver.

20   Michael Thompson, Lecture presented at Graland Country Day School, Denver, Colorado (n.d.).

21   For more information on RULER or the Yale Center for Emotional Intelligence, see http://ei.yale.edu/ruler/.

22   Scott Raab, "Will Smith on Kids, His Career, Ferguson, and Failure," *Esquire*, February 12, 2015, http://www.esquire.com/entertainment/interviews/a9938/will-smith-interview-0315/.

23   Thompson, Lecture presented at Graland Country Day School, Denver.

24   Margaret Atwood, *Cat's Eye* (New York, NY: Anchor Books, 1998), 213.

25   Robert Emmons, "Why Gratitude Is Good," *Greater Good Magazine*, November 16, 2010, https://greatergood.berkeley.edu/article/item/why_gratitude_is_good.

26   Noah Kagan, "Episode 74" [interview], Podcast with Lance Armstrong on *The Forward*, https://soundcloud.com/user-411867241/episode-74-noah-kagan-the-forward-podcast-with-lance-armstrong.

Chapter 15

1   Sihyun Park and Karen G. Schepp, "A Systematic Review of Research on Children of Alcoholics: Their Inherent Resilience and Vulnerability," *Journal of Child and Family Studies* 24, no. 5 (2015): 1222-1231. doi:https://doi.org/10.1007/s10826-014-9930-7.

2   Evan Imber-Black, Janine Roberts, and Richard A. Whiting, eds., *Rituals in Families and Family Therapy* (New York, NY: Norton, 1988).

3   Barbara H. Fiese, Thomas J. Tomcho, Michael Douglas, Kimberly Josephs, Scott Poltrock, and Tim Baker, "A Review of 50 Years of Research on Naturally Occurring Family Routines and Rituals: Cause for Celebration?" *Journal of Family Psychology* 16, no. 4 (2002): 381.

4   Park and Schepp, "A Systematic Review of Research on Children of Alcoholics."

5   Richard Louv, *Last Child in the Woods: Saving Our Children From Nature-Deficit Disorder* (Chapel Hill, NC: Algonquin Books of Chapel Hill, 2005.)

6   Borba, *UnSelfie*, 216.

7   Paul K. Piff, et al., "Higher Social Class Predicts Increased Unethical Behavior," *Proceedings of the National Academy of Sciences* 109, no. 11 4086-4091.

8   Michael Thompson, *Homesick and Happy: How Time Away From Parents Can Help a Child Grow* (New York, NY: Ballantine, 2012).

9   Nathaniel Branden, "Self-Esteem," *Talk of the Nation* February 4, 2002, http://www.npr.org/templates/story/story.php?storyId=1137494.

10 Branden, "Self-Esteem."

11 For more quotes from the Dalai Lama, see https://www.brainyquote.com/quotes/quotes/d/dalailama446763.html.

12 Reno Boyd, "Longmont High School Football Team Visits the TODAY Show," September 5, 2014, http://www.9news.com/story/sports/high-school/2014/09/05/longmont-football-on-today-show/15152847/.

13 Jason Beaubien, "St. Thomas Residents Welcome Relief Flights After Irma," *Morning Edition*, National Public Radio News September 15, 2017, http://www.npr.org/2017/09/15/551184466/st-thomas-residents-welcome-relief-flights-after-irma.

14 Jennifer King Lindley, "How to Raise Happy Kids: Commit Acts of Kindness," *Parents*, (n.d.), http://www.parents.com/fun/activities/how-to-raise-happy-kids-commit-acts-of-kindness/.

15 Sonja Lyubomirsky, *The How of Happiness: A Scientific Approach to Getting the Life You Want* (New York, NY: Penguin, 2008).

16 Lindley, "How to Raise Happy Kids."

17 Emma Seppala, Timothy Rossomando, and James R. Doty, "Social Connection and Compassion: Important Predictors of Health and Well-Being," *Social Research: An International Quarterly* 80, no. 2 (2013): 411-430. doi:10.1353/sor.2013.0027.

18 Muzafer Sherif et al., "The Robbers Cave Experiment" (1954), http://www.age-of-the-sage.org/psychology/social/sherif_robbers_cave_experiment.html.

19 Sherif et al., "The Robbers Cave Experiment."

20 See https://startempathy.org/changemaker-schools/ for more information.

21 Craig Knippenberg, "Crying for Columbine," in *Ordinary Men, Extraordinary Lives: Defining Moments,* ed. Jim Sharon (Energy for Life, 2011).

22 Craig Knippenberg, "Enough!" [Editorial], *Denver Post,* April 20, 2007.

23 USADA, "The Road Less Traveled: Jeremy Bloom," November 24, 2014, https://www.usada.org/the-road-less-traveled-jeremy-bloom/.

24 Steve Levitt and Stephen Dubner, "The Economist's Guide to Parenting (Rebroadcast)," *Freakonomics,* July 5, 2018, http://freakonomics.com/podcast/the-economists-guide-to-parenting-rebroadcast/.

25 Levitt and Dubner, "The Economist's Guide to Parenting."

26 Levitt and Dubner, "The Economist's Guide to Parenting."

27 Bo Jackson, "December 12, 2016" [interview], Podcast with Lance Armstrong on *The Forward,* http://theforwardpodcast.libsyn.com/bo-jackson.

INDEX

Symbols